IMMIGRANTS TO NEW ENGLAND 1700-1775

Ethel Stanwood Bolton

HERITAGE BOOKS
2007

HERITAGE BOOKS
AN IMPRINT OF HERITAGE BOOKS, INC.

Books, CDs, and more—Worldwide

For our listing of thousands of titles see our website
at
www.HeritageBooks.com

A Facsimile Reprint
Published 2007 by
HERITAGE BOOKS, INC.
Publishing Division
65 East Main Street
Westminster, Maryland 21157-5026

Originally published
Salem, Massachusetts
1931

— Publisher's Notice —
In reprints such as this, it is often not possible to remove blemishes from the original. We feel the contents of this book warrant its reissue despite these blemishes and hope you will agree and read it with pleasure.

International Standard Book Number: 978-0-7884-2059-7

PREFACE

The following list of immigrants includes many of those who came to New England between the years 1700 and 1775, with additions at either end. The list is the accumulation of years and has had the help of many people, too numerous to mention by name, for whose assistance I am most grateful. It comes from many sources, some accurate and some inaccurate, and I have, in only a few instances, gone back of the printed record. Inevitably, therefore, there will be mistakes, which I hope time and friendly people may gradually eliminate. In some cases, mostly in the records of ships entering Boston, those may have been included as immigrants who were merely returning from a trip to New York, or even a trip abroad. All of these may not have been discovered and taken out.

The list is only intended to be a guide toward further investigation, and as such it is hoped that it will prove useful to many.

E. S. B.

POUND HILL PLACE,
SHIRLEY, MASSACHUSETTS.

IMMIGRANTS TO NEW ENGLAND, 1700-1775.

By Ethel Stanwood Bolton.

AARSHAL, John, of Boston, Mass.; from Great Britain, before 1719; m. Susanna Holton in Boston, Oct. 8, 1719.—*Boston Rec. Com., Vol. 28, p.* 98.

ABERCROMBIE, Rev. Robert, of Pelham, Mass.; from Scotland, cir. 1742; b. 1712; grad. University of Edinburgh; first minister of Pelham; m. Margaret Stevenson; Children: David, Andrew, Margaret, Samuel, John, William, Sarah, Robert, Isaac, Mehitable, James; d. March 7, 1780.—*Sheldon's Deerfield, Vol. 2, p.* 5; *Wall's North Worcester, p.* 50.

ABERCROMBIE, Robert, of Pelham, Mass.; from Scotland before 1742; b. in Scotland; first minister of Pelham; Child: Isaac.—*Parmenter's Pelham, pp.* 72, 437.

ADAMS, John, of Boston, Mass.; painter, came from England with his servant, with Captain Osborn, on December 7, 1717; petition to ply his trade rejected by selectmen; warned out Jan. 27, 1718.—*Boston Record Com. Vol. 13, pp.* 32, 33.

ADAM, Richard, of Weare, N. H.; from England in 1775; a teacher; Child: Jenny; removed to Canada. —*Little's Weare, N. H.*

ADAMS, Robert, of Londonderry, N. H.; came before 1730.—*Coll. Me. Hist. Soc., Vol. II, p.* 24.

ADAMS, William, of Londonderry, N. H., from Ireland, cir. 1719-1721; said to have been born in Argyleshire; m. Mary ———; d. Oct. 4, 1755, aet. 61; Children: James, Jonathan, Samuel, William, David; Samuel moved to Boothbay; William had a brother James; d. Nov. 1, 1761 at 72.—*Parker's Londonderry, p.* 254, *and Greene's Boothbay, p.* 487.

AIKEN, Edward, of Londonderry, N. H.; from Ireland, 1720; b. 1660; m. Barbara Edwards; Children: Nathaniel, James, William; d. 1747 in Londonderry. —*Parker's Londonderry, p.* 255, *Whiton's Antrim, p.* 52, *Bedford, p.* 279, *Secomb's Amherst, p.* 487.

AIKEN, James, of Londonderry, N. H.; from Ireland, cir. 1720; son of Edward; m. Jean Cochran, 1725; Children: John, James, Elizabeth, one son and two daughters.—*Vital Records of Londonderry, Parker's Londonderry, p. 256.*

AIKEN, John, of Chester, N. H.; from Ireland, cir. 1724; b. 1689; m. —— Karr; Children: John, James, Margaret, Martha, Jane, Elizabeth, Mary; d. 1750. —*Chase's Chester, p. 462.*

AIKIN, Nathaniel, of Londonderry, N. H.; from Ireland, cir. 1720; son of Edward; m. Margaret Cochran, 1726; Children: Edward, John, James, Thomas, William.—*Parker's Londonderry, p. 256, Vital Records of Londonderry.*

AIKEN, Samuel, of Chester, N. H.; from Ireland, cir. 1736; brother of John; m. —— Young; Children: William, James, Peter, Sarah, Samuel.—*Chase's Chester, p. 462.*

AIKEN, William, of Londonderry, N. H.; from Ireland, cir. 1720; son of Edward; m. Janet Wilson, 1725; Children: Agnes, Edward, Mary, Jonathan, Martha, William.—*Vital Records of Londonderry, Parker's Londonderry, p. 256.*

ALEXANDER, James, of Windham, N. H.; from Ireland; brother of John and Alexander; m. Mary ——; Children: Agnes, Joseph; d. 1731.—*Morrison's Windham, N. H., p. 305.*

ALEXANDER, James, of Pelham, Mass.; from Ireland, before 1738.—*Parmenter's Pelham, p. 17.*

ALEXANDER, John, of Londonderry, N. H.; from Ireland; brother of James; Children: Robert, James, Ann; d. 1763.—*Morrison's Windham, p. 305.*

ALEXANDER, John, of Worcester, Mass.; from Ireland, before 1733.—*Perry's Scotch-Irish, p. 14, Parmenter's Pelham, p. 17.*

ALEXANDER, Randall, of Londonderry, N. H.; from County Antrim, Ireland, 1718; m. Janet ——; Children: Robert, Mary, Isabel, David, John, Samuel, William, Isabel; petitioner to Shute.—

Parker's Londonderry, p. 44, Morrison's Windham, N. H., p. 305.

ALEXANDER, William, of Lunenburg, Mass.; from Ireland, before 1743; m. Elizabeth Bradley, 1743; Children: John, Franice, William.—*Lunenberg Records, pp.* 223, 272.

ALEXANDER, William, of Deerfield, Mass.; from Londonderry, 1765(?); warned out of Deerfield, 1765; Children: John, Gin, Lydia.—*Sheldon's Deerfield, Vol.* 2, *p.* 8.

ALFORD, Jabez, Boston, Mass.; from Carolina, 1705; warned out.—*Boston Rec. Com., Vol.* 11, *p.* 48.

ALLANE, Thomas, of Georgetown, Me.; from ———, April 1718.

ALLD, William, of Peterborough, N. H.; from Ireland; b. 1723; m. Lettuce ———; Children: John, Benjamin, Jenny, Samuel; d. 1805, aged 82.—*Smith's Peterborough, pt.* 2, *pp.* 7, 8.

ALLEN, Andrew, Boston; from Virginia, to Cape Ann, to Billerica, to Boston; warned out May 3, 1708.—*Boston Rec. Com., Vol.* 11, *p.* 72.

ALLEN, George, Boston, Mass.; from Ireland, with Captain Dennis, Nov. 1719.—*Boston Record Com., Vol.* 13, *p.* 64.

ALLEN, Humphrey, Boston, Mass.; 1730; late from New York; convicted of stealing.—*Court of Sessions of the Peace, p.* 298.

ALLEN, Margaret, of Boston, Mass.; 1722; from Ireland, 1717; John Langdon of Boston Innholder paid £18 for 4 years service.—*Court of Sessions of the Peace, 1715-18, Vol. I, p.* 184.

ALLEN, Richard, of Boston, Mass.; from England; has opened a brew-house here, 1791.—*Centinel, May,* 1791.

ALLEN, Robert, Boston, Mass.; from Ireland, with Captain Dennis, Nov. 1719.—*Boston Record Com., Vol.* 13, *p.* 64.

ALLEN, William; from London, 1716; merchant.—*Boston Rec. Com., Vol.* 29, *p.* 233.

ALLISON, Samuel, of Londonderry, N. H.; from Ireland (?), 1718.—*Parker's Londonderry, p. 44.*

AMBREY, Dr. Frederick, of Bradford, Vt.; from Germany, before 1759; m. Sally ———; removed to Pennsylvania.—*McKeen's Bradford, p. 392.*

AMORY, Thomas, of Boston, Mass.; from Limerick to So. Carolina and Boston, 1721.—*Cullen's Irish in Boston, p. 53.*

ANDERSON, ———, of Warren, Me.; from Scotland, 1753; removed to Falmouth.—*Eaton's Warren, pp. 85, 120.*

ANDERSON, Allen, of Londonderry, N. H.; from Ireland, cir. 1718; d. without issue.—*Parker's Londonderry, p. 259.*

ANDERSON, Archibald, of Warren, Maine; from Bannockburn, Scotland, 1753; m. Anne Malcolm; Children: James, Archibald, John, Samuel; d. 1783.—*Eaton's Warren, pp. 85, 120, 122, 375.*

ANDERSON, Jacob, of Freeport, Maine; from Dungannon, Ulster County, Ireland, cir. 1710; Child: Jacob.—*Wheeler's Brunswick, p. 827.*

ANDERSON, James, of Londonderry, N. H.; from Ireland, cir. 1718; Children: Samuel, Robert, James, Thomas, David, Jane, Nancy.—*Parker's Londonderry, pp. 307, 398, Morrison's Windham, N. H., p. 308.*

ANDERSON, John, of Londonderry, N. H.; from north of Ireland, cir. 1725; Children: John, James, Robert, Jane.—*Parker's Londonderry, p. 260, Morrison's Windham, N. H., p. 307.*

ANDERSON, John, of Danbury, Conn.; "from the parish of Dunfarm by Lime (Dumfermlime?) in ye Shire of Feife in North Britton"; will, probated March 6, 1740, mentions mother, Margaret Henderson; sister, Elizabeth Anderson.—*Bailey's Danbury, p. 15.*

ANDERSON, Joseph, of New Boston, N. H.; from England, 17--; m. Margaret Foster.—*Cogswell's Henniker, N. H.*

ANDERSON, Thomas, of Chester, N. H.; from Ireland, cir. 1745; m. Jean Craige; Children: William, Joseph,

John, Thomas, Agnes, Joseph, Allen, Samuel, Margaret, David; d. 1804.—*Chase's Chester, p.* 464.

ANDERSON, William, of Deerfield, Mass.; from Dunfermline, Scotland in 1758; m. Abigail Hitchcock of Brimfield; Children: William, Solomon, John, Sarah, Fanny, William, Fanny; d. 1810.—*Sheldon's Deerfield, Vol.* 2, *p.* 30.

ANDDENSON, see Anderson.

ANDREWS, John, of Boston, Mass.; from Ireland, with Captain Dennis, Nov. 1719.—*Boston Record Commission, Vol.* 13, *p.* 64.

ANDREWS, Rev. Samuel; from England to New England, Oct. 8, 1761, (sailing).—*Money Book* 48-155, *Emigrant Ministers to America, p.* 11.

ANNAN, David, of Peterborough, N. H.; from Cupar of Fife, Scotland; b. 1754; son of John; m. Sarah Smith; Children: Sarah, David S., John, Mary, Robert, James, Jane, Amelia; d. 1802, in Ireland.—*Parker's Londonderry, p.* 188, *Smith's Peterborough, pt.* 2, *p.* 14.

ANTHOINE, Nicholas, of Marblehead, Mass.; from Isle of Jersey, cir. 1750; m. 1. Anne Hawkes, Dec. 3, 1755; m. 2. Rebekah LeGrow; Children: Anna, John, Rachel, Nicholas.—*Marblehead Vital Records, Cochran's Antrim, p.* 341.

APTHORP, Charles, of Boston, Mass.; from England; b. 1698; son of John and Susan Apthorp; m. 1726, Grizzell Eastwick; Children: Charles Ward, Grizzell, Susan, John East, James, Anne, Henry, Stephen, Joseph, Elizabeth, Thomas, Catharine, George, Robert, Rebecca, William, Catharine.—*Bridgman's Memorials, p.* 276.

ARBUCKLE, ———, of Merrimack, N. H.; from Ireland, before 1748; Children: William, Sarah, and a daughter.—*Secomb's Amherst, N. H., p.* 485.

ARCHELAUS, Henry, of Weare, N. H.; Hessian Soldier; m. ———, Paige; Children: Sally, Olive, Charles, Henry.—*Little's Weare, N. H.*

ARCHIBALD, John, Londonderry, N. H.; from Ireland, before 1730; m. Margaret ———; Children: Robert,

Elenor, Elizabeth, John, James.—*Coll. Me. Hist. Soc., Vol.* 11, *Vital Records of Londonderry.*

ARGENT, William, Boston, Mass.; farmer; from London, with Capt. Norris, June 1717, with intent to return in the spring; warned out Feb. 11, 1718.—*Boston Rec. Com., Vol.* 13, *p.* 33.

ARMINGTON, George, lately arrived in Boston from Ireland, 1718, ship "St. George Merchant," George Brown commander.—*Court of Sessions of the Peace,* 1715-18, *Vol.* 2, *p.* 213.

ARMSBY, John, of Medfield, Mass.; before 1704; m. Mehitable Boyden; Children: Mehitable, Joshua.— *Tilden's Medfield, p.* 306.

ARMSTRONG, John, of Boston, Mass.; lately arrived in Boston from Ireland, 1718, in the brigantine "Robert," James Ferguson commander; wife and four children.—*Court of Sessions of the Peace, p.* 210.

ARMSTRONG, Deacon John, of Windham, N. H.; from Londonderry, Ireland; b. 1713 (near Londonderry, Ireland); son of Robert Armstrong; m. Janet Wiley, d. October 12, 1772; Children: Janet, Agnes, Ann, John, Robert, David, Mary, John, David; d. May 6, 1795.—*Morrison's Windham, N. H., p.* 318, *American Ancestry, Vol.* 3, *p.* 3, *N. H. Genealogy, p.* 935.

ARMSTRONG, Robert, of Londonderry, N. H.; from County Londonderry, Ireland; see his son John.— *N. H. Genealogy, p.* 935.

ARMSTRONG, James, of Cape Elizabeth, Maine; from Ireland, in 1718; Children: Thomas, John, James.— *Smith's and Dean's Journal, p.* 60, *Willis's Portland, p.* 788.

ATKINS, Henry; from Bristol, England, 1716, "sail maker."—*Boston Rec. Com., Vol.* 29, *p.* 233.

ATKINS, Joseph, of Boston, Mass.; from Cork, Ireland, with Capt. Benedict Arnold, Aug. 1736; for Philadelphia.—*Boston Record Com., Vol.* 13, *p.* 312.

ATKINSON, Mrs. E., of Boston, Mass.; from London, dressmaker; "now at Mr. Edward Oakes's in Cornhill St.," 1729.—*News Letter,* 27 *March* 1729.

ATTWOOD, Thomas, of Boston, Mass.; from Bristol, England, 1716; gentleman.—*Boston Rec. Com., Vol.* 29, *p.* 233.

AUCHMUTY, ———, of Warren, Me.; from Scotland, 1753; removed to Boston.—*Eaton's Warren, pp.* 85, 121.

BABBIDGE, James, of North Yarmouth, Maine; from Uffculme, Devonshire, England, before 1730; b. 1697; son of James and Prudence.—*N. E. Hist. Gen. Reg., Vol.* 14, *p.* 30, *Wheeler's Brunswick, p.* 828.

BADGER, George; from Island of Jersey, husbandman; b. abt. 1718; volunteer against the West Indies, 1740. —*Colonial Wars* 1799.

BAGE, James, Boston, Mass.; butcher; from England, July-August 1716; warned out, Sept. 29.—*Boston Rec. Com. Vol.* 13, *p.* 11.

BAILEY, Thomas; clerk from England to "Naraganzett," 1712.—*Emigrant Ministers to America, p.* 12.

BAKER, George, Boston; upholsterer; from London, Enggland, 1699.—*Suffolk Court of Common Pleas,* 1699-1701, *p.* 64.

BAKER, James, Boston; from Great Britain, 1713; warned out, June 9, 1714.—*Boston Rec. Com., Vol.* 11, *p.* 186.

BAKER, John, of Concord, Mass.; came from Bristol, England, cir. 1720; m. Elizabeth ———; Child: John. —*Haywood's Westminster, Mass.*

BAKER, John, of Waltham, Mass.; from England, 1738; Child: Richard; removed to Killingly, Conn.— *Cochran's Antrim, p.* 346.

BALDERSON, Thomas; convict assigned to Apthorp and Hancock, July 18, 1747. From Wm. Cookson of Hull.

BALES, William, Wilton, N. H.; from Wales; impressed, deserted at Salem, Mass.; Child: William.—*Livermore and Putnam's Wilton, p.* 303.

BALLOCH, James, of Cornish, N. H.; from Scotland, 1796; b. 1761, in Antwerp, Stirlingshire, Scotland; m. Sarah Chase of Cornish, Nov. 10, 1796 (b. 1775,

d. 1840); Children: James, George W., Mary Francis, Allen, Margaret, Charles, Sarah J., Janette, William; d. Feb. 27, 1831.—*Child's Cornish, II, p. 15.*

BANISTER, Samuel; from London, 1716, with Mad^m Banister; merchant.—*Boston Rec. Com., Vol. 29, p. 233.*

BANUM, James, Boston; from ———, with Capt. Gerrish; warned out Feb. 1794.—*Boston Rec. Com., Vol. 11, p. 31.*

BARBER, ———, of Westerly, R. I.; from England.—*Thomas's History of Printing, Vol. 2, p. 82.*

BARBOUR, James, of Portland, Me.; from Ireland, 1718; son of John, Sr.; m. ——— Gibbs, widow; Children: Andrew, Mary.—*Smith's and Dean's Journal, p. 57.*

BARBOUR, John, Sr., of Portland, Me.; from Ireland, in 1718; Children: John, James, Hugh; drowned Jan. 19, 1719.—*Smith's and Dean's Journal, p. 57.*

BARBOUR, John, of Portland, Maine; from Ireland, in 1716 or 1717; son of John Barbour, q. v.; Children: Adam, Mary, Anne, Hannah.—*Smith's and Dean's Journal, p. 57, Willis's Portland, p. 788.*

BARBOUR, Matthew, of Western, now Warren, Me.; also of Westfield and Pelham, Mass.; m. 1726-7, Mrs. Mary (Gray) Blair, widow of William; Children: Mary, Robert, Sarah, Lydia.—*Leavitt's Blair Family, p. 139.*

BARBOUR, Robert, of Weston and Worcester, Mass.; from Ireland in 1718; b. Parish of Koppro, Co. Tyrone, Ireland; m. in Weston, Feb. 26, 1725-6, Sarah Gray of Worcester: she b. 1704, Co. Tyrone; d. June 9, 1790; Children: James, Elizabeth, Sarah, John, Matthew; d. Sept. 27, 1769, at Worcester, aged 68; a clothier; Robert is said to have had a brother Hezekiah of Westfield.—*Lincoln's Worcester, p. 49, E. D. Barbour's notes.*

BARCLAY, Andrew, of Boston, Mass.; from Scotland, cir. 1764.—*Thomas's History of Printing, Vol. 2, p. 230.*

BARCLAY, William, from England to New England, 1703; clerk.—*Emigrant Ministers to America, p. 12.*

BARNES, see also Barron.
BARNES, John, of Concord, Mass.; from England, 1730; b. 1708; m. —— Heselton, of Boston; Children: Joseph, Josiah, John, Amos, and three daughters; soldier at Quebec; d. 1762, at Quebec.—*Ancient Wethersfield, p.* 46.
BARNES, Robert, Boston, Mass.; from England, with Captain Eves, Dec. 24, 1716; a butcher; warned out June 4, 1717.—*Boston Rec. Com., Vol.* 13, *p.* 20.
BARNET, James, Boston; from Ireland, in ship Elizabeth; warned Nov. 3, 1719.—*Boston Rec. Com., Vol.* 13, *p.* 63.
BARNET, John, of Londonderry, N. H.; from County Antrim, Ireland, 1719; schoolmaster; m. Joan Seaford, 1721.—*Parker's Londonderry, pp.* 44, 90, *Williamson's Belfast, p.* 91.
BARNS, Mark, of Providence, R. I.; from Waterford, Ireland, cir. 1775.—*Murray's Irish Rhode Islanders, p.* 33.
BARR, Gabriel, of Nutfield, N. H.; from Ireland, cir. 1720; and unmarried after a courtship of forty years.—*History of Bedford, N. H., p.* 864, 100*th Anniversary of Bedford, p.* 289.
BARR, James, of Londonderry, N. H. and Goffstown, N. H.; from Ireland, cir. 1720; b. 1705 in Ballymoney, County Antrim; nephew of Gabriel, John and Samuel; m. Ann McPherson; b. 1708, in Ballymoney; d. 1798; Children: John, Sarah, James, Samuel, Molly; d. May 1, 1788.—*History of Bedford, pp.* 864, 865, *Hadley's Goffstown, p.* 26, 100*th Anniversary of Bedford, p.* 289.
BARR, James, of New Ipswich, N. H.; from Kilbrachan, Renfrewshire, Scotland, cir. 1773; b. Dec. 12, 1752; m. 1783 Molly Cummings, b. 1764, d. 1845; Children: James d. e., Nancy, Sarah, James, George, Caroline-Matilda, Cummings, Robena, Charlotte, William, Mary Whitehill, John, Esther, Jane, Charles, d. e.; d. March 7, 1829.—*Chandler and Lee's New Ipswich, p.* 208.

BARR, John; from Ballymoney, County Antrim, Ireland, cir. 1720; m. Jean ———, d. Nov. 11, 1737, in 66 years of her age & "17 years in this land"; he was in the Siege of Londonderry, Ireland, 1688-9.— *History of Bedford, N. H., p.* 863, 100*th Anniversary of Bedford, p.* 289.

BARR, Samuel, of Londonderry, N. H.; from Ireland, cir. 1720; m. ———; Child: Jean, b. Jan. 4, 1744; m. Daniel Hall, of Chester, N. H.; moderator, Selectman, 1741-2, Representative and 1761-1767 Colonel of the Regiment.—100*th Anniversary of Bedford, p.* 289.

BARRON, Elias, of Concord and Surry, N. H. ["Barnes"]; from Ireland, cir. 1750; brother of William.—*Kingsbury's Surry, p.* 437.

BARRON, Oliver; from Ireland, cir. 1750; brother of William.—*Kingsbury's Surry, p.* 437.

BARRON, William, of Concord, Mass., Keene, and Surry, N. H.; m. Isabel Larrabee, of Lunenburg, 1753; d. 1770; daughter of Samuel Larrabee; m. 2. Tabitha Williams, 1770; d. 1775; m. 3. Jemima ———; b. 1739; Children: Lucy, Isabel, Marion, William, Bethuel, Bethany, Leonard; d. 1796.—*Kingsbury's Surry, p.* 437.

BARTLETT, Henry, of Marlborough, Mass.; from Wales. —*Reed's Rutland, p.* 108.

BARTLEY, Robert, M. D., of Londonderry, N. H.; from Armagh, Ireland, cir. 1790; educated at Dublin University and Edinburgh; Children: Hugh, John McC., Robert, Nancy McC.; d. 1820.—*Parker's Londonderry, p.* 215, *Morrison's Windham, N. H., p.* 334.

BATLEY, John, of Worcester, Mass.; from Ireland, in 1718; there was a Nathaniel, of Dedham, in 1730.— *Lincoln's Worcester, p.* 49.

BARTHELEME, Claudius, of Derby, Conn.; from France, cir. 1750; b. 1737; m. Susanna Plumb, daughter of Samuel; b. 1744; d. Jan. 16, 1818; Children: Anne, Mary, Jerrod, Susanna, Joseph, Sarah, Anne, Henrietta, Claudius; d. October 10, 1824 aet 87.— *Orcutt's, Derby Conn., p.* 694.

BASKER, Joseph, Boston, Mass.; from Bristol, England, before 1715; wool comber; came in the "Marlborough" Galley; Samuel Peard, master asks for his liberty.—*Court of Sessions of the Peace, 1715.*

BAS, Joseph, of Dresden, Me.; from France.—*Huguenots in Dresden, p. 18.*

BATTERSON, George, of Fairfield, Conn.; from Scotland; m. Mary Oysterbanks; Child: George.—*American Ancestry, Vol. 3, p. 4.*

BATTESON, James; clockmaker, Boston; from Pennsylvania, August, 1707; warned out.—*Boston Rec. Com., Vol. 11, p. 64.*

BEAL, George, of Willington, Ct. or Deerfield, Mass.; from England, cir. 1726; graduate of Oxford; m. 1. ———; m. 2. 1742, Mary Hinsdale, widow; Children: William, Matthew; d. 1761.—*Sheldon's Deerfield, p. 79.*

BEAL, Zachariah, Portsmouth, N. H.; from England; Children: Zachariah and others.—*Fitt's Newfields, p. 434.*

BEARD, Andrew, of New Boston, N. H.; from Ireland, in 1766; Child: Joseph; d. 1798 aged 88.—*Cogswell's New Boston, p. 380.*

BEATH, John, Boothbay, Maine; from Derry, Ireland, cir. 1718; son of Walter; m. Margaret Fullerton, 1739, d. Oct. 13, 1818; Children: Margery, Joseph, Elizabeth, Mary, Margaret; d. Dec. 9, 1798.—*Greene's Boothbay, p. 498.*

BEATH, Walter, of Lunenburg, Mass., and Boothbay, Me.; from Derry, Ireland, in 1718; b. in Derry or Tyrone, 1681; Children: John, b. 1710, Jeremiah; d. June 11, 1759, aged 79; his sister Jennet m. Wm. Fullerton, Sr.—*Greene's Boothbay, p. 497, Maine Hist. Soc. Coll., 2d Series, Vol. 9, p. 289.*

BECKETT, Giles, of Bradford, Vt.; from England, 1774, (Yorkshire); Children: Edward and three others.—*McKeene's Bradford, p. 292.*

BELL, Aaron, Boston; from Ireland on ship "Elizabeth"; warned out Nov. 3, 1719; farmer.—*Boston Record Com., Vol. 13, p. 63.*

BELL, John, of Londonderry, N. H.; from Ireland, cir. 1719; b. 1679, at Ballymoney; probably son of Matthew; m. Elizabeth Todd, abt. 1712; daughter James and Rachel Todd; Children: Letitia, Naomi, Samuel, Elizabeth, Mary, John; d. July 8, 1743, abt. 64 yrs. of age.—*Morrison's Windham, p. 336. Chase's Chester, p. 468, Codman's Francistown, p. 515, Boston Evening Transcript, Feb. 20, 1907, Parker's Londonderry, p. 262.*

BELL, John, of Bedford, N. H.; from Ireland, cir. 1736; wife, Katherine ———, b. 1697, d. 1746; Children: Mary, John, Joseph, Susanna; d. Feb. 28, 1763.— *100th Anniversary of Bedford, p. 291.*

BELL, John, of Bedford, N. H.; from Ireland, in 1739, with his mother; son of John and Katherine Bell; b. 1732, in Ireland; m. 1. Jane Carr; m. 2. Sarah Bell, of Londonderry, N. H.; Children: Joseph, John, Rachel, Susanna, Mary and six others who died in infancy.—*History of Bedford, p. 869.*

BELL, Joseph, of Bedford and Halifax, Mass.; came from Ireland, 1739; son of John and Katherine Bell; b. in Ireland.—*History of Bedford, N. H. 869.*

BELL, Thomas, of Noddle's Island, Mass.; from Ireland, 1718.—*Cullen's Irish in Boston, p. 51.*

BELL, William, of Chester, N. H.; from Scotland, before 1780; b. Paisley, Scotland; m. Beatress Barr of Glasgow; Children: William, George, Elizabeth; d. 1817.—*Chase's Chester, p. 471.*

BENNER, Henry, of Broad Bay, Maine; from Germany, before 1760.—*Miller's Waldoboro, p. 51.*

BERKELEY, George, of Newport, R. I.; from Kilkenny, Ireland, 1729.—*Murray's Irish Rhode Islanders, p. 29.*

BERRY, Edward, of Boston, Mass.; from London, cir. 1766; removed to New York.—*Thomas's History of Printing, Vol. 2, p. 230.*

BERRY, William, of Boston, Mass.; from Ireland; "Printer of Painted Paper"; living with Dr. Nazro.— *Boston Rec. Com., Vol. 15, p. 69.*

BETHELL, Jarvice, Boston, Mass.; from Ireland by way of Newfoundland, August, 1714; wife; admitted an inhabitant.—*Boston Rec. Com., Vol.* 11, *p.* 220.

BETTON, James, of Windham, N. H.; from Scotland before 1753; b. 1728; m. Elizabeth Dickey; Children: Samuel, Martha, Sarah, Agnes, Ruth, Jannet, Elizabeth, Mary, John, Silas; d. Oct. 9, 1802.—*Morrison's Windham, N. H., p.* 337.

BETTY, John, of Worcester, Mass.; weaver; d. intestate, 1748; m. Rebecca ———; bondsman William Crawford "Physician," John McKinstrey, witness.—*Worcester Probate.*

BEVERAGE, ———, of Warren, Maine; from Scotland, 1753.—*Eaton's Warren, p.* 85.

BILL, Thomas, of Boston, Mass.; from New York; warned April 27, 1724.—*Boston Record Com., Vol.* 13, *p.* 127.

BILLOW, John, of Boston; from Ireland, 1717; in ship "Alexander," Thomas Spencer; he was "an infirm person," "sickley man very Poor who came from Barbadoes" with Capt. Thomas Spencer.—*Boston Rec. Com., Vol.* 13, *p.* 41, *Court of Sessions of the Peace,* 1715-18, *Vol.* 2, *p.* 199, *Suffolk Court Files* 12463.

BIRD, Andrew, of Warren Maine; from Scotland 1753; m. ——— Hathorne; children: Jane, Agnes, Alexander; removed to Cushing; killed by a tree.—*Eaton's Warren, pp.* 85, 122, 377, 505.

BISCETT, George, of Rhode Island; from England, 1767. —*Emigrant Ministers to America, p.* 14.

BISHOP, James, of ———, R. I.; from Dublin, Ireland, before 1775.—*Murray's Irish Rhode Islanders, p.* 28.

BISHOP, Richard, Boston, Mass.; from Brooklyn, April 21, 1727; warned out July 11.—*Suffolk Court Files,* 20510.

BISSELL, Samuel, of Newport, R. I.; "anvil smith," late of England, 1717.—*Advertisement in Boston News Letter, March* 11, 1717.

BLACK, John, of Barre, Mass., and Chesterfield, N. H.; from Ireland, October, 1740; b. Jan. 29, 1730, in Ireland; m. Isabella Moore, Nov. 27, 1760, b. Rutland, March 4, 1741; children: William, Margaret. —*Randall's Chesterfield, N. H., p. 229, Kingsbury's Surry, p. 455.*

BLACK, Josiah, of Kittery, Me.; probably from Ireland. —*Saco Valley Families, p. 465.*

BLACK, Samuel, of Boston, Mass.; from Ballylin, Donegal, Ireland; mariner; m. Elizabeth Fulton; d. before 1752.—*Goldthwaite Records, Ms. Boston Athenaeum.*

BLAIR, see also Blare.

BLAIR, Abraham, of Worcester, Mass., and Londonderry, N. H.; from Aghadowey, Ireland, in 1718; children David, Hannah, Sarah, Lydia, Jenet, Mary; in defense of Londonderry 1689; he was an uncle of Robert Blair of Worcester.—*Lincoln's Worcester, p. 49, Leavitt's Blair Family, p. 147.*

BLAIR, John, of Londonderry, N. H.; from Ireland in ship "Elizabeth"; warned from Boston, Nov. 8, 1719; son of David and brother of James; m. Jennett (McCloud?); children: William, b. 1726; Ann, b. 1727-8; Elizabeth, b. 1731; son, b. 1734-5; David, b. 1737; Margaret, b. 1738; Robert, b. 1741; will probated Oct. 30, 1754.—*Cogswell's New Boston, p. 352, Boston Rec. Com., Vol. 13, p. 63, Leavitt's Blair Family, p. 151.*

BLAIR, Robert, of Worcester, Mass.; from Ireland before 1733; b. at Aghadowey about 1683; m. Isabella, daughter of David Rankin; Children: Matthew, David, b. 1708-9, John, Sarah, Dolly, William, James, Robert, Elizabeth, Mary, Joseph; he was a nephew of Abraham Blair of Londonderry and brother of William of Shrewsbury; d. in Worcester, Oct. 14, 1774.—*Perry's Scotch-Irish, Leavitt's Blair Family, p. 22, 29.*

BLAIR, William, of Framingham and Shrewsbury, Mass.; from Aghadowey, Ireland, 1718; elder brother of Robert Blair of Worcester, and nephew of Abraham

Blair; m. Mary, sister of William Gray of Worcester; Children: William, John, Robert, Elizabeth, Mary, Samuel b. 1724; d. in Framingham and bur. Aug. 23, 1724.—*Leavitt's Blair Family, p. 139.*

BLANCHER, Nicholas, Boston, Mass.; from North Carolina, with Christopher Tilden; tenants of Dr. Josias Byles; "wife and 3 or 4 children."—*Boston Rec. Com., Vol. 15, p. 55.*

BLARE, see also Blair.

BLARE, Elizabeth, daughter of David Blair, from Ireland, Aug. 17, 1718; sister of John, James, and Rachel; if the granddaughter of Abraham Blair she had returned to Ireland before 1733.—*Leavitt's Blair Family, p. 150, Suffolk Court Files, 12620, Cullen's Irish in Boston, p. 51, Boston Rec. Com., Vol. 13, p. 46.*

BLARE, Lieutenant James, of Londonderry, N. H.; from Ireland, Aug. 17, 1718; son of David Blair; m. Isabella ———; Children, James, David, b. 1729, Alexander, b. 1731, Rebecca, Margaret; James Blare of Nutfield warned from Boston Jan. 23, 1723; will probated Feb. 26, 1745-6.—*Leavitt's Blair Family, p. 151, Suffolk Court Files 12620, Cullen's Irish in Boston, p. 51, Boston Rec. Com., Vol. 13, p. 46.*

BLARE, Rachel, from Ireland, Aug. 17, 1718; daughter of David and sister of John, James, Elizabeth; m. probably Robert Love of Boston.—*Leavitt's Blair Family, p. 150, Suffolk Court Files 12620, Cullen's Irish in Boston, p. 51, Boston Rec. Com., Vol. 13, p. 46.*

BLAZO, William, of Epsom, N. H.; from France.—*Curtis's Epsom, N. H., p. 1.*

BLENCOE, Richard; from London to Boston on the ship "Mary Ann," 1774; husbandman, æt. 25, "for employment."—*N. E. Hist. Gen. Reg., Vols. 62-64.*

BOARDSLEE, John; from England to New England, 1761.—*Emigrant Ministers to America, p. 15.*

BOGGS, Samuel, of Warren, Me.; from Ireland, 1753; m. Anna ———; Children: William, John, Samuel,

Anne, Mary, dau.; d. 1783.—*Eaton's Warren, pp.* 378, 379.

BOIES, James, of Milton, Mass.; from Ireland; b. 1702; m. 1. ———; m. 2. Elizabeth Smith, daughter of Jeremiah, 1759; Child: Jeremiah Smith; d. July 11, 1798.—*Teele's Milton, p.* 397.

BOHONON, Andrew, of Salisbury, N. H.; from Scotland before 1734; son of ——— and ——— (Johnson) Bohonon; impressed at 14; b. 1709; m. Tabitha Flanders, daughter of Jacob, 1734/5, d. Feb. 18, 1810, aet. 101; Children: Sarah, Andrew, John, Jacob, Ananiah; d. cir. 1803.—*Dearborn's Salisbury, N. H., p.* 485 *et seq.*

BOLSTER, Isaac, of Uxbridge, Mass., and Rumford, Me.; from England, before 1732; m. 1. Abigail ———; m. 2. Hepsibah ———, d. July 20, 1742; Child: Isaac; d. April 28, 1753.—*Lapham's Rumford, p.* 307.

BOLTON, Agnes, of Palmer, Mass.; from Ireland; b. 1728; m. Hugh Smith, son of James, 1754; Children: Elizabeth, Joseph, Matthew, Elihu, Agnes, Mary, John; d. 1805.—*Temple's Palmer, p.* 535.

BOLTON, Dr. Hugh, of Colrain, Mass.; from Tamlaght O'Crilly, Ireland, cir. 1730; m. Elizabeth Patterson, a sister-in-law of Jerome Bonaparte; Children: Hugh, Matthew, John, Nancy, Joseph; d. June 8, 1772, aged 85.—*Ms. owned by C. K. Bolton.*

BOLTON, Thomas, of Gorham, Me.; from Tamlaght O'Crilly, Ireland, cir. 1720; m. Mary (McLellan) Craige; Children: William, Mary, Martha, Agnes; d. before 1788, aged 90.—*McLellan's Gorham, p.* 404, *Ms. owned by C. K. Bolton.*

BOLTON, William, of Windham, N. H.; from Tamlaght O'Crilly, Ireland; m. Elizabeth ———; Children: John, David, James, Grizel, Agnes; d. Apr. 22, 1755 (?), aged 73.—*Morrison's Windham, p.* 347.

BOLTON, according to the will of Samuel Bolton of Tamlaght O'Crilly, Hugh, Thomas and William were his brothers.—*Ms. owned by C. K. Bolton.*

BLACKLE, Thomas, Portsmouth, N. H.; from Haverton, Devon, before 1730; m. Mary Blackston of Dover, Jan. 14, 1731.—*N. E. Hist. Gen. Reg., Vol.* 25, *p.* 118.

BOAG, John, Portsmouth, N. H.; from Kirkwell, County of St. Magnis, Scotland, before 1724; m. Elizabeth Preston, Dec. 24, 1724.—*N. E. Hist. Gen. Reg., Vol.* 24, *p.* 18.

BLAZO, William, of Epsom, N. H.; from France.—*Curtis's Epsom, N. H., p.* 1.

BLENCOE, Richard, from London to Boston on the ship "Mary Ann," 1774; Husbandman aet 25. "for employment."—*N. E. Hist. Gen. Reg., Vols.* 62-64.

BOARDMAN, Jacob, Boston, Mass.; from Great Britain, before 1715; int. m. Philadelphia Clark, June 14, 1715.—*Boston Rec. Com., Vol.* 28, *p.* 94.

BOARDSLEE, John, from England to New England, 1761. —*Emigrant Ministers to America, p.* 15.

BOGGS, Samuel, of Warren, Maine; from Ireland, 1753; m. Anna ——; Children: William, John, Samuel, Anne, Mary; d. 1783.—*Eaton's Warren, pp.* 375, 378.

BOIES, James, of Milton, Mass.; from Ireland; b. 1702; m. 1——; m. 2 Elizabeth Smith, daughter of Jeremiah, 1759; Child: Jeremiah Smith; d. July 11, 1798.—*Teele's Milton, p.* 397.

BOHONON, Andrew, of Salisbury, N. H.; from Scotland, before 1734; son of —— and —— (Johnson) Bohonon; impressed at 14; b. 1709; m. Tabitha Flanders, daughter of Jacob, 1734/5; d. Feb. 18, 1810; aet. 101; Children: Sarah, Andrew, John, Jacob, Ananiah; d. cir. 1803. — *Dearborn's Salisbury, N. H., p.* 485 *et seq.*

BOLSTER, Isaac, of Uxbridge, Mass., and Rumford, Me.; from England, before 1732; m. 1, Abigail ——, m.

2, Hepsibah ——, d. July 20, 1742; Child: Isaac; d. April 28, 1753.—*Lapham's Rumford, p.* 307.

BOLSTER, Isaac, Boston, Mass.; from Great Britain, before 1715; int. m. Elizabeth Press, Nov. 3, 1715.—*Boston Rec. Com., Vol.* 28, *p.* 95.

BOLTON, Agnes, of Palmer, Mass.; from Ireland; b. 1728; m. Hugh Smith, son of James, 1754; Children: Elizabeth, Joseph, Matthew, Elihu, Agnes, Mary, John; d. 1805.—*Temple's Palmer, p.* 535.

BOLTON, Dr. Hugh, of Colrain, Mass.; from Tamlaght O'Crilly, Ireland, cir. 1730; m. Elizabeth Patterson, a sister-in-law of Jerome Bonaparte; Children: Hugh, Matthew, John, Nancy, Joseph; d. June 8, 1772, aged 85.—*Ms. owned by C. K. Bolton.*

BOLTON, Thomas, of Gorham, Maine; from Tamlaght O'Crilly, Ireland, cir. 1720; m. Mary (McLellan) Craige; Children: William, Mary, Martha, Agnes; d. before 1788, aged 90.—*McLellan's Gorham, p.* 404; *Ms. owned by C. K. Bolton.*

BOLTON, William, of Windham, N. H.; from Tamlaght O'Crilly, Ireland; m. Elizabeth ——; Children: John, David, James, Grizel, Agnes; d. Apr. 22, 1755 (?) aged 73.—*Morrison's Windham, p.* 347.

BOLTON, according to the will of Samuel Bolton of Tamlaght O'Crilly, Hugh, Thomas and William were his brothers.—*Ms. owned by C. K. Bolton.*

BOLTON, William, of Reading, Mass.; from Ireland, 1718; warned from Andover Jan. 30, 1718-19; m. Elizabeth White, 1720; Children: William, John; d. 1725.—*Bolton Genealogy, pp.* 4-6; *Andover Vital Records, Vol.* 2, *p.* 59; *Reading Vital Records, Vol.* 1, *p.* 29.

BOND, Robert, Portsmouth, N. H.; from Saint Mary Offerey, Devonshire, before 1722; m. Mercy Ham, Dec. 14, 1722.—*N. E. Hist. Gen. Reg., Vol.* 24, *p.* 16.

BONE, Stephen, Boston, Mass.; from Canada 1736; baker; a deserting soldier given liberty to tarry by His Excellency the Governor.—*Boston Record Com., Vol.* 13, *p.* 318.

BONNER, James, Boston, Mass.; from Virginia, before 1710; int. m. Eliza Dillarock, Jan. 3, 1711; "Forbid by ye sd Philip Dillarock.—*Boston Rec. Com., Vol.* 28, *p.* 33.

BOODY, Zechariah, of Medbury, N. H.; from France before 1716; m. Elizabeth ——, abt. 1716/7; Children: Elizabeth, Charity, Mary, Sarah, Azariah, Hannah, Abigail, Keziah, Betsy; d. cir. 1755. — *Boody Genealogy, pp.* 123-4; *Stackpole and Mason's Durham, N. H., p.* 31.

BOOKER, John, of York, Me.; from England, cir. 1707; m. Hester Adams, daughter of Thomas Adams of York, Me.; Children: James and seven others; d. after 1753.—*Wheeler's Brunswick, p.* 830; *Maine Wills, p.* 387.

BOOTHBY, Henry, of Kittery, Me.; from Ireland 1720; Children: Thomas, Samuel, James(?); perhaps removed to Scarborough, Me.—*Saco Valley Families, p.* 477; *Bourne's Wells and Kennebunk, p.* 313.

BOOTHBY, Thomas, of Wells, Me.; from Ireland, by way of Halifax, before 1720; m. ————; Children: Richard, John(?) and Henry.—*Saco Valley Families, p.* 477.

BORLAND, John, of Boothbay, Me.; from Ireland about 1778; b. Ireland 1752; m. Mrs. Sarah Campbell; Children: Sally, John, Samuel, James, Polly, Betsey C.; d. at Damariscotta Mills, 1814.—*Greene's Boothbay, p.* 409.

BOSDELL, Isaac, Portsmouth, N. H.; from London, before 1719; m. Mary Powell of Stratham, N. H.; in Portsmouth, July 27, 1719.—*N. E. Hist. Gen. Reg., Vol.* 24, *p.* 13.

BOSDET, Barnard, Portsmouth, N. H.; from London, before 1719; m. Sarah Thompson, Sept. 17, 1719.— *N. E. Hist. Gen. Reg., Vol.* 24, *p.* 13.

BOTHWELL [Bothell], Alexander of Rutland, Mass.; from Ireland, November, 1719, with Captain Dennis; m. ————; (church members); Children: Alexander, m. Margaret Kennedy, Feb. 20, 1734-5; Elijah(?).—*Vital Records of Rutland, pp.* 17, 116;

Boston Hecord Com., Vol. 13, *p.* 64; *Reed's Rutland, p.* 82.

BOWEN, Peter, Boston, Mass.; "from Engd in ye Allen" 1716 in May last with Capt. Timo Asten; warned out July 13.—*Boston Rec. Com., Vol.* 13, *p.* 5; *Suffolk Court Files* 10961.

BOWSER, William, from London to Boston on the "Success" 1774 to settle; merchant, aet 22.—*N. E. Hist. Gen. Reg., Vol.* 63, *p.* 24.

BOYCE, John, of Londonderry, N. H.; from Londonderry, Ireland; Child: Samuel.—*Lyford's Canterbury, N. H., Vol.* 2, *p.* 32.

BOYD, Adam, of New England; from Ballymoney, Ireland, in 1723; b. 1692; m. Janet Craighead; Children: Margaret, John, Janet, Agnes, Thomas, Mary, Adam, Andrew, Hannah, Elizabeth, Samuel; removed to Delaware and Pennsylvania; d. 1768.—*Sprague's Annals of the American Pulpit, Vol.* 3, *p.* 130; *Craighead Family, p.* 6.

BOYD, Rev. Alexander, of Georgetown, Me.; from Scotland, 1748; educated at Glasgow University, preached at Palmer for a time in 1748.—*Sprague's Annals of the American Pulpit, Vol.* 3, *p.* 29; *Green's Boothbay, p.* 177.

BOYD, Andrew, of East Greenwich, R. I.; (perhaps two Andrews); from Antrim, Ireland, before 1775.— *Murray's Irish Rhode Islanders, p.* 31.

BOYD, Archibald, of Palmer, Mass.; from north of Ireland; in Palmer 1742.—*Temple's Palmer, p.* 126.

BOYD, George, of Boothbay, Me.; from Ireland 1750; b. County Antrim, Ireland; m. Margaret ———, 1765; Children: Thomas; George W.; a brother of Samuel of Bristol, and Thomas of Boothbay.— *Greene's Boothbay, p.* 504.

BOYD, James, of Bristol, Maine, and Worcester, Mass.; m. Jean ———; Children: Samuel, John, James, Andrew, Margaret, William, Thomas, Joseph, Eliza. —*Boston Evening Transcript; Worcester Vital Records, p.* 31.

BOYD, Samuel, of Bristol, Me.; from Ireland, 1750; b.

County Antrim, Ireland; m. ———; Children: Thomas, called "the surveyor" to distinguish him; brother of Thomas and George of Boothbay.—*Greene's Boothbay, p.* 504.

BOYD, Thomas, of Boothbay, Me.; from Ireland 1750; b. parish of Dunt— and town of Bu-foot, County Antrim, 1732; m. 1758; Child: Adam, of Back Narrows; d. 1792; a brother of Samuel of Bristol and George of Boothbay.—*Greene's Boothbay, p.* 504.

BOYD, Rev. William, from Ireland in 1718; returned 1719(?); son of ——— Boyd of Dungiven, Derry.—*Leavitt's Blair Family, p.* 24.

BOYD, Capt. William, of Londonderry, N. H.; from Ireland in 1719; m. Alice Hunter; Children: Joseph, William, Isaac, John, Alice, James; d. 1789, aged 70; he brought over fourteen ship-loads of Scotch-Irish.—*Cochran's Antrim, p.* 371.

BOYDELL, John, of Boston, Mass.; from England, 1716; d. 1739.—*Thomas's History of Printing, Vol.* 2, *p.* 225.

BOYES, William, of Rehoboth, Mass.; aged 19 in 1724; servant of John Lym(?) of Rehoboth; runaway.—*News-Letter, Feb.* 27, 1724.

BRADFORD, James, Boston, Mass.; from New York; warned out August 31, 1723.—*Boston Rec. Com., Vol.* 13, *p.* 120.

BRADFORD, John, Portsmouth, N. H.; from London, Middlesex, before 1718; m. Dorcas Hudson, Dec. 10, 1718.—*N. E. Hist. Gen. Reg., Vol.,* 23, *p.* 395.

BRAMLEY, Benjamin, Boston, Mass.; joiner, from England with Capt. Wentworth, May, 1710; with wife; warned out.—*Boston Rec. Com., Vol.* 11, *p.* 122.

BRANCH, James, Boston, Mass.; from New York; warned out Sept. 26, 1723.—*Boston Rec. Com., Vol.* 13, *p.* 120.

BREAKENRIDGE, James, of Palmer, Mass.; from Ireland July 16, 1727; b. Scotland 1696; moved to Ireland; m. Sarah ———, 1720, d. Nov. 17, 1773, aet 79; Children: James*, William*, Francis (d. on voy-

* Members Provincial Congress, 1775.

age), Francis, Sarah, Esther, George, Margaret; d. April 5, 1767; aet. 72; James, Jr., settled in Ky. and was the ancestor of politicians.—*Temple's Palmer, p.* 415.

BREST, Mary, Boston, Mass.; from New York; warned out July 11, 1727.—*Suffolk Court Files* 20510.

BREWSTER, Isaac, of Londonderry, N. H.; from Ireland; Child: James.—*Cochran's Francestown, p.* 541.

BRIARD, John, Portsmouth, N. H.; from "Santelin in South Hamshier in Jersey," before 1726; m. Agnis Leby, Dec. 1, 1726.—*N. E. Hist. Gen. Reg., Vol.* 24, *p.* 358.

BRICKHEAD, William, from London, 1716; upholsterer. —*Boston Rec. Com., Vol.* 29, *p.* 234.

BRIDGE, Thomas, of Boston, Mass.; from England, 1704; b. Hackney, England, 1656; fourth minister of King's Chapel; m. Elizabeth ———; Children: Anna, Sarah, Thomas, Elizabeth, Ellen, Lydia, Copea; d. 1715.—*Bridgman's Memorials, p.* 260.

BRIERS, William, Boston, Mass.; labourer from London with Capt. Eves, August, 1717; warned out 23 Nov. —*Boston Rec. Com., Vol.* 13, *p.* 32.

BRIESLER, Buckhart, of Braintree, Mass., (now Briesner); "Germantown," 1757.—*Pattee's Braintree, p.* 481; *Mass. Archives, Vol.* 15a.

BRIESLER, George, of Braintree, Mass., (now Briesner); "Germantown," 1757; m. Elizabeth Hardwig, 1753. —*Pattee's Braintree, pp.* 480, 557, 478; *Mass. Archives, Vol.* 15a.

BRIMMER, Martin, of Boston, Mass.; from Hanover, Germany, before 1726; m. Susanna Sigourney, 1726; Children: Herman, Martin, Andrew, John Baker, Mary, Susanna, Elizabeth, Martin. — *Mass. Hist. Soc. Proceedings* 1858-60, *p.* 351; *Boston Record Commission, Vols.* 24, 28.

BRINLEY, Francis, of Roxbury, Mass.; from London 1710; b. London, England, son of Thomas; grad. Eton Coll.(?); m. Deborah Lyde, April 13, 1718, daughter of Edward and Catherine Lyde of Boston; Children: Thomas, Frances, Edward, Nathaniel,

Deborah, Catherine, George; d. 1742 in Roxbury.—*Temple's Framingham, Mass., p.* 484.

BRISON, John, of Warren, Maine; from Scotland 1753; no male children.—*Eaton's Warren, pp.* 85, 121.

BRITHUNE, Elizabeth, of Boston; "from New York six months since," 1733; warned out Feb. 10.—*Boston Record Com., Vol.* 13, *p.* 229.

BROCKWELL, Rev. Charles, from England to New England 1737.—*Emigrant Ministers to America, p.* 16.

BRODERICK, Thomas, of Boston, Mass.; from London before 1708; int. m. Sarah Breens, Feb. 3, 1708.—*Boston Rec. Com., Vol.* 28, *p.* 31.

BROMLEY, James, Boston, Mass.; from Ireland before 1720; int. m. Mary Boyce Sept. 24, 1720; forbid by Samuel Boyce, her father.—*Boston Rec. Com., Vol.* 28, *p.* 98.

BROOK, Edward, Portsmouth, N. H.; from Ramsgate, St. Lawrence Parish; m. Catherine Tobey, April 17, 1735.—*N. E. Hist. Gen. Reg., Vol.* 25, *p.* 122.

BROUSE, James, of Boston, Mass.; felt maker from London; admitted an inhabitant Nov. 27, 1727.—*Boston Record Com., Vol.* 13, *p.* 170.

BROWN, Mrs., from London to Boston on the "Boston Packet" to settle, 1774; lady aged 30.—*N. E. Hist. Gen. Reg., Vol.* 63, *p.* 234.

BROWN, Rev. Arthur, of Providence, R. I.; from England 1729; b. Drogheda, Ireland, 1697; son of Rev. John B. Brown.—*Emigrant Ministers to America, p.* 17.

BROWN, David, of North Bridgewater; from Ireland 1740; m. Janet Miller (m. 2 Simon Griffin); Children: Ann, John, James, Elizabeth, Ann, John, James; d. Apr. 9, 1753.—*Kingman's North Bridgewater, pp.* 456, 460.

BROWN, James, Boston, Mass.; from Great Britain, before 1717; int. m. Elizabeth Skinner, July 8, 1717. —*Boston Rec. Com., Vol.* 28, *p.* 96.

BROWN, John, Boston, Mass.; "a mariner stranger," 1709; int. m. Susana Rich, Oct. 28, 1709.—*Boston Rec. Com., Vol.,* 28, *p.* 32.

BROWN, John, of Warren, Maine; from Scotland 1753; said to have been killed by Indians.—*Eaton's Warren, pp.* 85, 122.

BROWN, Matthew, of Palmer, Mass.; from Ireland; b. 1676; Children: Thomas, William, Robert, James; d. Apr. 30, 1766, aged 80.—*Temple's Palmer, p.* 412.

BROWN, Richard, of Boston, Mass.; from London; cutler; admitted an inhabitant, and liberty to open a shop, &c. Aug. 3, 1728; m. Sarah Seadon, 1732.—*Boston Record Com., Vol.* 13, *p.* 178.

BROWN, Samuel, Middleborough, Mass., and Oxford, Maine; from England before 1775; m. Ruth, daughter Josiah and Mary Dean of Taunton, Mass.; Children: Celia, Anna, Esther, Samuel, Clarissa, Henry, Jacob Dean, Ruth Dean, Mary Staples, John, Leonard, Cyrus.—*Annals of Oxford, Mass., p.* 148.

BROWN, Timothy, Boston, Mass.; "a sick man that came from St. Martin's, belonging to Ireland, sent to the alms-house on the Province Charge."—*Boston Record Com., Vol.* 13, *p.* 275.

BROWN, Walter, Boston, Mass.; from London, August, 1715; barber; warned out in October. — *Suffolk Court Files,* 12463.

BROWNING, James, of Rutland, Mass.; came from Ireland cir. 1720; b. in Scotland, g. s.; m. Elizabeth —— in Rutland June, 1720; Children: William, Elizabeth, James, Trustram, Margaret, Joseph, Mary, John, Samuel, Martha; d. Feb. 3, 1749, aged 77.—*Hyde's History of Brimfield, p.* 380.

BROWNING, John, of Rutland, Mass.; from Ireland before 1740; m.—*Reed's Rutland, p.* 82.

BRUCE, Robert, from Scotland to New England in the "Amherst" 1774; "to settle"; carpenter, aged 34.—*N. E. Hist. Gen. Reg., Vol.* 63, *p.* 234.

BRUCE, Timothy, of Bolton, Mass.; from Scotland; m. Susanna Joslin; Child: Timothy, and perhaps Thomas, Samuel and William.—*Hayward's Gilsum, N. H., p.* 278; *Bolton Vital Records, pp.* 171, 196, 197.

BRUSH, Richard, Boston, Mass.; cordwainer from London 1731; admitted an inhabitant with liberty to open a shop 1731.—*Boston Record Com., Vol.* 13, *p.* 211.

BRYANT, Benjamin, from Bristol, England, 1716; carpenter.—*Boston Rec. Com., Vol.* 27, *p.* 233.

BUDDY, Nicholas, from Jersey cir. 1730; "whereas one Nicholas Buddy an Idle and Poor man resided in this Town for several years past, and is in danger of becoming a charge to the Town . . . and there being an offer of some of his friends of sending him to Jersey his native country &c." — *Boston Rec. Com., Vol.* 15, *p.* 33; *Proceedings of Mass. Hist. Soc.* 1859-60, *p.* 343.

BUGNON, Jacques, of Dresden, Maine; from France before 1703.—*Huguenots in Dresden, p.* 19.

BURCKHARDT, Jacob, of Braintree, Mass.; "Germantown," 1757.—*Mass. State Archives; Pattee's Braintree, p.* 480.

BURGER, Joseph, Boston, Mass.; from Great Britain, before 1716; int. m. Ann Pilsbury Oct. 17, 1716.—*Boston Rec. Com., Vol.* 28, *p.* 96.

BURK, Tobias, of ——, R. I.; from Limerick, Ireland; b. cir. 1755.—*Murray's Irish Rhode Islanders, p.* 29.

BURKMAR, Thomas, of Shirley, Mass., and Duck Trap, Maine; from Germany?; m. Mary ——; d. April 26, 1832, aet. 90; Children: Joseph, Thomas, George, John, David, Nancy, Samuel; d. May, 1826, aet 84, at Duck Trap (North port).—*Bolton's Shirley, pp.* 329-30.

BURNE, Ralph, Portsmouth, N. H.; from Shadwell, Middlesex, before 1716; m. Martha Beal, June 24, 1716. —*N. E. Hist. Gen. Reg., Vol.* 23, *p.* 392.

BURNS, George, of Milford, Mass.; from Ireland, 1736; b. 1734, son of John Sr. (below); m. Jane McQuaid, d. Nov. 30, 1814; Children: Anna, Sarah, Susannah, Hannah, Jemima, Esther, Elizabeth.; d. March 7, 1805.—*Ramsdell and Colburn's Milford, N. H., p.* 609.

BURNS, John, of Hudson and Milford, N. H.; from Londonderry, Ireland, 1736; born in Scotland cir. 1701, son of Thomas & Margaret (Leslie) Burns; came

with wife and three children; Children: Mary, John,
George, Jane, Betsy, Thomas, Martha, Sarah. —
N. H. Genealogies, p. 312; *Hadley's Goffstown, p.*
59; *Ramsdell and Colburn's Milford, N. H., p.* 608.

BURNS, John, Milford, N. H.; from Londonderry, Ireland, 1736; b. March 28, 1732, son of John (above);
m. Elizabeth Jones, 1761, daughter of Jonathan and
Elizabeth Jones of Wilmington, Mass., d. April 26,
1782; Children: John, Daniel, Elizabeth, Moses,
Joseph, Mary, Joshua; d. Jan. 16, 1825.—*N. H.
Genealogies, p.* 312; *Ramsdell and Colburn's Milford, p.* 608.

BURNS, John, of Bedford, N. H.; from Londonderry,
Ireland, 1740; m. 1, ———, d. July 9, 1745, aet.
21, no children; m. 2, Anna McQuisten of Litchfield;
Children: Robert, Margaret, William, Ann, James,
Sarah, Elizabeth, John; d. March 26, 1788, aet 77.
—*100th Anniversary of Bedford, p.* 293; *History of
Bedford, pp.* 875, 876.

BURNSIDE, ———, of Londonderry, N. H.; from Ireland
1719.—*Lincoln's Worcester, p.* 201.

BURTON, Benjamin, of Cushing, Me., from Ireland; m.
Alice Lewis; Children: Rebecca, Agnes, Mary, Alice,
Benjamin, John, Sarah, Elizabeth, Thomas, William, Jane; d. March 20, 1763.—*Eaton's Warren,
pp.* 381, 512-13.

BURTON, Mary, Boston, Mass.; from Ireland with Capt.
John Carrell, 1736; admitted.—*Boston Rec. Com.,
Vol.* 15, *p.* 3.

BURVELL, George, Boston, Mass.; from Great Britain,
before 1734; int. m. Mary Moore, June 13, 1734.
—*Boston Rec. Com., Vol.* 28, *p.* 222.

BUTLER, Jonathan, of Saybrook, Conn.; from Ireland before 1726; b. about 1700; m. Temperance Buckingham 1726; Children: Ezekiel of Branford; d. 1760,
aged 60.—*Amer. Ances., Vol.* 3, *p.* 7.

BUTLER, Malachi, of Windham, N. H., and Woodbury,
Conn.; from England, cir. 1720; m. Jemima Daggett; Children: Benjamin, Silas, Solomon, Zephe-

niah, Thankful, Susannah, Margery, Lydia, Mary.—
Cogswell's Nottingham, N. H., p. 171.

CABOT, George, of Boston, Mass.; from St. Heliers in Island of Jersey cir. 1700; bapt. 10 Feb. 1677; son of Francis and Susanne (Gouchy); m. Abigail Marston of Salem, daughter of Benjamin; d. 9 Oct. 1709; Children: Abigail, Marston; d. 1717.—*Ms. in possession of George C. Cabot; Ms. in possession of N. E. Hist. Gen. Soc.*

CABOT, John, of Salem, Mass.; from St. Heliers, Island of Jersey cir. 1700; bapt. 7 April 1680, son of Francis and Susanne (Gouchy); m. Anna Orne, daughter of Joseph, 29 Oct. 1702, d. 1772, aet. 94; Children: Susanne, John, Esther, Mary, Ann, Margaret, Elizabeth, Francis, Joseph; d. 7 June 1742, in Salem.—*Ms. in possession of George C. Cabot; Ms. in possession of N. E. Hist. Gen. Soc.*

CAKLE, Roger, came with Alexander Ralston 1773.—*Wyman's Charlestown, p.* 163.

CALDER, Robert, Boston, Mass.; from Great Britain before 1720; int. m. Hannah Lawrence of Charlestown, Feb. 3, 1720. — *Boston Rec. Com., Vol.* 28, *p.* 98.

CALDERWOOD, James, of Londonderry, N. H.; from Londonderry, Ireland, November, 1725; m. Margaret ———; Children: Jane b. Ireland, John, Robert.—*Eaton's Warren, Me., p.* 514.

CALDERWOOD, John, of Vinal Haven, and Warren, Me.; from Ireland, 1725; b. Ireland Feb. 15, 1725; son of James; parents settled in Londonderry, N. H.; m. Elizabeth McCordy; Children: Thomas, Jesse, and eleven others; d. 1808.—*Hundredth Anniversary Vinal Haven, Me., p.* 48; *Eaton's Warren, Me., p.* 514.

CALDWELL, William, of Worcester, Mass.; from Ireland in 1718; in defense of Londonderry 1689; church member in Worcester 1733.—*Lincoln's Worcester, p.* 49; *Perry's Scotch-Irish, p.* 14.

CALL, Philip, of Salisbury, N. H.; from England before 1733; m. ————; Children: Stephen, Sarah; d.

before Nov. 28, 1763.—*Dearborn's Sailsbury, pp.* 518-9.

CALLWELL, Alexander, Portsmouth, N. H.; from Clough, County Antrim, before 1741; m. Margaret McGregor of Londonderry, N. H., at Portsmouth Nov. 4, 1741.—*N. E. Hist. Gen. Reg., Vol. 27, p. 13.*

CALWELL, Hannah. See James Wason.

CALWELL, John, Portsmouth, N. H.; from Ireland before 1734; b. at Clough, County Antrim; m. Isabel Wasson of the same County, in Portsmouth, March 20, 1735.—*N. E. Hist. Gen. Reg., Vol. 25, p. 122.*

CAMPBELL, Alexander, of Danville, N. H.; from Ireland 1728; b. Ulster, Ireland; Child: Annas.—*Cogswell's Henniker, p. 478.*

CAMPBELL, Alexander, of Georgetown, Me.; from Scotland 1729; m. Frances Drummond. — *Wheeler's Brunswick, p. 840.*

CAMPBELL, Archibald, of Oxford, Mass.; from ——— 1750; Children: Alexander, Edward R.—*Randall's Chesterfield, p. 240.*

CAMPBELL, Daniel, of Rutland, Mass.; from Scotland 1716; b. Scotland 1696; killed March 8, 1744, by Edward Fitzpatrick, an employee.—*Reed's Rutland, p. 183; Monumental Inscriptions, Rutland, p. 10.*

CAMPBELL, David, of Litchfield, N. H.; from Scotland; Child: William; d. 1777, aged 85.—*Cochran's Francestown, p. 565.*

CAMPBELL, Elizabeth of Boston; from Glasgow to Boston in 1716 with her mother and four daughters, in snow "Amity."—*Boston Rec. Com., Vol. 29, p. 232.*

CAMPBELL, Henry, of Londonderry, N. H.; from Londonderry, Ireland, 1733; b. 1697; m. Martha Black; Children: William, Samuel, James, John, Henry, Daniel and a daughter; d. 1785 aged 88.—*Secomb's Amherst, p. 526; Morrison's Windham, p. 356; Merrill's Ackworth, p. 194; Cogswell's Henniker, p. 484.*

CAMPBELL, Hugh, of New Salem, N. H.; from England before 1755; m. Margaret Kelso; Children: James, John, Robert, William, Polly. — *Whiton's Antrim, p. 61.*

CAMPBELL, James, of Londonderry, N. H.; from Ulster, Ireland, in ship Elizabeth; warned from Boston Nov. 3, 1719; b. about 1690 in Ulster, son of William of Campbelltown, Argyleshire, and Londonderry, Ireland; m. in Ireland Jane or Jennet Humphrey; Children: John, William, James, Elizabeth; James had a brother Samuel; James moved to Cherry Valley, N. Y., in 1741. — *Alexander's Alexander Family; Boston Record Com., Vol.* 13, *p.* 63.

CAMPBELL, John, of Boston; sent back to Ireland, old and disabled, in the brigantine "Friends Adventure," Jan. 12, 1769.—*Boston Rec. Com.*

CAMPBELL, John Gillis, of Boston; from Scotland; m. Jeannette Baird; d. Warren, Me., 1809.—*Eaton's Warren, p.* 412.

CAMPBELL, Patrick, Boston, Mass.; from Great Britain before 1711; int. m. Susanna Griffin July 9, 1711. —*Boston Rec. Com., Vol.* 28, *p.* 91.

CAMPBELL, Robert, of New London, Conn.; from Ireland cir. 1719; b. in Ulster, Ireland, 1673; m. Janet, d. 1729; Children: Charles and five others; d. 1725. —*Hadley's Goffstown, N. H., p.* 73.

CAMPBELL, Robert, of Townsend, Mass., and Londonderry, N. H.; from Ireland, before 1730; m. Elizabeth Waugh; Child: Robert; d. 1792.—*Cogswell's New Boston, p.* 412; *Documentary History of Maine, p.* 24.

CAMPBELL, Robert, of New Ipswich, N. H.; from Scotland before 1760; m. (?) 2, Margaret ——; d. Nov. 1, 1810, aet 51 years; Children: Caleb and probably others; d. after 1791.—*Chandler and Lee's New Ipswich, p.* 289; *New Ipswich Epitaphs Ms., p.* 27.

CANELL, Philip, of Portland, Pearsontown and Standish, Me.; from Isle of Man before 1770; m. Jane ——; Children: Nancy, Thomas, Philip, Jane, Joseph, Ellen; d. 1824 aet 81 years.—*Saco Valley Families, p.* 127; *McLellan's Gorham, p.* 422.

CARGIL, David, of Londonderry, N. H. [called David Calgik]; from north of Ireland, 1718; selectman at Londonderry 1719. — *Supplement to Morrison's Wind-*

ham, p. 64; *Documentary History of Maine*, Vol. 11, p. 24.

CARGILL, James, of Mendon, Mass.; clothier; will probated Nov. 7, 1753; m. Sarah ——; Children: Mary Arnold, Benjamin, Chloe [m. a Gilson], Lucy, James; [Seth Arnold exr.].—*Worcester Probate*.

CARLETON, Joseph, of Newton, Mass.?; from England before 1715; m. Abigail Osgood; Children: David, Jonathan, Moses, Jeremiah, Mary, Abigail.—*Cochran's Francestown*, p. 568.

CARLISLE, Alexander, of Boston, Mass.; from Scotland cir. 1743.—*Thomas's History of Printing*, Vol. 2, p. 226.

CARLO, Phillip, Boston, Mass.; from "Philadelphy" 1734; wife and two children warned out April, 1734. —*Suffolk Court Files*.

CARLOR, Jacob, of Dresden, Maine; from France, *Huguenots in Dresden*, p. 18.

CARNOT, John, Londonderry, N. H.; from Londonderry, Ireland, before March 17, 1730.—*Documentary History of Maine*, Vol. 11, p. 20.

CARPENTER, Samuel, Boston, Mass.; from Great Britain before 1715; int. m. Martha Smallage Sept. 8, 1715. —*Boston Rec. Com.*, Vol. 28, p. 94.

CARR, ——, see also Karr.

CARR, Thomas, Boston, Mass.; from Great Britain before 1715; int. m. Elizabeth Clay Oct. 22, 1715.—*Boston Rec. Com.*, Vol. 28, p. 96.

CARSON, John, of New Boston and Francestown, N. H.; from the Highlands of Scotland before 1756; son of John Carson; m. (?) Mary Livingston, d. March, 1773; Children: John, Simon, Robert; d. 1792 aged about 90.—*Cochran's Francestown*, pp. 569, 570.

CARSON, William, of Francestown and Lyndboro, N. H.; from the Highlands of Scotland before 1770; son of John, and brother of John above; m. Issable Johnson of Lyndborough; Children: Robert, William, Mary, Asa; d. 1818 aet 96 years.—*Cochran's Francestown*, pp. 572-574.

CARSWELL, John, of Warren, Maine; from Scotland, 1753.—*Eaton's Warren, pp.* 85, 122.
CARTER, James, from London before 1740; ropemaker; b. cir. 1697; volunteer against the West Indies 1740. —*Colonial Wars,* 1899.
CARTER, Miles, from Ireland, tanner, before 1740; b. cir. 1700; volunteer against the West Indies, 1740.— *Colonial Wars,* 1899.
CARTY, Francis, Boston, Mass.; from Dublin on the ship "Globe," 1717; "Irish seaman." "of about 18 years, being a slender man, full of freckles in his Face, wears his own Curled Bushy Brown hair."—*Boston News Letter Sept.* 30-*Oct.* 7, 1717.
CARULESS, Nathaniel, Boston, Mass.; arrived from northern Ireland, 1718, in the ship "William," Robert Montgomery, master; wife and four children. — *Court of Sessions of the Peace.*
CASEY, John, of Groton, Mass.; from Ireland, cooper, about 21 in 1754; he ran away from his master John Blair of Groton.—*Boston Evening Post. Oct.* 7, 1754.
CASTNER, Anthony, of Waldoboro, Maine; from Germany, cir. 1764; to North Carolina after 1770.—*Miller's Waldoboro, p.* 67.
CASTNER, Wilbaldus, Broad Bay, Waldoboro, Maine; from Germany before 1764; m. Justina ———. — *Miller's Waldoboro, p.* 64.
CASWELL, Miss Susannah, Boston, Mass.; from London, April 25, 1727; warned out July 11 (return).— *Suffolk Court Files* 20510; *Boston Rec. Com., Vol.* 13, *p.* 167.
CATES, Joseph, of Gorham, Maine; from Greenwich, England, before 1745; m. Deborah Cobb at Cape Elizabeth, 1745; Children: James, Abigail, Benjamin, Joseph, Deborah, Elizabeth, Sarah, Andrew, Ebenezer, Lydia; d. 1810 aged 89.—*McLellan's Gorham, p.* 424.
CAVALEAR, Louis, of Frankfort, Me.; from France in 1752; Child: Mary m. Louis Houdlette q. v.—*Maine*

Hist. Soc. Coll. 2nd Series, Vol. 3, p. 356; Huguenots in Dresden, p. 18.

CEARL, Joseph, of Boston, Mass.; from Bristol, England, in 1716; cordwainer.—*Boston Rec. Com., Vol. 29, p. 232.*

CHANDLER, John, of Worcester, Mass.; before 1738.—*Parmenter's Pelham, p. 17.*

CHANDLER, R., Boston, Mass.; from London on the "Minerva" 1774 to settle; gentleman aged 25.—*N. E. Hist. Gen. Reg., Vols. 62-64.*

CHANDLER, William, Portsmouth, N. H.; from Dedford, Kent, before 1714; m. Elizabeth Lucy of Portsmouth Dec. 2, 1714.—*N. E. Hist. Gen. Reg., Vol. 23, p. 271.*

CHISIEL, John, of Worcester, Mass.; from Ireland before 1733.—*Perry's Scotch-Irish, p. 14.*

CHRISTIE, Jesse, of Londonderry, N. H.; from Ireland before 1727; m. 1 ———, m. 2 Mary ———; Children: Peter, George.—*Hadley's Goffstown, p. 85.*

CHRISTIE, Peter, of Londonderry, N. H.; from Ireland before 1727; b. 1710 in Ireland, the son of Jesse; m. Jane Moer of Londonderry; Child: Jesse.—*Hadley's Goffstown, p. 85.*

CHURCH, George, Portsmouth, N. H.; from Rumford, Essex, before 1732; m. Mary Stevens Dec. 26, 1732. —*N. E. Hist. Gen. Reg., Vol. 25, p. 119.*

CHUTE, Thomas, of Portland, Me.; from London to Marblehead after 1700; b. 1692; m. Mary ———; Children: Abigail and others.—*Smith's and Dean's Journal, p. 112.*

CILLY, ———, of "Broad Bay," Me.; from Germany cir. 1768; removed to North Carolina. —*Eaton's Warren, p. 134.*

CINAE, Honora, Boston, Mass.; from Ireland with Captain John Carrell, 1736; wife of Dinish Cinae; Children: James, Peter; admitted Sept. 18, 1736.—*Boston Rec. Com., Vol. 15, p. 3.*

CLAGGETT, Wyseman, of Dunstable, Mass., and Portsmouth, N. H.; from Bristol, England, cir. 1758; b. 1721; in 1748 of Antigua; m. Lettice Mitchel, 1759; Children: Martha, Clifton, Wentworth, Edward, Ritta, John, William, John K.; d. Litchfield Dec. 4, 1784.—*Secomb's Amherst, p.* 533; *Fox's Dunstable, p.* 221.

CLARIDGE, Ambrose, Boston, Mass.; from Great Britain before 1718; int. m. Tabitha Mitchell, Aug. 13, 1718.—*Boston Rec. Com., Vol.* 28, *p.* 97.

CLARK, Archibald, of Londonderry, N. H.; from Ireland before 1730.—*Documentary History of Maine, Vol.* 11, *p.* 24.

CLARK, James, of Londonderry and Windham, N. H.; from Ireland before 1730; m. ———; Children: John, Matthew, Eleanor, Samuel, George.—*Morrison's Windham, p.* 377; *Documentary History of Maine, Vol.* 11, *p.* 24.

CLARK, James, of Rutland, Mass.; from Ireland in 1718; m. Mary ———; Children: George, John and five more; killed Aug. 3, 1724, "an oldish man."—*Lincoln's Worcester, p.* 49; *Worcester Soc. Ant., Vol.* 7, *p.* 77; *Worcester Vital Records.*

CLARK, John, of Worcester and Colrain, Mass.; from Ireland 1718 or 1719; m. Agnes Adams; Children: Jane, Matthew, Thomas, John, James, William, Samuel, Elizabeth, George; will probated 1750; d. in South Hadley, Mass.—*McClellan's Colrain, p.* 66; *Wall's Reminiscences of Worcester, p.* 128.

CLARK, John, of Rutland, Mass.; from Ireland before 1726; John Clark "a North Brittain" of Rutland warned from Boston July 15, 1726; m. Mary McIein Feb. 26, 1730; Children: Elizabeth, Isabell, James.—*Perry's Scotch-Irish, p.* 14; *Rutland V. R., pp.* 26, 125; *Boston Record Com., Vol.* 13, *p.* 154.

CLARK, Joseph, of Worcester, Mass.; from Ireland before 1733; m. Sarah ———; Children: Joseph, Sarah (m.

Jerathneel Wilder), Mary (m. William Stone), Easter (m. Solomon Bixby), Priscilla (m. Aaron Wilder); d. betw. Dec. 1767 and June 11, 1772.—*Perry's Scotch-Irish, Worcester Probate, Series A,* 12160.

CLARK, Matthew, of Worcester, Mass., and Londonderry, N. H.; from Ireland before 1733; m. Jennette ———; Children: Jane, John, Alexander, Agnes.—*Perry's Scotch-Irish, p.* 14; *Documentary History of Maine, Vol.* 11, *p.* 24; *Worcester Vital Records.*

CLARK, Matthew, of Lancaster, Mass.; from Ireland, before 1740; "Matthew Clark and wife in communion with the Irish Church in Worcester. Probably son of John of Worcester; m. Elizabeth ———; Children: James, Mary, Elizabeth, Matthew, William, Mary, John, Daniel, Sarah; d. July 9, 1761. —*Lancaster Vital Records, pp.* 285, 289, 290, 293-298, 323, 324: *Worcester Probate, Series A.,* 12223.

CLARK, Rev. Matthew, of Londonderry, N. H.; from Ireland cir. 1729; second minister in Londonderry; m. Mrs. James McGregor, Jan. 9, 1733, in Boston; d. Jan. 25, 1735, aged 76.—*Parker's Londonderry, p.* 137.

CLARK, Moses, from England to New England, 1720.—*Emigrant Ministers to America, p.* 20.

CLARK, Robert, of Londonderry, N. H.; from Ireland cir. 1725; m. Letitia Cockran; Children: William, John, Samuel, Ninian, Jane, Letitia, Agnes, Elizabeth; d. 1775.—*Parker's Londonderry, p.* 265.

CLARK, Samuel, of Brunswick, Me.; from Ireland before 1739; m. probably in Boston Martha ——— also from Ireland.—*Wheeler's Brunswick, p.* 830.

CLARK, Thomas, of Boston, Mass.; from London, before 1764; shop at the south side of the Court House, 1764.—*Boston Gazette, Nov.* 12, 1764.

CLARK, William, Boston, Mass.; from New York, with wife and three children; warned August 12, 1724.—*Boston Rec. Com., Vol.* 13, *p.* 134.

CLARK, William, of Boston, Mass.; from London, before 1729; brush maker; admitted an inhabitant, and liberty to open a shop &c. March 5, 1729.—*Boston Record Com., Vol. 13, p. 180.*

CLARK, William, from England to New England, 1769. —*Emigrant Ministers to America, p. 20.*

CLARKE, Edward, Portsmouth, N. H.; from London before 1725; m. Christian Buskby, of Boston, widow, Oct. 18, 1725.—*N. E. Hist Gen. Reg., Vol. 24, p. 359.*

CLARRICK, William, of Deerfield, Mass.; from Bordeaux France, 1745; captured off Louisburg 1745 and sent to Boston; d. Dec. 24, 1808, aet 75.—*Sheldon's Deerfield, Vol. 2, p. 125.*

CLAYLAND, Mrs. Elizabeth, Peterboro, N. H.; "Thomas Little m. Susanna Wallace, daughter of William and Elizabeth"; Elizabeth Clayland was Susanna's grandmother; she came from Ireland with the Wallaces and was buried at Peterborough, N. H.—*Smith's Peterborough, p. 133.*

CLAYTON, William, Boston, Mass.; from Great Britain before 1714; int. m. Margaret Clap, Oct. 13, 1714. —*Boston Rec. Com., Vol. 28, p. 94.*

CLENDENIN, Archibald, of Londonderry, N. H.; from County Antrim, Ireland, 1718, one of the sixteen original settlers. — *Parker's Londonderry, p. 44; Williamson's Belfast, p. 92.*

CLINTON, Francis, of Boston, Mass.; from Ireland 1730; joyner.—*Cullen's Irish in Boston, p. 54.*

CLOUSE, George, of Broad Bay, Maine; from Germany before 1760; Ann Elizabeth; d. Waldoboro, Maine, 1805, aged 88 years.—*Miller's Waldoboro, p. 52.*

CLYDE, Daniel, of Windham, N. H.; from Ireland, 1730; joyner; admitted inhabitant of Boston, September 9, 1730; b. 1683, Clydesdale, Scotland; m. Esther Rankin; Children: Joseph, Hugh, John, Daniel, Ann, Samuel, Mary, Nancy, Agnes; d. June, 1753. —*Morrison's Windham, p. 380; Boston Record Com., Vol. 13, p. 200.*

CLYDE, Hugh, of Windham, N. H.; b. Ireland 1724,

son of Daniel; m. Sarah ———; Children: Joseph et als.; d. 1800, in Windham.—*Hayward's Gilsum, p.* 288.

COAD, Stephen, Boston, Mass.; from Great Britain before 1714; "now Reserd. [resident.] in Boston"; int. m. Mary Woodcock of Dedham, Dec. 3, 1714.—*Boston Rec. Com., Vol.* 28, *p.* 94.

COAN, John, Boston, Mass.; butcher, with wife and one child from Philadelphia by land, abt. Nov., 1717; warned out Dec. 24, 1717.—*Boston Rec. Com., Vol.* 13, *p.* 32.

COBBIT, Phillip, from the Island of Jersey; laborer; b. cir. 1707; volunteer against the West Indies, 1740. —*Colonial Wars*, 1899.

COCHRAN, James, of Topsham, Maine; from Londonderry, Ireland, 1720; m. Letitia Patten; Children: Thomas, Peter, Molly, and one other; d. soon after arrival.—*Cogswell's New Boston, p.* 356.

COCHRAN, James, of Amherst, N. H.; from Belfast, Ireland, before 1744; Children: Jonathan(?), Robert (?), John.—*Secomb's Amherst, p.* 539.

COCHRAN, John, of Brunswick, Maine; from Ireland, 1717; m. Lily Kilgore; Children: James, Joseph, Thomas, Nathaniel, Samuel, Elizabeth, Susannah. —*Cogswell's New Boston, p.* 363.

COCHRAN, John, of Windham, N. H.; from Londonderry, Ireland, cir. 1719; b. 1704; m. Jennie McKeen, 1734; Children: John, Isaac, James, Elizabeth, Mary; d. 1788.—*Morrison's Windham, p.* 393; *Deed of Belfast, Maine,* 1769; *Cochran's Antrim, p.* 421.

COCHRAN, John, Portsmouth, N. H.; from Dunbo, Londonderry, Ireland, before 1731; m. Issabella Smith, also of Dunbo, in Portsmouth, Feb. 20, 1731.— *N. E. Hist. Gen. Reg., Vol.* 25, *p.* 118.

COCHRAN, John Ninian, of Francestown, N. H.; from Ireland, cir. 1775; Children: James, William and others.—*Cochran's Francestown, p.* 588.

COCHRAN, Thomas, of New Boston, N. H.; from Londonderry, Ireland, cir. 1720; b. Londonderry, cir

1703; son of James, q. v.; m. Jennet Adams; d. June 7, 1784, aet 76; Children: James, John, Robert, Peter, Thomas, Letitia, Elizabeth; d. November 20, 1791 aet 89.—*Cogswell's New Boston, pp.* 356, 357.

COCHRAN, William, Londonderry, N. H.; from Ireland, before March 17, 1730; m. Elizabeth MacKertney, Nov. 26, 1730.—*Documentary History of Maine, Vol* 11, *p.* 20, *Vital Records of Londonderry, N. H., p.* 197.

COCKLE, John, British soldier and deserter, 1775; impressed; Child: Polly.—*Merrill's Ackworth, p.* 280.

COCKS, Philip, Portsmouth, N. H.; from "Dratwitch," Worcestershire, before 1722; m. Jane Carter, Sept. 13, 1722.—*N. E. Hist. Gen. Reg., Vol.* 24, *p.* 15.

COD, Henry, of Amherst, N. H.; from Ireland, cir. 1744; m. Sarah Wilkins of Middletown, Mass.; Children: Henry, Sarah.—*Secomb's Amherst, p.* 540.

COFFEEN, Michael, of Topsfield, Lunenburg, and Winchendon, Mass.; from Ireland; b. before 1718; m. Lydia; Children: John, Eliezer, Lydia, Amone, Henry, Daniel, Abigail, Priscilla; d. Winchendon. —*Stearns' Rindge, N. H., p.* 478, *Lunenberg Vital Rec., p.* 280.

COFFIRAM, William, Boston, Mass.; from Ireland on the ship "Elizabeth"; warned out Nov. 3, 1719.—*Boston Rec. Com., Vol.* 13, *p.* 63.

COJAN, "Mr. Laughlin," Boston, Mass.; "an Irish seaman, being sickly, a slender man of about 26 years old, with his own Brown Hair"; came on the ship "Globe," from Dublin, 1717.—*News Letter, Sept.* 30-*Oct.* 7, 1717.

COLE, Phebe, at Boston, Mass.; with her four children "Imported into this Town in November last [1735] from New York by Capt. Griffeth."—*Boston Record Com., Vol.* 13, *p.* 298.

COLE, Robert, Boston, Mass.; from Great Britain, before 1714; int. m. Abigail Tenny April 9, 1715.— *Boston Rec. Com., Vol.* 28, *p.* 94.

COLE, Thomas, of Boston, Mass.; from London; victualer; admitted an inhabitant with liberty to open a shop, December 13, 1727.—*Boston Record Com., Vol. 13, p. 171.*

COLLINGS, George, of Kittery, Me.; from England, before 1737; m. ———; Child: Mary; sister, Elizabeth Heard of Clindleigh, Devon; d. 1737—will.— *Maine Wills, pp. 562-3.*

COLTEN, Rev. Jonathan, from England to New England, 1752.—*Emigrant Ministers to America, p. 21.*

COLTER, James, Boston, Mass.; from London with his wife and one child and Mary Newberry, single woman; 1722, admitted inhabitant on bond of Capt. James Starling, August 27, 1722.—*Boston Rec. Com., Vol. 13, pp. 1, 103.*

COMB, John, Boston, Mass.; from Great Britain before 1711; int. m. Dorothy Davis, Mar. 4, 1712.—*Boston Rec. Com., Vol. 28, p. 91.*

CONN, George, of Harvard, Mass.; from Ulster about 1720; b. cir. 1716; son of John; m. Mary ———; d. May 19, 1783 aet 70 yrs.; Children: Anne, John, George, Andrew, Rosanna, Elizabeth, Mary, Margaret, Thomas; d. Feb. 21, 1796 aet 80.—*N. E. Hist. Gen. Reg., Jan., 1927, pp. 27, 28, Stearns' Ashburnham, p. 644, Nourse's Harvard, pp. 483, 535, Cochran's Antrim, p. 435, Harvard Vital Records.*

CONNAN, Phillip, from Ireland, before 1746; husbandman; b. cir. 1716; volunteer against the West Indies, 1740.—*Colonial Wars,* 1899.

CONNOR, Charles, Boston, Mass.; with wife and child, from Philadelphia, 1732; warned out Sept. 18, "bin in Boston Six weekes."—*Boston Record Com., Vol. 13, p. 64.*

COOK, Mark, Portsmouth, N. H.; from Virginia, before 1740; b. York, Va.; m. Sarah Maddin from Limerick, Ireland, in Portsmouth, Dec. 22, 1740.—*N. E. Hist. Gen. Reg., Vol. 27, p. 9.*

COOPER, Boice, of Warren, Maine; from Ireland, cir. 1740; m. 1. Katherine Kellyhorn; m. 2. Lydia

North; Children: Boice, Elizabeth, Catherine; d. 1795 aet 75.—*Eaton's Warren, p.* 384.

COOPER, James, from London, before 1740; rope maker; b. cir. 1707; volunteer against the West Indies, 1740.—*Colonial Wars,* 1899.

COOPER, Samuel, Boston, Mass.; from Great Britain before 1719; int. m. Elizabeth Bowen of Roxbury, Sept. 3, 1719.—*Boston Rec. Com., Vol.* 28, *p.* 98.

COPLEY, Richard, of Boston, Mass.; from County Clare, Ireland, 1737; m. Mary Singleton; Child: John Singleton, the portrait painter, father of Lord Lyndhurst; d. 1737.—*Cullen's Irish in Boston, p.* 190.

CORDINER, William, from England, 1706; "clerk."—*Emigrant Ministers to America, p.* 21.

CORLEW, Edward, of Scituate, Mass.; from England, cir. 1730; m. Abigail Russell, 1732; Children: John, Edward, Thomas, William, Daniel.—*Deane's Scituate, p.* 243.

CORNISH, Walter, Boston, Mass.; from Great Britain before 1720; int. m. Elizabeth Mason June 2, 1720. —*Boston Rec. Com., Vol.* 28, *p.* 98.

CORSER, John, Boscawen, N. H.; from Scotland, before 1716; b. 1678; m. Tabitha Kenney of Newbury, 1716 or 17; Children: John, Nathan, Tabitha, Polly, Sarah, William, Hannah; d. 1776.—*Coffin's Boscawen, N. H., p.* 497.

COSSIT, Rev. Ranna, from England to New Hampshire, 1773.—*Emigrant Ministers to America, p.* 21.

COTTER, Darby, from Ireland, before 1740; laborer; b. cir. 1702; volunteer against the West Indies, 1740. —*Colonial Wars,* 1899.

COTTON, Robert, Boston, Mass.; from Great Britain, before 1717; int. m. Anna Man, Aug. 23, 1717.— *Boston Rec. Com., Vol.* 28, *p.* 96.

COUCH, Joseph, of Newburyport, Mass., and Boscowen, N. H.; from Wales, cir. 1740; m. 1. Elsie Rowell; m. 2. Mrs. Mary Webster; m. 3. Mrs. Muzzey; Children: (1) John, Elsie, Benjamin, Joseph; (2) Mary.—*Coffin's Boscawen, N. H., p.* 510.

COW, Peter, Portsmouth, N. H.; from Jersey, before

1735; m. Mary Long, Nov. 4, 1735.—*N. E. Hist. Gen. Reg., Vol.* 25, *p.* 122.

COWAN, Ephraim, of Worcester and Pelham, Mass.; from Ireland, before 1738.—*Parmenter's Pelham, pp.* 17, 442.

COWDIN, James, of Lunenburgh and Holden, Mass.; from Ireland, 1728; a barrister of Dublin; m. 1. "Lady Polly Connor"; m. 2. Janet Craig, she m. 2. Captain James Craig, d. 1776; Children: David, Thomas, Margaret, William, Samuel, Elizabeth, Robert, John, James; d. 1748 [will].—*Fitchburg Hist. Soc.,* 1897-9, *pp.* 19-24; *Worcester Probate, Series A,* 13830.

COWDIN, Thomas, Lunenburg and North Worcester, Mass.; from Ireland, 1728; b. 1720, son of James; m. 1. Experience Gray of Worcester, 1748; d. 1760; m. 2. Hannah Craig of Rutland, 1761, d. 1822; Children: Thomas, Experience, Hannah, Joseph, Angier, Daniel, James; d. 1792.—*Fitchburg Hist. Soc.,* 1897-8, *p.* 14-38, *Old Records of Fitchburg, Vol.* 2, *Worcester Probate, Series A,* 13856.

COWEE, James, of Westminster, Mass.; from Great Britain, cir. 1745; b. cir. 1726; m. Mary, dau. John Pearson of Rowley, Mass., March 3, 1757; d. March 11, 1813, aet 83; Children: John, Sarah, Mehitable, David, James, Mary, Rebecca, Nathan, Rhoda, Joel, Pearson; d. Apr. 29, 1801, aet 74 [will].—*Heywood's Westminster, p.* 590, *Worcester Probate, Series A,* 13883.

COWES, James, Boston, Mass.; from Virginia; warned out July 7, 1726.—*Boston Record Com., Vol.* 13, *p.* 153.

COWLING, Thomas, of Wells, Me.; from England, and Annapolis Royal, N. S.; brother, William, in Great Britain; cousin, Martha Davis of Annapolis Royal; cousin, John Harris, brick layer of Annapolis Royal; d. 1751, will.—*Maine Wills, pp.* 649-650.

Cox, Edward, of Boston, Mass.; from London, cir. 1766; removed to New York.—*Thomas's History of Printing, Vol.* 2, *p.* 230.

Cox, T., of Boston, Mass.; from England, cir. 1733.—*Thomas's History of Printing, Vol. 2, p. 225.*

CRAFTS, Lydia, Roxbury, Mass.; "Thomas Bedonah, a negro man belonging to Roxbury and Lydia his wife, formerly Lydia Crafts, an Englishwoman," presented for fornication before marriage, 1704.—*Court of Sessions of the Peace, 1702-12, p. 32.*

CRAIG, Alexander, of Chester, N. H.; from Ireland, 1724 or 5; Children: Alexander, Andrew, Agnes; d. in 1750.—*Chase's Chester. p. 496.*

CRAIG, Hugh, of Gorham and Windham, Maine; from Ireland, 1729 or 1730; son of ———— and Mary Craig, q. v.; b. cir. 1723; m. Elizabeth Warren in Falmouth, Nov. 11, 1749, d. 1810 aet 83; Children: Betty, Mary, Thomas, Rebecca, John, Jane, Hugh, Martha; d. March 19, 1777 aet 54.—*Lewis's Gorham, pp. 404, 405, Springvale, Me., Advocate, Oct. 2, 1903.*

CRAIG, John, of Boston, Mass.; from Ireland, cir. 1730; m. (?) Rachel Clark, April 8, 1740, at Boston.—*McLellan's Gorham, p. 404, Boston Record Com., Vol. 28, p. 214.*

CRAIG, Mary (McLellan), of Gorham and Windham, Me.; from Ireland, 1729-30; sister of Hugh McLellan of Gorham, Me., and James McLellan of Saco, Me.; m. 1. ———— Craig; Children: Jane, Hugh, (stepson John of Boston); m. 2. Thomas Bolton in Boston, d. cir. 1788; Children: William, Martha, Mary, she d. cir. 1788 aet 89.—*Lewis's Gorham, pp. 404, 406.*

CRAIGE, Robert, of Chester, N. H.; from Ireland, cir. 1736; m. Margaret Crossett; Child: Thomas; d. 1790.—*Chase's Chester, p. 497.*

CRAIGHEAD, Rev. Thomas, of Freetown, Mass.; came from Donegal, Ireland, in 1715; son of the Rev. Robert Craighead of Londonderry, Ireland; m. Margaret ————; Children: Thomas, Andrew, Alexander, John, Jane; d. April, 1739, Newville, Pa.—*Craighead Family, Craighead, pp. 35-40 et seq.*

CRAIGUE, William, of Ashby and Chelmsford, Mass.; from County Cumberland, England, cir. 1775; b. cir. 1759; m. Esther Adams, cir. 1787; Child: Samuel A.—*Contributed by Ellery L. Perkins.*

CRAMY, Dennis, of Boston, Mass.; a wigmaker from Ireland, before 1730; admitted an inhabitant and to open a shop, Dec. 11, 1730.—*Boston Record Com., Vol. 13, p. 64.*

CRANCH, Richard, of Braintree, Mass.; from England, 1746; b. in Knightsbridge, Devon, 1712; son of John Cranch; m. Mary, daughter of the Rev. William Smith of Weymouth, 1762, d. 1818; d. Oct. 16, 1811.—*Pattee's Braintree, pp. 490-492.*

CRAWFORD, Aaron, of Rutland, Mass.; from Ireland, before 1721; b. about 1677; m. Agnes ———, d. Dec. 10, 1760 aet. 82; Children: Alexander, Samuel, Martha, Mary, Moses; Brother-in-law, Samuel Orr of Pennsylvania; d. Aug. 6, 1754 aet 77 [will].—*Reed's Rutland, p. 82; Monumental Descriptions, Rutland, Mass., pp. 8, 9; Worcester Probate, Series A, 13980.*

CRAWFORD, John, of Rutland, Mass.; from Ireland with Captain Dennis, Nov., 1719; warned out of Boston, Jan., 1720; m. Isabell ———; Children: Margaret, John; tythingman, 1722. — *Reed's Rutland, p. 82, Boston Record Com., Vol. 13, p. 64.*

CRAWFORD, John, of Stirling, Me.; from Scotland, 1753; b. 1717; Children: John, Anne, James, Archibald, Alexander; d. 1809, aged 88.—*Eaton's Warren, pp. 85, 122, 387.*

CRAWFORD, Robert, of Worcester and Royalston, Mass.; from Ireland in 1718; m. Elizabeth Leitch of Lunenburg, Jan. 13, 1763; warned from Boston, 1724; Children: Elizabeth, William, James, Reuben, John Green, Joseph Warren, Manasses, Robert; d. betw. June and Oct., 1785; [will].—*Lincoln's Worcester, p. 49, Wall's Reminiscences of Worcester, p. 128, Worcester Probate, Series A, 14025.*

CRAWFORD, William, of Chester, N. H.; from Ireland, cir. 1730; m. 1. Mary Graham; m. 2. Jean ———;

Children: Robert, William, John.—*Chase's Chester, p.* 498.
CRAWFORD, Dr. William, of Worcester, Mass.; m. Martha ———; Children: Robert, John, William, Joseph, Elizabeth, Mary, Margaret, Sarah; grandson, William Crawford; brother, John Crawford; will probated June 6, 1761.—*Worcester Probate Records, Series A,* 14036.
CREAMER, Jacob, of Broad Bay, Maine; from Germany, before 1760.—*Miller's Waldoboro, p.* 51.
CREIGHTON, David, of Waldoboro, Me.; see also *Criton*; from Ireland; m. ———; Children: Abraham, Samuel, David; d. 1744, killed by Indians.—*Eaton's Thomaston, p.* 190, *Eaton's Warren, p.* 529.
CRELLIUS, Joseph, of Boston, Mass.; from Franconia, Germany, cir. 1749; removed to Philadelphia.—*Pattee's Braintree, p.* 473 *et seq.*
CRESTE, John, Boston, Mass.; from Ireland with Captain Dennis, Nov., 1719; warned out 1720.—*Boston Record Com., Vol.* 13, *p.* 64.
CRIE, John, of Martinicus, Me.; from Scotland; Children: Eben, John, Reuben.—*Eaton's Thomaston, p.* 190.
CRISTY, John, Boston, Mass.; from Great Britain, before 1717; int. m. Elizabeth Bishop, Nov. 7, 1717.—*Boston Rec. Com., Vol.* 28, *p.* 96.
CRISTY, Captain John, of Windham, N. H.; from Scotland or Ireland, cir. 1746; m. 1. Elizabeth ———; m. 2. Jane ———; m. 3. Mary ———; Children: Elizabeth, Moses; d. 1766.—*Morrison's Windham, p.* 409.
CRITON, John, of Boston; see also Creighton; from Ireland, 1719.—*Cullen's Irish in Boston, p.* 51.
CROLLEY, Anne, Boston, Mass.; from Great Britain, before 1718; int. m. Philip Alman, Feb. 21, 1719.—*Boston Rec. Com., Vol.* 28, *p.* 97.
CROMBEY, Andrew, convict assigned to Apthorp and Hancock, July 18, 1747, from Wm. Cookson of Hull.

CROMBIE, Benjamin, of Rowley, Mass., and Chester, N. H.; from Ballymore, Ireland; half-brother of John; m. Rebecca Davis of Ipswich, May 6, 1741; Children: Moses, Amos, and nine others.—*Chase's Chester, p. 500, Ipswich Vital Records, Vol. 2, p. 117.*

CROMBIE, John, of Londonderry, N. H.; from Ireland, cir. 1720; m. Joan Rankin, Nov. 17, 1721; Children: Hugh, William, James, John, Elizabeth, Mary, Jane, Nancy, Ann.—*Parker's Londonderry, pp. 90, 266, Chase's Chester, p. 500.*

CRONER, Rev. Frederic, of Waldoboro, Me.; from Germany; m. Mary Ulmer; Children: Catherine, Frederic, Hannah; left the country.—*Eaton's Thomaston, p. 195.*

CROOK, Thomas, of Falmouth, Maine; from Ireland, 1719.—*Mass. Resolves, 1719-20.*

CROSBEY, John, Boston, Mass.; from Great Britain, before 1711; int. m. Esther Palmer, Jan. 1, 1712.—*Boston Rec. Com., Vol. 28, p. 91.*

CROSS, John, Boston, Mass.; from Great Britain, before 1717; int. m. Martha Morris, July 12, 1717.—*Boston Rec. Com., Vol. 28, p. 96.*

CROSS, William, Portsmouth, N. H.; from Bideford, in Great Britain, before 1715; m. Abigail Briard, Jan. 2, 1716.—*N. E. Hist. Gen. Reg., Vol. 23, p. 392.*

CROSSETT, James, of Chester, N. H.; from Ireland, cir. 1736; m. ——— Young, "sister of Aiken's wife"; Children: James, John.—*Chase's Chester, pp. 500, 501.*

CROSSETT, Mrs. Martha (Hamilton), from Ireland in 1716; Children: John, Archibald, William, all of Pelham, Robert of Rutland. — *Rutland Vital Records, p. 127.*

CROU, William, of ———, R. I.; from County Waterford, Ireland; b. cir. 1755.—*Murray's Irish Rhode Islanders, p. 29.*

CROUSE, Jacob, of Warren Me.; [Kraus]; from Germany (Hessian soldier), 1775; m. ——— in Waldoboro, d. December 27, 1845; Children: Jacob, Sarah,

Elizabeth, Theresa; d. March 4, 1832.—*Eaton's Warren, pp.* 389, 531.

CUCKERSON, Thomas, from London to Boston in the ship "London," 1774, aged 17, "gentleman" for pleasure.—*N. E. Hist. Gen. Reg., Vol.* 63, *p.* 21.

CUMMING, Thomas, of Portland, Me.; from Scotland, in 1773; Children: Robert, Margaret, Eleanor. — *Smith's and Deane's Journal, p.* 375.

CUMMINS, Mr. Thomas, of Lancaster, Mass.; from Ireland; died March 24, 1784.—*Lancaster Vital Records, p.* 329.

CUNNINGHAM, James, of Rutland, Me.; from Ireland, in 1737; b. in County Derry, Ireland, in 1713; m. Mary ——, d. Dec. 29, 1821 aet 91; d. Feb. 20, 1786, aged 73.—*Rutland Vital Records, p.* 221, *Monumental Inscriptions, Rutland, p.* 9.

CURRIL, John, Boston, Mass.; from Great Britain, before 1719; int. m. Sarah Wye, March 31, 1719; forbid by Sarah Wye.—*Boston Rec. Com., Vol.* 28, *p.* 97.

CURTICE, William, baker, Boston, Mass.; from England, with Captain Pitts, 1706; warned out Oct. 8, 1706. —*Boston Rec. Com., Vol.* 11, *p.* 54.

CUSCADIN, Alexander, of Boston, from Londonderry, Ireland; d. April 16, 1811, aged 26 years.—*Copps Hill Burying Ground, Gravestone.*

CUTLOVE, William, Boston distiller; from London, before 1715; warned out May 10, 1715.—*Boston Rec. Com., Vol.* 11, *p.* 227.

CUTTEN, John, Boston, Mass.; from Barbadoes, before 1712; int. m. Mary Needham, Oct. 9, 1712.—*Boston Rec. Com., Vol.* 28, *p.* 92.

DALBEE, Richard, Boston, Mass.; fisherman, with wife and two children from Newfoundland, with John Webber, Nov., 1717; warned out Dec. 9, 1717.— *Boston Rec. Com., Vol.* 13, *p.* 32.

DALTON, Edward, from London to New England in the "Venus," 1774, taylor, aged 28, "to settle."—*N. E. Hist. Gen. Reg., Vol.* 63, *p.* 234.

DANFORTH, Jeddediah, from Scotland; laborer; volunteer against the West Indies, 1740. — *Colonial Wars,* 1899.

DANIELSON, John, of Brimfield, Mass.; perhaps from Scotland; m. Margaret Mighill, 1727; Children: John, Nathaniel, Margaret, Timothy, Mary, Sarah. *Hyde's Brimfield, pp.* 393-396.

DARRAH, Robert, of Litchfield, N. H.; from Ireland, 1738; m. 1. J—— McKean; m. 2. —— Blood; Children: Elizabeth, Robert, John, James, Polly, Peggy, Jane, Naomi, David, Samuel.—100*th Anniversary of Bedford, p.* 297.

DARRANCE, Samuel, of Johnstowne, Conn.; believed to have sailed to America from Belfast, 1719; entered Glasgow, 1709; licensed Dunbarton, Scotland, 1719. *Ulster Journal of Archael., Vol.* 3, *p.* 208.

DASCOMB, ———, Watertown, Mass.; from England cir. 1725; Children: Thomas, James, one daughter.— *Livermore and Putnam's Wilton, p.* 359.

DASSETT, John, Boston, Mass.; from London, 1716; shoe maker.—*Boston Rec. Com., Vol.* 29, *p.* 234.

DAVENPORT, Francis, of Boston, Mass.; from "West Jersie," before 1708; int. m. Martha Newbery, June 2, 1708.—*Boston Rec. Com., Vol.* 28, *p.* 31.

DAVIDSON, John, of Boston, Mass.; from Ireland, before 1769; a weaver.—*Deed of Belfast, Maine.*

DAVIDSON, William, of Woburn and Tewksbury, Mass.; from Menemore, Ireland, 1728; b. Menemore, Ireland; m. 1. Mary Alexander, d. 1738 in Woburn; m. 2. Margaret McCartney; Children: Robert, Nathaniel, William, John, George, Elizabeth, Jane; Alexander, Francis, Mary, Peggy; d. 1757, in Tewksbury.—*Morrison's Windham, p.* 423, *Hadley's Goffstown, p.* 111, *Merrill's Ackworth, p.* 206.

DAVIDSON, Rev. William, of Londonderry, N. H.; from Ireland; University graduate of Scotland; m. Frances (Cummings) Thompson in 1733; Children: two sons and two daughters; d. 1791, aged 77. — *Parker's Londonderry, p.* 159, *Morrison's Windham, p.* 608.

DAVIES, Rev. Thomas, from England, 1761; b. 1736, Kington, Herefordshire; d. May 12, 1766.—*Emigrant Ministers to America, p.* 23.

DAVIS, Ephraim, from England, 1730; Child: Jonathan. —*Merrill's Ackworth, p.* 207.

DAVIS, Jane, widow, Boston, Mass.; from Ireland in the ship "Elizabeth"; warned from Boston, Nov. 3, 1719.—*Boston Rec. Com., Vol.* 13, *p.* 63.

DAVIS, John, Portsmouth, N. H.; from Bristol, England, before 1718; m. Mary Gooding of Nechowanuck, in Portsmouth, Oct. 23, 1718.—*N. E. Hist. Gen. Reg., Vol.* 23, *p.* 395.

DAVISON, John, of Peterborough, N. H.; from Ireland. —*Smith's Peterborough, pt.* 2, *p.* 50.

DAVISON, Thomas, of Peterborough, N. H.; from Ireland; b. 1722; m. Anna Wright, 1757, daughter of Matthew, d. 1823; Children: Thomas, Charles, Mary, Sarah, William, Betsy, John, Robert, Anna, Hannah; d. 1823, aged 88.—*Smith's Peterborough, pt.* 2, *pp.* 50, 51, 52.

DAWLEY, James, Boston, Mass.; "an Irishman from Lisbon," May 3, 1727; warned out July 11 (return), 1727.—*Suffolk Court Files* 20510, *Boston Rec. Com., Vol.* 13, *p.* 167.

DEAN, Rev. Barzillai, from England to New England, 1745.—*Emigrant Ministers to America, p.* 24.

DECAMP, David, of Charlestown, N. H.; a Hessian soldier, who deserted in New Jersey and m. in New Jersey; he and his wife came on foot to Charlestown, N. H., bringing with them the first "wine apple" tree to Charlestown; Children: Mary, Deborah, John, David.—*Sanderson's Charlestown, N. H., p.* 324.

DE LANGLOISERIE, Louis Hector Piot, Boston, Mass.; from Montreal, before 1740; int. m. Esther Bridge, Aug. 14, 1740.—*Boston Rec. Com., Vol.* 28, *p.* 234.

DEMARY, ———, of Boston, Mass.; from France, before 1728; Children: John, Ezekiel, (there were Demarys born in Boston as early as 1700, so perhaps this is a guess, or they came earlier).—*Stearns' Rindge, N. H., p. 507.*

DEMPSEY, Thomas, of Kennebunk Port, Me.; from Ireland; m. 1. ———; m. 2. ——— Wildes, widow of Nathaniel Wildes; Children: Margaret, Hephzibah; d. before 1775.—*Bradbury's Kennebunk Port, p. 238.*

DEMUTH, Martin, of Broad Bay, Maine; from Germany, before 1760.—*Miller's Waldoboro, p. 51.*

DENIO, Aaron (Réné De Noyon), of Deerfield, Mass.; from Canada; b. Dec. 26, 1704, at Boucherville, P. Q.; m. Anna Combs, dau. John and Elizabeth Coombs of Northampton, July 8, 1730, living in 1759, "very old"; Children: Aaron, Anna, Joseph, Seth, Abigail, Eli, Baptist, Sarah, Elizabeth, Dorothy, Sebarah, Solomon; d. Apr. 5, 1774, at Deerfield, Mass.—*Denio Genealogy, 1926, pp. 40-53.*

DENMAN, Peter, Boston, Mass.; from England with Capt. Wentworth, May, 1710; silversmith; warned out.—*Boston Rec. Com., Vol. 11, p. 122.*

DENNY, Major ———, of Georgetown, Me.; from England about 1728.—*Sullivan's District of Maine, p. 175.*

DENSMORE, Samuel, from Ireland, before 1740; husbandman; b. cir. 1721; volunteer against the West Indies, 1740.—*Colonial Wars, 1899.*

DESENNE, Boston, Mass.; from Great Britain, before 1713; int. m. Ann Chardon, April 29, 1714.—*Boston Rec. Com., Vol. 28, p. 93.*

DEW, Jacob, of Broad Bay, Waldoboro, Maine; from Germany, before 1752.—*Mass. Archives, Vol. 15a, pp. 240-2.*

DEWIND, Francis, Boston, Mass.; from Great Britain, before 1719; int. m. Katherin Hart, Dec. 8, 1719. —*Boston Rec. Com., Vol. 28, p. 98.*

DICK, Thomas, of Pelham, Mass.; from Ireland? before 1738.—*Parmenter's Pelham, p. 17.*

DICKEY, David, of Chester, N. H.; from (prob.) Ireland; m. Isabella ———; Children: John, David. *Chase's Chester, p. 503.*

DICKEY, John, of Londonderry, N. H.; from Londonderry, Ireland, 1729; m. Margaret ———; Child: Adam.—*Merrill's Ackworth, p.* 209.

DICKEY, John, of Warren, Maine; from Stirling, Scotland, 1753; b. 1730; m. Nancy Patten; Children: John, William, Waldo, James, Margaret, David; d. April 4, 1800, aged 70.—*Eaton's Warren, p.* 85, 120, 391, *New Edition, p.* 535.

DICKEY, William, of Warren, Maine; from Scotland, 1753; b. Stirling, Scotland, 1750, son of John and Nancy (Patten) Dickey; m. Martha Melony, d. July 26, 1818; Children: James, William, Sarah, Lois, David, Martha, John, Rachel; d. February 16, 1822.—*Eaton's Warren, p.* 535.

DIKE, Samuel, of Hamilton and North Bridgewater, Mass.; from Scotland; b. June 14, 1722; weaver; m. Mary Perkins, d. Dec. 25, 1816; Children: Samuel, Anthony, John, Mary, Sarah, Anna, Abigail, Nathaniel, Veren; d. Oct. 22, 1800, aged 79.— *Kingman's North Bridgewater, p.* 488.

DIMUTH, Johi Heinrich, of Broad Bay, Waldoboro, Maine; from Germany, before 1752.—*Mass. Archives, Vol.* 15A, *pp.* 240-2.

DINSMOOR, Thomas, of Bedford, Mass., and Hollis, N. H.; from Ireland, before 1725; weaver; m. Hannah ———; Children: Abram, Abel.—*Amer. Ances., Vol.* 3, *p.* 116.

DINSMORE, David, of Chester, N. H.; from Londonderry, Ireland, cir. 1745; b. 1714; m. Widow Elizabeth Kennedy, d. 1807 aet. 97; Children: Samuel, James, David, Thomas, Arthur, Robert, Mary. — *Chase's Chester, p.* 510, 1926 *Ed., p.* 303.

DINSMORE, John, of Londonderry, N. H.; from Bally Wattick, Ireland, (Belly Waitche) County Antrim; mason by trade; m. ———; Children: Robert Elizabeth, John; d. 1741 aet 99 years.—*Cochran's Francestown, p.* 629, *Morrison's Windham, p.* 437,

Cochran's Antrim, p. 453, Hadley's Goffstown, pp. 119, 120.

DISHILL, John, Boston, Mass.; from Maryland, before 1734; int. m. Elizabeth Linehan, April 25, 1734.—*Boston Rec. Com., Vol. 28, p. 221.*

DITTY, Francis, Portsmouth, N. H.; from Winbird, Dorsetshire, before 1715; m. Elizabeth Furber, May 26, 1715.—*N. E. Hist. Gen. Reg., Vol. 23, p. 272.*

DIVERS, William, Portsmouth, N. H.; from Crediton, Devon, before 1725; m. Sarah Nason, Aug. 18, 1725.—*N. E. Hist. Gen. Reg., Vol. 24, p. 357.*

DIX, Samuel, of Boston, Mass.; wigmaker from London, 1730; admitted an inhabitant and to open a shop, Dec. 16, 1730.—*Boston Record Com., Vol. 13, p. 202.*

DOAK, James, Boston, Mass.; from Virginia; warned out, July 17, 1725.—*Boston Record Com., Vol. 13, p. 141.*

DODS, Thomas, Boston, Mass.; from North Britain [Scotland], before 1712; int. m. Elinor Black, Dec. 30, 1712.—*Boston Rec. Com., Vol. 28, p. 92.*

DOKE OR DOAK, Robert, [Londonderry, N. H.]; from Ireland in ship "Elizabeth"; warned, Nov. 3, 1719; proprietor of Londonderry, 1722. — *Boston Record Com., Vol. 13, p. 63, Parker's Londonderry, p. 325.*

DOHERTY, Michael, of Providence, R. I.; from Donegal, Ireland, cir. 1777; b. cir. 1755.—*Murray's Irish Rhode Islanders, p. 35.*

DOMETT, Captain Joseph, of Boston, Mass.; came probably from Devonshire, before 1743; b. 1720; m. Ann ———; Children: John, Joseph, Philobeth, Ann, George (Christ Church, Salem St., Boston); d. 1762.—*Contributed by Miss Winifred L. Holman.*

DOOLINTY, Philip, of ———, R. I.; from Kilkenny, Ireland, before 1775; b. cir. 1753.—*Murray's Irish Rhode Islanders, p. 29.*

DORHLERMANN(?), Paulus, of Broad Bay, Waldoboro,

Maine; from Germany, before 1752.—*Mass. Archives, Vol.* 15A, *pp.* 240-2.

DOUGLAS, John, of Middleborough, Mass.; from Scotland, cir. 1707; kidnapped and brought to Boston aet 12; b. cir. 1695; m. Eunice Rattliff; Children Elijah, John, George; d. Nov. 12, 1795, aged 90. —*Amer. Ances., Vol.* 3, *p.* 194, *Larned's Windham Co. Comr., Vol. II, p.* 69, *Wheeler's Brunswick, pp.* 831, 832.

DOUGLASS, Samuel, of Townsend, Mass., and Brookline, N. H.; from Scotland cir. 1730; b. May 18, 1699; son of Samuel and Hepzibah (Farrar) Douglass; m. Hepzibah Richardson, 1723, in Scotland; Children: Samuel, Hepzibah; d. after 1793 in Littleton, N. H. —*Parker's Brookline, p.* 499.

DOVE, William, Boston, Mass.; from Great Britain before 1714; int. m. Dorcas Wakefield June 14, 1715.— *Boston Rec. Com., Vol.* 28, *p.* 94.

DOWNE, John, from Dublin, Ireland, cordwainer, before 1740; b. cir. 1601; volunteer against the West Indies, 1740.—*Colonial Wars,* 1899.

DOWNES, Edward, of Canton, Mass.; from —— cir. 1724; m. Ruth Puffer 1724; Children: Ruth, Sarah, Hannah, Miriam, Abigail, Edward. — *Cochran's Francistown, p.* 641.

DOWNIE, Walter, of N. Bridgewater; from Scotland, cir. 1735; m. ————; d. aet 100 yrs.; Children: William, Isabel; returned to Scotland. — *Kingman's North Bridgewater, p.* 490.

DREW, see also Drue.

DREW, Catherine, Portsmouth, N. H.; from Dedford, England, before 1723; m. John Seward, Nov. 14, 1723.—*N. E. Hist. Gen. Reg., Vol.* 24, *p.* 17.

DREW, Charles, Portsmouth, N. H.; from the Parish of "St. Sover," Jersey, before 1738; m. Mary Montgomery Nov. 27, 1738.—*N. E. Hist. Gen. Reg., Vol.* 26, *p.* 379.

DREW, Francis, Portsmouth, N. H.; from "Sansover," Jersey, before 1727; m. Sarah Hunking March 21,

1727; (see Charles Drew).—*N. E. Hist. Gen. Reg., Vol.* 24, *p.* 359.

DREW, Martha, Portsmouth, N. H.; from Dedford, England, before 1728; m. James Abitt, Jan. 11, 1728; (see Catherine Drew).—*N. E. Hist. Gen. Reg., Vol.* 24, *p.* 360.

DRISCOLL, Catherine, Boston; from Ireland, in ship "Catherine," Capt. Robert Waters; spinster — accepted.—*Boston Rec. Com., Vol.* 15, *p.* 54.

DRISCOLL, Cornelius, of Providence, R. I.; from Kinsale, County Cork, Ireland, before 1781.—*Murray's Irish Rhode Islanders, p.* 34.

DRISKILL, Daniel, Boston, Mass.; from Great Britain before 1714; int. m. Abigail Waters, July 24, 1714.—*Boston Rec. Com., Vol.* 28, *p.* 93.

DROUGHT, Robert, Portsmouth, N. H.; from King's Co., Ireland, before 1733; m. Elizabeth Hinds Oct. 8, 1733.—*N. E. Hist. Gen. Reg., Vol.* 25, *p.* 120.

DRUE, Valentine, Boston, Mass.; from Great Britain before 1721; int. m. Elizabeth Stevens May 3, 1721.—*Boston Rec. Com., Vol.* 28, *p.* 158.

DRUMMOND, Patrick, of Bath, Me.; son of Alexander who came with family in 1729; he had many children; lived in Phippsburg, see grave stone there.—*Reed's Bath, p.* 316.

DUDLEY, John, Boston, Mass.; from South Carolina, with —— Pitts July 8, 1719; warned out July 24, 1719. —*Boston Rec. Com., Vol.* 13, *p.* 57.

DUNANT, Abraham, Boston, Mass.; from Geneva, before 1735; int. m. Sarah Armstrong Sept. 11, 1735.—*Boston Rec. Com., Vol.* 28, *p.* 223.

DUNBAR, Col. David, of Pemaquid, Me.; from Ireland 1729; Sagadahoc territory. — *Greene's Boothbay, p.* 109.

DUNCAN, George, of Londonderry, N. H.; from Ireland cir. 1740; son of George Duncan of Ireland; m. 1. ——————; m. 2. Margaret Cross; Children: John, George, William, Robert, Abraham, Esther, James. *Parker's Londonderry, p.* 269; *Merrill's Ackworth, p.* 212; *Cochran's Antrim, p.* 468; *Chase's Haverhill, p.* 628.

DUNCAN, George, of Londonderry, N. H.; from Ireland cir. 1740; b. cir. 1720-25; son of George and Margaret (Cross); m. Letitia Bell; Children: John, George, James, Josiah, Elizabeth, Letitia; d. 1780-5 aet cir. 70.—*Parker's Londonderry, p. 270.*

DUNCAN, John, of Worcester, Mass. (also called Dunkin); from Ireland in 1718; Children: Simeon, John, Samuel, Daniel, a daughter; son-in-law James Hawes, weaver; will probated Feb. 5, 1739/40.— *Worcester Probate Records; Lincoln's Worcester, p. 49.*

DUNCAN, John, of Londonderry, N. H.; from Ireland, cir. 1740; b. before 1720; son of George and —— Duncan (above); m. Rachel Todd; Children: John, George, Abraham, William, James, Naomi, Polly, Rachel, Rosanna.—*Parker's Londonderry, p. 270.*

DUNCO, William, Boston, Mass.; from Ireland, with Captain Dennis, Nov. 1719; farmer. — *Boston Record Com., Vol. 13, p. 64.*

DUNDAS, James, Salem, Mass.; from Scotland before 1762; m. Elenor Shaddock of Marblehead, Nov. 13, 1762.—*Salem Vital Records, Vol. 4, p. 297.*

DUNLAP, Alexander, of Deering and Windham, N. H.; from Scotland and Nova Scotia before 1740; Child: Samuel G. — *Little's Weare, N. H.; Morrison's Windham, p. 519.*

DUNLAP, Archibald, of Chester, N. H.; from Ireland, before 1741; m. Martha Neal, daughter Joseph, of Chester, 1741; Children: Joseph, James, John, Mary, William, Sarah, Samuel, Martha.—*Hadley's Goffstown, p. 131.*

DUNLAP, Robert, of Palmer, Mass.; from the North of Ireland in 1718; Grantee, 1733, "Had pitched earlier"; "Robert Dunlap, with his wife & four children are come into this Town from Springfield, were to go over to Capt. Temple's at Noddle's Island the next day" Jan. 22, 1735.—*Boston Rec. Com., Vol. 13, p. 265; Temple's Palmer, p. 127.*

DUNLAP, Robert, of Topsham, Maine; from Ireland, cir. 1730; Children: John, Jane, Margaret.—*Wheeler's Brunswick, p. 832.*

DUNLAP, Rev. Robert, of Brunswick, Maine; from County Antrim, Ireland, in 1736; b. Aug. 1715, in Barilla, Antrim, son of John and Jane Dunlap; m. Jane Allison; Children: John, Elizabeth, Samuel, Robert, Hugh, Jane; d. June 26, 1776.—*Wheeler's Brunswick, p.* 832; *Alexander's Alexander Family, pp.* 70, 71, 110.

DUNLOP, William, Boston, Mass; from Ireland, before 1713; int. m. Sarah Boon, late of Great Britain Jan. 1, 1714.—*Boston Rec. Com., Vol.* 28, *p.* 93.

DUNN, Edward, of Shirley, Mass.; from Belfast, Ireland, before 1788; m. Elizabeth ———; d. January 2, 1820; Children: Mary, Alexander, Nancy, Andrew; d. June 8, 1796.—*Middlesex Probate, Series A* 4475; *Bolton's Shirley, p.* 336.

DUNNING, Andrew, of Brunswick, Maine; from (Ashburton, Devonshire?) England in 1717, landed at Georgetown; m. Susan Bond; Children: William, David, Andrew, Robert, James, David deposed in 1767, that on or about 1718, he came to Boston in vessel with Andrew McFadden.—*Wheeler's Brunswick, p.* 832; *Pejepscot Papers.*

DUNSMORE, "old father," member of the church in Ireland of which Mr. Clark of Westfield was pastor (Kilrea); received in full communion at the church in Lancaster, Mass.—*Lancaster, Mass., Vital Records, p.* 285.

DURRELL, Philip, of Kennebunk Port, Me.; from Guernsey, cir. 1700; Children: Philip, Benjamin, John, Rachel, Susan, Elizabeth, Lydia, Sarah, and one other.—*Bradbury's Kennebunkport, p.* 241.

DWIGHT, Rev. Daniel, M. A.; from England to New England, 1729.—*Emigrant Ministers to America, p.* 25.

DYER, John Henry, Boston, Mass.; from London, before 1751; a cooper near the South Market House.—*Boston Gazette, July* 30, 1751; *Old-Time New England, Vol.* 18, *p.* 37.

DYER, Thomas, Boston, Mass.; from Great Britain before 1714; int. m. Eliza. Proctor Dec. 9, 1714.—*Boston Rec. Com., Vol.* 28, *p.* 94.

EAGER, Thomas, from England to New England, 1712; "clerk."—*Emigrant Ministers to America, p.* 25.

EAKINS, John, Boston, Mass.; from Carolina, before 1722; int. m. Mary Bason July 16, 1722.—*Boston Rec. Com., Vol.* 28, *p.* 159.

EALS, John, Portsmouth, N. H.; from the Isle of Wight, before 1715; m. Sarah Hix, June, 1715.—*N. E. Hist. Gen. Reg., Vol.* 23, *p.* 272.

EDGELL, EDGEHILL, William, of Boston and Westminster, Mass.; came from England cir. 1720-5; m. Elizabeth, daughter of John and Sara Norman of Marblehead, Aug. 2, 1725; Children: William, John, Simon, Benjamin; lived in Marblehead, Woburn, Lexington; d. in England. — *Heywood's Westminster, Mass.; Marblehead Vital Records, Vol. I, p.* 366; *Vol. II, p.* 306.

EDSWORTH, Abigail, Boston, Mass.; from New York, before 1724; warned from Boston, April 27, 1724.— *Boston Rec. Com., Vol.* 13, *p.* 126.

EDWARDS, John, Boston, Mass.; mariner, from Newfoundland, with Sanders, 1716; wished to settle and be a butcher; warned from Boston Oct. 23, 1716; a John Edwards m. Mary Needham June 7, 1717, in Boston.—*Boston Rec. Com., Vol.* 13, *p.* 11; *Vol.* 28, *p.* 70.

EICHHORN, Jacob and Michael of Broad Bay, Waldoboro, Maine; from Germany before 1760.—*Miller's Waldoboro, p.* 52.

ELBORTON, Elbert, Portsmouth, N. H.; from New York, before 1717; b. in New York; m. Lydia Meder of "Oysteriver," Dec. 22, 1717.—*N. E. Hist. Gen. Reg., Vol.* 23, *p.* 394.

ELDER, Robert, of Cape Elizabeth, Maine; from Ardmore, County Antrim, Ireland.—*McLellan's Gorham, p.* 481.

ELDER, Samuel, of Gorham, Maine, from Ardmore, County Antrim, Ireland; m. —— Huston; Children: Margaret, William, Isaac, Elizabeth, Eunice, Samuel, Jane.—*McLellan's Gorham, p.* 481.

ELDING, Read, Boston, Mass.; from Barbadoes, before

1696; int. m. Hannah Pemberton Jan. 29, 1696.—*Boston Rec. Com., Vol.* 28, *p.* 349.

ELDRIDGE, Obadiah, Boston, Mass.; shoe-maker, from Virginia, April, 1720; warned out June 20, 1720. —*Boston Rec. Com., Vol.* 13, *p.* 72.

ELLARD, Mr. Benjamin, Boston, Mass.; from Cork, Ireland, with Capt. Benedict Arnold, Aug. 16, 1736; m. ————; Children: James, John, Elizabeth; he also brought a maid servant with him.—*Boston Record Com., Vol.* 13, *p.* 312.

ELLISON, A————, of Boston, Mass.; from England cir. 1771.—*Thomas's History of Printing, Vol.* 2, *p.* 233.

ELTON, John, Boston, Mass., and wife, now lodging at ———— Thorn's, from Newfoundland, with Captain Arnold, October, 1716; warned out, Nov. 26, 1716. —*Boston Rec. Com., Vol.* 13, *p.* 13.

EMERSON, Thomas, of Thomaston, Me.; from Dublin, Ireland, before 1789; m. Lydia Morse; Child: John; d. in Ireland.—*Eaton's Thomaston, p.* 213.

ENSTONE, Edward, Boston, Mass.; from Great Britain, before 1715; "set up and kept a school for music and dancing without allowance and approbation of the Selectmen," fined 40/.—*Court of Sessions of the Peace,* 1715-18, *vol.* 2.

EPES, William, Esq., of Salem, Mass.; from Chesterfield, Virginia, before 1750; m. Abigail Pickman, April 5, 1750; Children: Abigail, William, Judith, William Isham, Love Rawlins.—*Salem Vital Records, Vol.* 1, *pp.* 282, 283; *Vol.* 8, *p.* 337.

ERICKSON, Ereck, Portsmouth, N. H.; from Philadelphia, before 1721; b. in Philadelphia; m. Mary Lambeth, Dec. 25, 1721.—*N. E. Hist. Gen. Reg., Vol.* 24, *p.* 15.

ERSKINE, John. See John Marr.

ERVEN, Samuel, of Salem, Mass.; from Bristol, England, before 1770; m. Lydia Chever, int. Jan. 13, 1770.— *Salem Vital Records, Vol.* 3, *p.* 338.

ERWIN, George, of Brimfield, Mass., called "George Arwin"; from Queenstown, Ireland, 1720, with the Shaws on ship "Elizabeth" to Boston; warned Nov. 3, 1719; Child: Jane, m. Seth Shaw.—*Temple's Palmer, pp.* 547, 548; *Boston Record Com., Vol.* 13, *p.* 63.

EVANS, Edward, of Chester, and Salisbury, N. H.; from Sligo, Ireland, cir. 1760; teacher, "medium height, spare built, active and sprightly in his movements, possessing a Scotch complexion, and was very good-looking"; m. Sarah Flagg, daughter of Ebenezer, 1769, d. July 29, 1831, aet 79; Children: Josiah, Richard, Mary, Lucretia, Nancy, Ebenezer, Sally, Betsy, Susan, Gardner, Edward, John; d. May 26, 1818, aet 82.—*Dearborn's Salisbury, p.* 553.

EVANS, William, of Boston, Mass.; from Antego, sick; warned out November 10, 1724.—*Boston Record Com., Vol.* 13, *p.* 134.

EWELL, Thomas, of Marblehead, Mass.; from Ramsgate, Kent, England, before 1735; m. Mary Bartlett, of Marblehead, July 5, 1735, in Newbury; Child: Deborah.—*Newbury Vital Records, Vol.* 2, *p.* 169; *Marblehead Vital Records, Vol.* 1, *p.* 169.

FADDEN, James, Portsmouth, N. H.; from Coleraine, County Antrim, Ireland, before 1726; m. Hannah Sante, April 8, 1726.—*N. E. Hist. Gen. Reg., Vol.* 24, *p.* 358.

FAGIN, John, Boston, Mass.; from Great Britain, before 1710; int. m. Elizabeth Porter, Nov. 1, 1710; Child: "William of John and Hannah," 1712.—*Boston Rec. Com., Vol.* 28, *p.* 33; *Vol.* 24, *p.* 82.

FAIRE, Martha, of Boston, Mass.; from Ireland, before 1734.—*Tyley Manuscript, Boston Athenaeum.*

FAREWELL, Absalom, of Bethel, Maine; English sailor and soldier, came first to Marblehead; Children: William, Hannah, Melvin, Molly, Samuel, Susan, Richard, Robert Foster.—*Lapham's Bethel, p.* 529.

FARRAND, Andrew, of Palmer, Mass.; from Londonderry, Ireland, in 1718; settled in Palmer about 1720; brother of Thomas Farrand, Jr. (?); m. 1. ———; Child: John, d. 1736 aet 16; m. 2. Sarah ———; Children: Mary, Jane, Barnard, Sarah, Margaret, Ann, William, Susannah, John; he and Robert Farrell built the grist mill. — *Lincoln's Worcester, p. 49; Temple's Palmer, p. 446; Wall's Reminiscences of Worcester, p. 128; Palmer Vital Records, pp. 30, 211.*

FARRAND, Thomas, Jr., of Palmer, Mass.; from Ireland; settled in Palmer 1720, at junction of Ware and Swift rivers; brother-in-law of Elisha Hall; m. Mary ———; Children: Mary, Jean, Thomas, Ruth, Elizabeth, Sarah, Andrew. — *Temple's Palmer, p. 446; Palmer Vital Records, p. 30.*

FARRELL, John, of Stillwater, Maine; from Ireland; kept a tavern; m. Catherine McNeil, daughter of Adam of Litchfield, Conn., 1772; no issue.—*Wyman's Charlestown, p. 645.*

FARRIN, Patrick, of Ipswich, Mass.; from Ireland, before 1721; m. Joanna Tuttle of Boston, Feb. 7, 1721 in Boston, d. May 8, 1733; Children: Edward, John, Edward, James, Richard, Richard, Richard. *Wheeler's Brunswick* gives John, who was patently born in Ipswich, as from Dublin, Ireland, before 1755. He evidently went to Brunswick at that time and was called an Irishman.—*Wheeler's Brunswick, p. 834; Ipswich Vital Records, Vol. I, p. 137; Vol. II, pp. 159, 552, 554; Boston Record Com., Vol. 28, p. 100.*

FARRIS, Adam, Boston, Mass.; from Philadelphia, April 18, 1727; warned out July 11 (return); warned April 18, 1727.—*Suffolk Court Files 20510; Boston Rec. Com., Vol. 13, p. 167.*

FAVOUR, Sarah, Boston, Mass.; from England, with Captain Mould, Dec. 1707; warned out.—*Boston Rec. Com., Vol. II, p. 78.*

FAVOUR, William, Boston, Mass.; from France, before

1717; int. m. Rachel Defew, March 26, 1718.—*Boston Rec. Com., Vol.* 28, *p.* 97.

FEATHERSTONE, George, of Boston, Mass.; grocer from London, 1742; "now living at the *Green Canister and two blue Sugar Loaves,*" Marlboro Street; m. Phebe Smith of Reading, Mass., Aug. 7, 1746.— *Boston News Letter, July* 29, 1742; *Boston Rec. Com., Vol.* 28, *p.* 245.

FELLOWS, John, Boston, Mass.; from Great Britain, before 1711; int. m. Sarah Batt, March 21, 1712.— *Boston Rec. Com., Vol.* 28, *p.* 91.

FELSTED, William, Boston, Mass.; iron monger from Jamaica, 1737; begged leave to open a shop; liberty granted him.—*Boston Rec. Com., Vol.* 15, *pp.* 23, 28.

FELT, Mr. John, of Portland, Me.; from "Gentha in Orkney"; d. March 23, 1760, aet 23, grave-stone, East Cemetery, Portland.—*Portland Price Current, July* 7, 1877.

FENTON, John, of Rutland, Wales, and Brimfield, Mass.; from Ireland; m. in Ireland; Child: John, of Palmer.—*Temple's Palmer, p.* 446.

FENTON, William, of Rutland, Mass.; from Ireland, before 1720; m. Ann ——; Children: William, Samuel, Agnes; surveyor of highways 1722; the son Samuel left a will in which he mentions his father William, his wife Jennet Barr, daughter of Matthew Barr of New Braintree; his children, Joseph, Anne, John, Samuel, Matthew; he may have been born in Ireland; the will was probated Aug. 7, 1754.— *Reed's Rutland, p.* 82; *Worcester Probate Series A* 20532.

FERGUSON, Henry, Boston, Mass.; in Boston before 1741; m. Jean Griffin, April 27, 1741.—*Boston Rec. Com., Vol.* 28, *p.* 339.

FERGERSON, James, of Worcester, Mass.; from Londonderry, Ireland, in 1718.—See *Lincoln's Worcester, p.* 47; *Wall's Reminiscences of Worcester, p.* 128.

FERGUSON, John, of Pelham, N. H.; from Scotland 1725; m. Ann Johnson Sept. 23, 1729 in Boston; Children: William, David, John; clothier.—*100th Anniversary* of Bedford, p. 299; *Brown's History of Bedford, N. H., p.* 896; *Boston Rec. Com., Vol.* 28, *p.* 149.

FERGUSON, John, of Peterborough, N. H.; from Ireland cir. 1736; b. 1704; school-master; m. Sarah McDaniel in Lunenburg, Mass., b. 1710, d. 1791; Children: Mary, Henry, Sarah, Catrin, John, Esther; d. 1769 aged 65.—*Smith's Peterborough, pt.* 2, *p.* 73 *et seq.*

FERGERSON, Roger, convict assigned to Apthrop and Hancock, July 18, 1747, from William Cookson of Hull. —*Suffolk Court Files.*

FERRELL, or FARREL, Robert, of Palmer, Mass.; from Ireland, with Jno. McMaster, 1720; b. about 1687; m. Elizabeth ——, b. about 1694, d. June 15, 1758, aet 64, "mother of 16 children"; Children: Robert, Isaac, Sarah, Josiah, Arad, Timothy, Jenny, Anna; d. Oct. 22, 1765 aet. 78.—*Temple's Palmer, p.* 458; *Palmer Vital Records, p.* 211.

FEUST, Peter, Boston, Mass.; from New York, 1727; warned out May 24, 1727; m. perhaps Susannah Gray April 23, 1728.—*Boston Rec. Com., Vol.* 13, *p.* 168; *Vol.* 28, *p.* 143.

FEYLER, Charles or Samuel, of Waldoboro, Maine; Child: Charles.—*Eaton's Warren, Maine; Miller's Waldoboro, p.* 52.

FIELD, Christopher, Boston, Mass.; from Great Britain, before 1714; int. m. Rebecca Maccarter Jan. 20, 1715.—*Boston Rec. Com., Vol.* 28, *p.* 94.

FIFE, John, of Pembroke, N. H.; from Ireland, before 1738; a John Fife m. Abigail Smith in Boston, Oct. 10, 1716, by the Rev. Mr. Benjamin Wadsworth "Presbyter." — *Carter's Pembroke, p.* 92; *Boston Rec. Com., Vol.* 28, *p.* 63.

FILES, William, of Gorham, Maine; from England, in 1728; m. Joanna (Gordon) Moore of Cape Cod, 1756; Children: Ebenezer, Samuel, William, Robert M., George, Joseph, Polly, Joanna, Elizabeth; d. 1823 aged 95.—*McLellan's Gorham, p.* 490.

FINCH, Richard, of Peterborough, N. H.; British soldier in 1775, and deserter; m. Hepzibeth Melendy, d. in Waltham, Mass., 1837, aet 83; Children: William,

Fanny, Sarah, Harriet, Mary.—*Smith's Peterborough, N. H., pt. 2, p. 83.*

FINCH, Thomas, Boston, Mass.; from New York, 1736; warned out October 5, 1736.—*Boston Record Com., Vol. 13, p. 53.*

FINLAY, Joseph, of Londonderry, N. H.; from Ireland cir. 1775; m. 1. Mrs. Jane Taylor; m. 2. Mrs. Elizabeth Logan; Children: Hugh, Samuel, Robert, Esther, Elizabeth.—*Merrill's Ackworth, p. 214.*

FISHER, Caleb, from Bristol, England, 1716; weaver.—*Boston Rec. Com., Vol. 29, p. 233.*

FISHER, Samuel, of Londonderry, N. H.; from Ireland, in 1740; m. Sarah Taylor; Children: James, Samuel, Ebenezer, John, and seven daughters who m. William Cunningham, David Ela, Matthew Archibald, Samuel Taylor, James Humphrey, —— Carson, David McQuesten; d. 1806, aged 83.—*Cochran's Antrim, p. 491; Truro, Nova Scotia History, N. E. Hist. Gen. Reg., Vol. 59, p. 112.*

FISHER, Thomas, of Boston, Mass.; from Manchester, England; d. June 27, 1805, aged 30.—*Copps Hill Burying Ground.*

FITTON, John, of Providence, R. I.; from Waterford, Ireland, cir. 1750; b. 1731; d. 1810.—*Murray's Irish Rhode Islanders, p. 54.*

FITZGERALD, Rev. Edward, of Worcester, Mass.; from Londonderry, Ireland, in 1719.—*Lincoln's Worcester, p. 163.*

FITZGERALD, Edward, of Boscawen, N. H.; from Ireland, before 1734; an original settler of Boscawen; m. Mehitable Uran; Children: Jane, Mary, Sarah, James, Rebekah, Edward, Susanna, Dorcas, Rachel, John, Martha.—*Coffin's Boscawen, p. 527.*

FITZGERALD, Edward, of Newport, R. I.; from Tipperary, Ireland, cir. 1775.—*Murray's Irish Rhode Islanders, p. 35.*

FITZGERALD, Elener, wife of Martin FitzGerald of Boston, Mass.; from Kilkenny, Ireland; sister of James Hennesy; d. Feb. 11, 1817 aet 25.—*Copps Hill Burying Ground.*

FITZGERALD, John, from Cork, Ireland, nailer; b. cir. 1703; m. perhaps Martha Merrow March 23, 1731; Martha, daughter of John and Martha Fitzgerald was b. in Boston Nov. 16, 1732; volunteer against the West Indies 1740.—*Colonial Wars* 1899, *Boston Rec. Com., Vol.* 24, *p.* 207; *Vol.* 28, *p.* 171.

FITZGERALD, Jane, see Joseph Scott.

FITZGERALD, John, of Warren, Maine; from Limerick, Ireland, before 1775; m. Sophia Schenk; Children: Lucy, Sarah, William, John, Margaret, Mary, Andrew, George, Sophia, Theresa; d. 1838 aged 86 and a half.—*Eaton's Warren, p.* 394; *new ed. p.* 541-2.

FITZGERALD, Patrick, of York, Maine; from Ireland, before 1738; m. ————; Child: David.—*Moody's History of York, pp.* 52, 53.

FITZGERALD, Thomas, Boston, Mass.; from Ireland, before 1717; m. Elizabeth Boulderson, Oct. 20, 1723. —*Boston Rec. Com., Vol.* 28, *pp.* 96, 113.

FITZPATRICK, Edward, Rutland, Mass.; from Ireland, before 1744; murdered Daniel Campbell, at Rutland, Dec. 8, 1744.—*Rutland Inscriptions, p.* 10.

FLAMONT, see Fleming.

FLEET, Thomas, of Boston, Mass.; from England, 1712; printer; m. Elizabeth Goose, June 8, 1715; Children: Thomas, Elizabeth, William, Isaac, Ann, Mercy, Thomas, John, Elizabeth.—*Thomas's History of Printing, Vol.* 1, *p.* 98; *Boston Record Commission, Vol.* 24, *pp.* 113, 134, 148, 165, 181, 192, 207, 216, 233; *Vol.* 28, *p.* 57.

FLEMING, John, of Boston, Mass.; from Scotland, 1764; d. in France.—*Thomas's History of Printing, Vol.* 1, *p.* 15.

FLEMING, Joseph, of Palmer, Mass.; from the North of Ireland 1718; b. 1673; from Conn. 1721; grantee, 1733; Children: David, William, Jane, Hannah, Joseph; d. Oct. 15, 1757, aged 84.—*Temple's Palmer, pp.* 128, 449; *Palmer Vital Records, p.* 212.

FLEMMING, Alexander, of Boston, Mass.; from Great Britain, before 1754; a dyer in Marlborough Street, Boston; m. Margaret Tusker, Oct. 2, 1755.—*Boston*

Gazette, May 14, 1754; *Old-Time New England, Vol.* 18, *p.* 37.

FLETT, John, of Portland, Maine; from Scotland; killed 1760.—*Smith's and Dean's Journal, p.* 184.

FLIN, John, from Ireland; laborer; b. cir. 1710; volunteer against the West Indies 1740.—*Colonial Wars,* 1899.

FLING, William, Portsmouth, N. H.; from the Parish of Killrich, Waterford, Ireland, before 1737; m. Jean Cook from County Tipperary, in Portsmouth, Dec. 18, 1737.—*N. E. Hist. Gen. Reg., Vol.* 26, *p.* 378.

FLYN, Patrick, Boston, Mass.; in Boston before 1721; m. Prudence Ward, June 20, 1721; Children: Mary, Martha, John, Nathan.—*Boston Rec. Com., Vol.* 28, *p.* 100; *Vol.* 24, *pp.* 155, 160, 170, 181.

FOGG, Rev. Daniel, from England to Massachusetts Bay, 1770.—*Emigrant Ministers to America, p.* 27.

FOLLETT, Thomas, Portsmouth, N. H.; from Jersey, before 1730; m. Susannah Coolbroth Oct. 1, 1730.—*N. E. Hist. Gen. Reg., Vol.* 25, *p.* 117.

FOLTON, Mather, Boston, Mass.; from England, with Capt. Richard Mayheer (Mahier), October, 1717; spoon maker; wife and three children; warned out Nov. 11.—*Boston Rec. Com., Vol.* 13, *p.* 32.

FONAPS, Charles, Boston, Mass.; from Amsterdam, before 1716; int. m. Emme Marshall May 29, 1716.—*Boston Rec. Com., Vol.* 28, *p.* 95.

FOOSHERON, see Jeree.

FORBES, Alexander, of Salem, Mass.; from Lynn, County Norfolk, before 1765; m. Mary Gautier, Jr., int. Sept. 21, 1765.—*Salem Vital Records, Vol.* 3; *pp.* 373, 407.

FORBUSH, James, Worcester, Mass.; from Londonderry, Ireland, 1718; Child: James; d. before 1762 (will). —*Wall's Reminiscences of Worcester, p.* 128; *Worcester Probate Series A,* 21880.

FORBUSH, Robert, of Rutland, Mass.; from Ireland, in 1718(?) Lieutenant; m. Mary Graham Oct. 31, 1745, d. Jan. 1776 aet. 53; m. 2. Margaret Graham, widow, Dec. 13, 1781; Children: Jane, Mary, James,

John, Katee, David (grad. at Dartmouth College);
d. Feb. 17, 1799, about 85 years.—*Lincoln's Worcester, p.* 49; *Worcester Probate Series A,* 21923; *Rutland Vital Rec., pp.* 42, 140.

FORSAITH, Matthew, of Chester, N. H.; from Ireland, cir. 1730; b. in Scotland, 1699; m. Esther Graham; Children: Matthew, Jonathan, David, Esther, Robert, Hannah, William, Josiah; d. 1791 cir. 90 years. —*Chase's Chester, p.* 524; *Hadley's Goffstown, p.* 155.

FOSTER, James, of Coventry, R. I.; from Dublin, Ireland, cir. 1775; b. cir. 1734.—*Murray's Irish Rhode Islanders, p.* 33.

FOSTER, John, from Durham, England, to Boston on the "Success," 1774, to settle; farmer, aged 40.—*N. E. Hist. Gen. Soc. Rec., Vol.* 63, *p.* 24.

FOSTER, William, Boston, Mass.; from Great Britain, before 1714; int. m. Bathshaba Hart of Rhode Island, "now residing in Boston," July 18, 1715 (see Barsheba Hart).—*Boston Rec. Com., Vol.* 28, *p.* 94.

FOUGHT, Philip, of Dresden, Maine; from France.—*Huguenots in Dresden, p.* 18.

FOWLER, ——, of Amesbury, Mass.; from Wales; Child: Thomas.—*Chase's Chester, p.* 525.

FOWLER, John, Boston, Mass.; from Great Britain, before 1713; int. m. Bathsheba Brikley April 27, 1714. —*Boston Rec. Com., Vol.* 28, *p.* 93.

FOWLER, John; convict assigned to Apthorp and Hancock, July 18, 1747, from Wm. Cookson of Hull.— *Suffolk Court Files.*

FRAKER, Thomas, of Boston, Mass.; from England; b. cir. 1720; m. 1. Jane Howard; 2. Sarah Cooper; 3. Susanna Tolman; Children: Jane, Thomas, Philip, Abigail, Hannah; d. about 1765.—*Contributed by Miss Winifred L. Holman.*

FRENCH, Samuel, Boston, Mass.; joiner from Great Britain with Captain Porter, cir. June 4, 1715; with a wife and two children; warned out June 14, 1715. —*Boston Rec. Com., Vol.* 11, *p.* 228.

FRIEND, John, Boston, Mass.; tailor, with his wife from

England, with Captain Odell, Dec. 31, 1717; warned out Feb. 4, 1718; m. 2. Ann Wakefield, in Boston June 20, 1725; Child: John.—*Boston Rec. Com., Vol. 13, p. 33; Vol. 24, p. 181; Vol. 28, p. 126.*

FRINK, Thomas, of Sudbury, Mass.; from —— before 1699; m. Sarah ——; Children: Sarah, Abigail, Peter, Thomas. — *Reed's Rutland, p. 98; Sudbury Vital Records, p. 47.*

FROST, Robert, Londonderry, N. H.; from Ireland, before 1730.—*Documentary History of Maine, p. 24.*

FRYLAND, William, of Boston, Mass.; joyner from Ireland, cir. 1730; "admitted as inhabitant, & Liberty to exercise calling" Sept. 9, 1730; m. int. Jane Little, June 10, 1731; m. Jance Miller, Sept. 26, 1732.— *Boston Record Com., Vol. 13, p. 200; Cullen's Irish in Boston, p. 32.*

FULLERTON, Robert, Boston, Mass.; in Boston before 1745; m. Jean McClure, Jan. 29, 1745. — *Boston Rec. Com., Vol. 28, p. 340.*

FULLERTON, William, of Boothbay, Me.; from County Tyrone, Ireland, 1728; b. about 1680; intended for Philadelphia, but put into the Kennebec at Arrowsic; went then to Pemaquid; m. Jennett Beath, sister of Walter Beath; Children: William, Margaret, and two sons in Philadelphia.—*Greene's Boothbay, p. 472.*

FULLERTON, William, of Boothbay, Me.; from Ireland, 1728; b. 1705, son of William (above); Children: James, Elizabeth, Margery, John, Margaret, Jennett, Marian, Catherine, Mary, Ebenezer. — *Greene's Boothbay, pp. 121, 473, 474; Boston Rec. Com., Vol. 28, p. 340.*

FULTON, Gowen, of Topsham, Maine; from Coleraine, Ireland, cir. 1730, with wife and one child; m. Margaret Caswell; she b. in Glasgow, Scotland; d. 1791 aet 96; Children: John, James, Robert.—*Wheeler's Brunswick, p. 834.*

FULTON, John, of Topsham, Maine; from Ireland, cir. 1730; son of Gowen and Margaret Fulton q. v.; m. Hannah Maxwell of Scarboro.—*Wheeler's Brunswick, p. 834.*

FUMEY, John, Newbury, Mass.; from Ross, England, before 1729; merchant; m. Hannah Gibbons, of Marblehead, Aug. 7, 1729, in Newbury.—*Newbury Vital Records, Vol.* 2, *p.* 193.

GALBRAITH, Matthew, from Ireland before 1740; husbandman; b. cir. 1772; volunteer against the West Indies 1740.—*Colonial Wars,* 1899.

GALE, Edward, Portsmouth, N. H.; from Waterford, Ireland, before 1733; m. Mary Arrixson (Erickson?) Dec. 9, 1733.—*N. E. Hist. Gen. Reg., Vol.* 25, *p.* 120.

GALLOT, or GALLOP, Peter, of Framingham, Mass.; from France before 1732; silk weaver; m. Priscilla Collar, Jan. 10, 1734; Children: Peter, Francis, James, John, John, Phinehas; d. about 1753.—*Temple's Framingham, p.* 557; *Framingham Vital Records, pp.* 82, 288.

GAMBLE, Archibald, of Warren, Me.; from Ireland before 1740; son of Thomas and Margaret (Scott) Gamble; m. Isabella (Ashwell) Galloway; Children: Anne, Thomas, Mary, Robert, Margaret, Elizabeth; d. cir. 1779.—*Eaton's Warren, pp.* 60, 395; *Eaton's Thomaston, p.* 234.

GAMBLE, John, of Boston, Mass.; "a servant man born in Ireland," "aged about twenty eight years, a smith by trade, and can work something at the carpenter trade; a Tall Fellow, of a stammering speech, inclining to the Scotch language, straight Hair, of a yellowish colour."—*Boston News Letter, Oct.* 14-21, 1717.

GAMBLE, William, of Chester, N. H.; from Londonderry, Ireland; m. the Widow Clark in Londonderry, N. H.; Children: Janet, Margaret; m. 2. Anne Stark; Children: William, Archibald; d. 1785, aged 77. — *Chase's Chester, p.* 530.

GAMMON, John, of Charlestown, Mass.; from Great Britain, March 7, 1721; "at Jonathan Green's," warned out.—*Records of the Middlesex County Sessions of the Peace; Wyman's Charlestown, p.* 399.

GAMMON, Joseph, of Gorham, Maine; from England, before 1763; m. Elizabeth ———; Children: Samuel, David, Daniel, Joshua, Joseph, Christiana, William, John, Mary, Abigail.—*McLellan's Gorham, p.* 511.

GAMMON, Philip, of Gorham, Maine; from England, before 1757; m. Joanna ———; Children: Philip, Nathaniel, Joseph, Ruth, Jonathan, Benjamin, Betsey; removed to Raymontown.—*McLellan's Gorham, p.* 510.

GARDENER, Phillip, periwig maker, Boston, Mass.; from New York, 1715; journey-man to Dr. Nazaro; warned out Nov. 15, 1715.—*Boston Rec. Com., Vol.* 11, *p.* 238.

GARDNER, Ebenezer, of Machias, Maine; from Cumberland, Nova Scotia, before 1776; m. Damaris Merrill, 1776; Children: Susan, Eunice, Hannah, Ebenezer, Samuel, Thomas, John, William. — 100*th Anniversary of Machias, p.* 162.

GARDNER, John, Portsmouth, N. H.; from Gloucestershire, before 1715; m. Mary Bowen Nov. 3, 1715.—*N. E. Hist. Gen. Reg., Vol.* 23, *p.* 272.

GARDNER, Robert, of Boston, Mass.; from Glasgow; wigmaker; admitted an inhabitant and liberty to open a shop &c. March 5, 1729; m. Mary ———; Child: David.—*Boston Record Com., Vol.* 13, *p.* 182; *Vol.* 24, *p.* 229.

GARDNER, Thomas, from London to Boston on the "Harmony," 1774, to settle; with wife Margaret ———, aged 43; Children: Margaret, Simon, Rebecca, Thomas; shoemaker, aged 44.—*N. E. Hist. Gen. Reg., Vol.* 63, *p.* 237.

GARNER, Philip, Boston, Mass.; from Great Britain, before 1718; int. m. Hannah Ball Aug. 2, 1718.—*Boston Rec. Com., Vol.* 28, *p.* 97.

GASTON, John, from Ireland; b. 1703; d. Voluntown, Conn., 1783. — *Matthew's American Armoury, p.* 187.

GATCOMB, Francis, of Boston, Mass.; from Wales before 1721; b. 1693; m. Rachel Partridge, Aug. 10, 1721; Children: Francis, Dorcas, Mary, Rachel, Elizabeth, Francis; d. July 30, 1744, aged 51 (will).—*Lin-*

coln's Worcester, p. 152; Worcester Inscriptions, p. 47; Boston Rec. Com., Vol. 24, pp. 155, 160, 170, 187, 221; Welch Genealogy, p. 11; The Granary Burying Ground, p. 106.

GAULT, Samuel, of Chester, N. H. [Gott, Gaat, Galt]; from Londonderry, Ireland, 1721; b. in Scotland; m. Elsie Carlton, of Wales; Children: Patrick, Samuel, Andrew, Matthew, Jane; d. after Jan. 29, 1789. —Chase's Chester, p. 530; Carter's Pembroke, p. 118; N. H. Genealogies, p. 1993.

GEAR, George, of Boston, Mass.; from Jersey before 1720; int. m. Mary Murriner, Oct. 20, 1720.—Boston Rec. Com., Vol. 28, p. 99.

GEDERY, Augustin; from France, 1722; warned from Boston, 1722, with a wife and family.—Boston Rec. Com., Vol. 13, p. 107.

GEDERY, Gload, from France, 1722; warned from Boston 1722, and his wife also.—Boston Rec. Com., Vol. 13, p. 107.

GEDERY, Paul, from France, 1722; warned from Boston, 1722, and his wife also.—Boston Rec. Com., Vol. 13, p. 107.

GENTHER, David, of Broad Bay, Waldoboro, Maine; from Germany before 1760.—Miller's Waldoboro, p. 52.

GENTHER, Frederick, of Broad Bay, Waldoboro, Maine; from Germany before 1760.—Miller's Waldoboro, p. 52.

GEROULD [or Jerould], Dr. James, of Medfield, Mass.; from Languedoc, France, before 1719; b. cir. 1680; m. Martha Dupee; d. March 25, 1763; Children: James, Martha, Gamaliel, Stephen, Dubee, Mary, Joanna, Susanna, and thirteen others; d. Oct. 25, 1760, aet. 73 (will.—Tilden's Medfield, p. 398; Hayward's Gilsum, p. 312; Hadley's Goffstown, p. 166 (mistakes b. date for emigration date!); Medfield Vital Records, pp. 54, 55, 150, 213.

GIBBS, Rev. William; from England to New England, 1744.—Emigrant Ministers to America, p. 29.

GIBSON, Samuel, of Hillsborough, N. H.; from Ireland,

before 1733; b. 1693 or 1694; m. Ann McAffee, in Boston, 1733; Children: Elizabeth, Samuel; d. in Merrimack, 1779.—*Cochran's Francestown, p.* 729; *Secomb's Amherst, p.* 600.

GIBSON, Widow, Boston, Mass.; arrived from Northern Ireland, 1718, in the ship "Friends' Goodwill," Edward Goodin, master, with two children.—*Court of Sessions of the Peace, Suffolk County.*

GIER, Thomas, Boston, Mass.; from Ireland in ship "Elizabeth"; warned out Nov. 3, 1719.—*Boston Rec. Com., Vol.* 13, *p.* 63.

GIFFORD, Samuel, Boston, Mass.; from London, upholsterer, September, 1717; warned out October 15, 1717.—*Boston Rec. Com., Vol.* 13, *p.* 29.

GILBERTSON, George, Portsmouth, N. H.; from Colraine, Ireland, before 1733; m. Dorothy Hill, March 14, 1734.—*N. E. Hist. Gen. Reg., Vol.* 25, *p.* 121.

GILCHRIST, Robert, of Chester, N. H.; from Ireland, cir. 1725; m. Agnes Kelso; Children: John, Alexander, William, Agnes, Elizabeth, Robert; d. 1746.—*Hadley's Goffstown, pp.* 167-8.

GILCHRIST, William, Andover and Lunenburg, Mass.; from Ireland, cir. 1725; brother of Robert Gilchrist (above); m. Elizabeth White, dau. of Patrick White, of Lunenburg, June 21, 1743.—*Lunenburg Records, p.* 250; *Hadley's Goffstown, p.* 167.

GILKEY, James, of Gorham, Me.; from Ireland, cir. 1748; m. Martha Morton, 1748; Children: Joseph, Rebecca, James; m. 2, Mrs. Margaret Watts; Children: Samuel, John, Isaac; d. 1790, aged more than 80 years.—*McLellan's Gorham, p.* 513.

GILLEN, Richard, at Boston, Mass.; a sailor from North Carolina, 1736, belonging to Capt. Philpot, "a poor stranger, hurt, supported by the Overseers of the Poor."—*Boston Rec. Com., Vol.* 13, *p.* 297.

GILLESPIE, Andrew, of Boston, Mass.; from London, before 1759; tobacconist at the North End of Boston.—*Boston Gazette, Sept.* 7, 1759; *Old Time New England, Vol.* 18, *p.* 93.

GILLIS, John, see Campbell, John Gillis.

GILLYARD, Peter, Portsmouth, N. H.; from Guernsey, before 1733; m. Ann Roberts of Newcastle, Me., in Portsmouth, March 7, 1733.—*N. E. Hist. Gen. Reg., Vol. 25, p. 120.*

GILMER, James, of Londonderry and Windham, N. H.; from Ireland before 1730, "Gent."—*Documentary History of Maine, p. 24; Deed of Belfast, Me., 1769.*

GILMORE, Robert, of Londonderry, N. H., from Coleraine, Ireland, cir. 1718; m. Mary Ann Kennedy; Children: William, Robert, John, James; aged 80 at death.—*Morrill's Ackworth, p. 218; Morrison's Windham, p. 534; Williamson's Belfast, p. 96.*

GILPATRICK, Thomas, of Wells, Me.; from Donaghedy, Barony of Strabane, Co. Tyrone, in 1720.—*Bounne's Wells and Kennebunk, p. 313.*

GIMISON, George, Boston, Mass.; from North Britain, before 1718; int. m. Mary Vale, Oct. 26, 1718.—*Boston Rec. Com., Vol. 28, p. 97.*

GINN, Thomas, of Vinal Haven, Me.; from Liverpool, England, cir. 1769; b. 1762; m. Sarah Young, of York, in 1786; Children, 10; d. aged 52 yrs. in Vinal Haven.—*Hundredth Anniversary of Vinal Haven, p. 42.*

GIVEN, David, of Brunswick, Maine; from Coleraine, Ireland, cir. 1719, with wife and three sons; Children: David, John, Robert, Martha, Jane, and two other daughters.—*Wheeler's Brunswick, p. 835; Boston Rec. Com., Vol. 28, pp. 206, 340.*

GLADE, Henry, of Boston, Mass.; from France, before 1756; petition to become a citizen, 1756, "from Boston goal."—*Mass. Archives, Vol. 15A.*

GLAN, William; from Scotland, gardener, before 1740; b. cir. 1713; volunteer against West Indies.—*Colonial Wars, 1899.*

GLASFORD, James, of Worcester, Mass.; from Ireland in 1718; m. Jennet ———, d. 1757 [will]; Children: James, John, Mary, Miriam, Annie, Paul; grandson, Nathaniel Carroll, son of Miriam Clogstone.—

Worcester Probate, Series A, 23891, 23892; Lincoln's Worcester, p. 49; Temple's Palmer, p. 393.

GLASFORD, James, Boston, Mass.; in Boston before 1727; m. Sarah Beninton, May 25, 1727.—*Boston Rec. Com., Vol.* 28, *p.* 138.

GLASFORD, John, of Palmer, Mass.; "had a house and lot on Ware river in 1741"; in 1749 to board the minister; Children: John, Paul; of Boston, 1726/7, when he bought 140 acres and house in Leicester, North part.—*Temple's Palmer, p.* 128.

GLIN, see also Glyn.

GLIN, George, Boston, Mass.; tailor, from South Carolina, Feb. 1719; warned out, Feb. 24.—*Boston Rec. Com., Vol.* 13, *p.* 52.

GLYN, ———, of Boston, Mass.; Child: Martha [a Martha m. David McClure, June 11, 1730, in Boston]; d. Boston.—*Chase's Chester, p.* 533; *Boston Rec. Com., Vol.* 28, *p.* 156.

GLYN, Anne, of Boston; spinster, from Dublin, 1721, in the brigantine "Anne and Rebecca."—*Mass. Archives, Petition, Vol.* 105, *Court of Sessions of the Peace, Vol.* 1 *p.* 117, 1715-18.

GODFREY, ———; from England, cir. 1756.—*Lyford's Canterbury, N. H., p.* 183.

GOLD, John, Boston, Mass.; from Barbadoes, 1704, with Mr. John Foster, wife and two children; warned out.—*Boston Rec. Com., Vol.* 11, *p.* 38.

GOLD, Philip, Boston, Mass.; from France, 1722, wife and family; warned from Boston, 1722.—*Boston Rec. Com., Vol.* 13, *p.* 107.

GOODMAN, Thomas, Boston, Mass.; from Great Britain, before 1712; int. m. Elizabeth Jackson, Jan. 13, 1714.—*Boston Rec. Com., Vol.* 28, *p.* 93.

GOODWIN, James; from Ireland, August, 1717, with Captain Douglas in the ship "Globe"; a James Goodwin m. Elizabeth Childs, March 7, 1719; warned out, Sept. 28, 1717.—*Irish in Boston, p.* 51: *Boston Rec. Com., Vol.* 13, *p.* 29, *Vol.* 28, *p.* 75; *Bolton's Scotch-Irish, p.* 318.

GOODWIN, John, Boston, Mass.; from England, 1711; b. at Savers Dock, near London, March 16, 1683; m. 1, ———; Children: 2 sons and a daughter, d. e.; m. 2, Lydia Sprague, daughter of Jonathan Sprague of Malden and Charlestown, d. 1739, aet. 57; Child: Samuel; m. 3, Elizabeth Willard, daughter of Jacob Willard of Salem, Mass.; Children: Samuel and six others.—*Huguenots in Dresden, Me., p. 23; Willis's History of the Law Courts and Lawyers of Maine.*

GOODWIN, William, of Boston, Mass.; spectacle maker from London; admitted an inhabitant, March 18, 1724; m.? Love Thing, March 25, 1725.—*Boston Rec. Com., Vol. 13, p. 124, Vol. 28, p. 126.*

GOODWIN, William, Rumford, Maine, *alias* William Redmond; from England or Ireland, deserter; m. Rachel Harper of Northampton, Mass.; Children: Rebecca, William Colman, Rachel, Betsy, Polly, James, Nancy, John, Harris Redmond, Sally, David Abbott. —*Lapham's Rumford, pp. 334-5.*

GORDON, Alexander, Boston, Mass.; from Ireland, with Captain Dennis, Nov. 1719, farmer; m. Elener Carmack, in Boston, Nov. 3, 1729.—*Boston Rec. Com., Vol. 13, p. 64, Vol. 28, p. 167.*

GORDON, John, of Shirley, Mass.; from County Tyrone, Ireland, in 1749; son of Nathaniel Gordon, q. v.; b. 1729; m. Mary Campbell, of Townsend, Mass., Oct. 28, 1762; Children: Josiah, Elizabeth, James, Daniel; d. in Peterborough.—*Chandler's Shirley, p. 426; Shirley Vital Records, pp. 36, 37, 128, 189.*

GORDON, John, of Antrim, N. H.; from the Highlands of Scotland, before 1770; m. 1, Mary Boyce; m. 2, Esther Snow; Children: Daniel, Margaret, John, James, Alexander, Samuel, William, Hannah; removed to Canada. —*Cochran's Antrim, p. 511; Whiton's Antrim, p. 53.*

GORDON, Nathaniel, of Shirley, Mass.; from County Tyrone, Ireland, in 1749; b. 1705; m. Sarah Martin, in Ireland; d. 1781; Children: John, James, Samuel, Hannah, Elizabeth; d. in Peterborough, 1789, aet. 83.—*Chandler's Shirley, p.* 426; *Woodbury's Bedford, p.* 308; *History of Bedford, N. H., p.* 642 *et seq.; Genealogy of the Rand Family* (1898), *pp.* 60, 61, 230.

GORDON, Samuel, of Shirley, Mass.; from Tyrone, Ireland, in 1749; son of Nathaniel Gordon, q. v.; b. 1732; m. Eleanor Mitchel, daughter of Larance and Elizabeth Mitchel, of Shirley; Children: Samuel, Sally, Elizabeth, Hannah, Nathaniel, Eleanor, Jane, Polly, Nehemiah, John, Nancy; d. Dec. 2, 1818, in Peterborough, N. H.—*Smith's Peterborough, Pt.* 1, *pp.* 93, 94; *Chandler's Shirley, p.* 426; *Shirley Vital Records, pp.* 36, 37.

GORDON, William, of Dunstable, Mass., from England before 1755; m. Temperance ———; Children: Elizabeth, James, Cosmo, Catherine.—*Smith's Peterborough, Pt.* 2, *p.* 93; *Dunstable Vital Records, p.* 39.

GORSS, John, Portsmouth, N. H.; from Tinmouth, Great Britain, before 1751; m. Sarah Cook, of Marblehead, Dec. 24, 1751.—*Marblehead Vital Records, p.* 176.

GORWOOD, Charles, Portsmouth, N. H.; from the Parish of Brigg, Lincolnshire, before 1737; m. Anna Alcock, Nov. 29, 1737.—*N. E. Hist. Gen. Reg., Vol.* 26, *p.* 378.

GOUD, Daniel, James, Jean George, of Dresden, Maine, Huguenots.—*Huguenots in Dresden, p.* 18.

GOULD, Mrs. Mary, wife of George Gould, of Boston, Mass.; from Bath, England; d. April 7, 1817, aged 37.—*Copp's Hill Burying Ground*

Gower, Robert, of Topsham, Me.; from Kent, England, cir. 1766; m. 1 Margaret Alexander; Children: Edward, William; m. 2 Mary Henry, 1770; Children: James, John, Samuel, George; d. Farmington, Me. —*Wheeler's Brunswick, p.* 835.

Gragg, Samuel,—see Gregg.

Graham, Duncan, of Rutland, Mass.; from Londonderry, Ireland, in 1718; m. Katherine ——, d. March 19, 1781, aged 91 y. 9 mo.; Children: Alexander, also perhaps William, John, Mary; d. at Rutland April 10, 1768.—*Lincoln's Worcester, p.* 49; *Wall's Reminiscences of Worcester, p.* 128; *Rutland Vital Records, p.* 229.

Graham, Francis, Boston, Mass.; from Ireland, with with Captain Dennis Nov. 1719, farmer; m. Mary Dickey Jan. 20, 1731.—*Boston Record Com., Vol.* 13, *p.* 64; *Vol.* 28, *p.* 171.

Graham, Robert, of Chester, N. H.; from Ireland, before 1733; m. Janet Hume; Children: Robert, Agnes, Jean, Esther, Mary, Ann; d. 1748 aged 80.—*Chase's Chester, p.* 534.

Graham, William, of Chester, N. H.; from Ireland; m. Margaret Aiken; Children: John, James, David, Sarah, Jane, Margaret, Martha and two others (daughters); d. 1789 aged 73.—*Chase's Chester, p.* 535.

Granger, Mr. Samuel, Boston, Mass.; late of London, who came with Capt. Brunton, 1720; admitted inhabitant of Boston Jan. 25, 1720; admitted "to keep School to teach writeing, Logick & Merchants Accots."; m. Susannah Peiret, March 20, 1726.—*Boston Record Com., Vol.* 13, *p.* 65; *Vol.* 28, *p.* 163.

Grant, Donald, of Newtown, Conn.; from near Inverness, Scotland, cir. 1760; m. ———; Child; Hannah.—*Amer. Ances., Vol.* 3, *p.* 161.

Grant, Lt. James, of Salem, Mass.; "of His Majestys 45 Regiment, 1762"; int. m. Mary Hicks, Jan. 2, 1762; Children: Hannah, Joshua Hicks, James, Patty.—*Salem Vital Records, Vol.* 1, *pp.* 379, 380; *Vol.* 3, *pp.* 495, 440.

Grater, Francis, of Marblehead, Mass.; from Barcelona, Spain, 1750; m. Jane Wilson, Jan. 24, 1779; Children: James H., Charity Wilson, George Wilson, Jenny, Francis, Francis, George Wilson, Francis, Jane; d. 1845 aged 94, in Amherst, N. H.—*Secomb's Amherst, p.* 606; *Marblehead Vital Recs., Vol. I, p.* 219; *Vol. II, p.* 181.

Graves, Rev. Matthew; from England to New England 1755.—*Emigrant Ministers to America, p.* 30.

Gray, Francis, of Boston, Mass.; from Ireland, 1719; m. ———; Children: three; warned from Boston, 1719.—*Cullen's Irish in Boston, p.* 51.

Gray, George, Boston, Mass.; from Jersey, before 1720; int. m. Mary Murriner Oct. 20, 1720.—*Boston Rec. Com., Vol.* 28, *p.* 99.

Gray, Hugh, Worcester, Mass.; from Ireland, 1718.— *Wall's Reminiscences of Worcester, p.* 128.

Gray, John, Holden, Mass.; from Ireland 1718; Children: John, Samuel, Matthew, Jonas, and probably Robert, Hugh, William and Mary.—*Holden Vital Records.*

Gray, John, Worcester and Pelham, Mass.; from Ireland, 1718; b. cir. 1707; son of John Gray (above); m. Isabel ———, d. 1799 aet 92; Children: Daniel, Isaac, John, Elizabeth, and perhaps Ebenezer; d. 1782, aet 82.—*Worcester Vital Records, pp.* 115, 116; *Wall's Reminiscences of Worcester, p.* 128; *Parmenter's Pelham, pp.* 17, 475; *Pelham Vital Records, p.* 41; *The Gray Family, Raymond, p.* 150.

Gray, Capt. John, of Biddeford, Me.; from London before 1720 [son of Joseph]; m. Elizabeth Tarbox, widow; Children: Elizabeth, Mary Alice; will 1752, mentions "annual income from England." — *Saco Valley Families, p.* 699.

Gray, John, Boston, Mass.; from Great Britain by way of St. Christophers, 1736; a sailor; fell from a yard arm, broke his breast bone and one of his legs; maintained at Province charge. — *Boston Record Com., Vol* 13, *p.* 293.

GRAY, Matthew, Worcester, Mass.; from Ireland, before
1717; b. 1710, probably son of John; m. Margaret
———; m. 2, Jean ———, b. 1716, d. Dec. 20, 1764 aet.
48; Children: Sarah, Jean, Elizabeth, Mary, Matthew, John, Moses, Aaron, Reuben, Easter, Isaac,
Jacob, Robert, Joseph, Susanna, Jemima, Sarah, Sarah; d. Feb. 16, 1783, aet 73.—*Wall's Reminiscences
of Worcester, pp.* 128, 204; *Lincoln's Worcester,
p.* 49; *Worcester Probate Records, Series A,* 25351,
25338; *Worcester Vital Records, pp.* 115, 116,117;
The Gray Family, Raymond, p. 161, et seq.

GRAY, Robert, of Hadwen Lane, Worcester, Mass.; from
Ireland, 1718; probably son of John Gray; b. 1697;
m. Sarah Wiley, who came in the same ship in 1718;
Children: Molly, [wife of Andrew Boyd], Sarah
[Gray], Moses Willey, Samuel, Experience [wife of
Thomas Cowdin], Robert, Joseph, John, Thomas;
d. January 16, 1766 [will].—*Lincoln's Worcester, p.*
49; *Wall's Reminiscences of Worcester, p.* 128; *First
Settlers of Northern Worcester, p.* 49; *Worcester
Vital Records, pp.* 115, 116, 117; *Worcester Probate
Records, Series A. p.* 25358; *The Gray Family, Raymond, p.* 156 et seq.

GRAY, Robert, of Biddeford, Me.; from Ireland, abt.
1718; at Biddeford, Me., 1739.—*Folsom's Biddeford.*

GRAY, Samuel, of Worcester, Mass.; from Ireland before
1728; m. Eleanor ———; Children: Eleanor, Elizabeth, Samuel, Patience.—*Perry's Scotch-Irish, p.*
14; *Parmenter's Pelham, p.* 17; *Worcester Vital
Records, pp.* 115, 116, 117.

GRAY, Thomas, Scituate, Mass.; from Ireland, before
1730; m. Sarah ———; Children: George, Sarah,
Elizabeth, William, Mary.—*N. E. Hist. Gen. Reg.,
Vol.* 59, *p.* 138; *Scituate Vital Records, p.* 164;
Dean's Scituate, p. 276.

GRAY, William, of Lincoln Street, Worcester and Pelham, Mass.; from Aghadowey, Ireland, in 1718;
[his sister Mary m. William Blair from Aghadowey,
John and Robert Gray, in 1724, sureties]; Chil-

dren: William, Hugh, Ann, Eliot, Eliot m. Jean ——, Esther, Jonathan, Lydia, Mary, Sarah.—*Lincoln's Worcester, p.* 49; *Wall's Reminiscences of Worcester, p.* 128; *Parmenter's Pelham, p.* 17; *First Settlers in Northern Worcester, p.* 47; *Worcester Vital Records, pp.* 115, 116, 117.

GRAY, William, of Lynn, Mass.; from Great Britain, before 1706; m. Hannah Scarlet, daughter of ——— and Hannah (Paul) Scarlet, Nov. 16, 1706, buried Oct. 28, 1756; Children: Joseph, William, Jeremiah, Abraham, Hannah, Benjamin, Joseph; d. June 7, 1743, in Lynn, Mass. [will].—*William Gray of Lynn, Mass. and Some of His Descendants, pp.* 1, 2; *Lynn Vital Records, Vol. I, pp.* 169, 170, *Vol. II, pp.* 162, 490.

GRAYNER, see GRYNER.

GREEK, William, Boston, Mass.; from New York with wife and child, August, 1710; in service at Annapolis Royal, dismissed; warned out, April 2, 1711.— *Boston Rec. Com., Vol.* 11, *p.* 128.

GREEN, John, of Gorham, Maine; from England, cir. 1743; m. 1760 Elizabeth Sharp, of Biddeford; Children: Jonathan, Thomas, Josiah, Moses, Cary, Isaac; m. 2. Elizabeth Rand; Child: Hannah; d. 1809, aged cir. 84.—*McLellan's Gorham, p.* 525.

GREEN, William, of Thomaston, Me.; from England, before 1775; m. 1. Barbara Deags; m. 2. Lucy Thomas; Children: Isaac, Lydia, John, Barbara, Betsey, Benjamin, William, also another; a large family; removed to New Brunswick. — *Eaton's Thomaston, p.* 244.

GREENLAW, William, of Warren, Me.; from Scotland, 1753; m. Jane ———; Children: Ebenezer, Charles, Jonathan, Alexander, William; settled at Deer Isle, Me.; four of the children went to St. Andrew's, N. B.; son William remained in Maine; removed to Boston and Deer Isle.—1*st ed. Eaton's Warren, pp.* 85, 121; 2*nd ed. Eaton's Warren, pp.* 132, 92; *Sabine's Loyalists.*

GREGG, David, of Windham, N. H.; from Londonderry, Ireland, 1722; b. 1685, son of John; m. Mary Nevins or Evans; Children: William, John, Jane, Mary, Hannah, Thomas, David.—*Parker's Londonderry, p. 275; Morrison's Windham, p. 544; Morrill's Ackworth, p. 223.*

GREGG, James, of Londonderry, N. H.; from Antrim, Ireland, cir. 1718; b. in Ayeshire, Scotland, in 1690; m. Janet Cargill; Children: William, John, Samuel, Thomas, Elizabeth.—*Parker's Londonderry, p. 274; Smith's Peterborough, pt. 2, p. 98.*

GREGG, John, Londonderry, N. H.; from Ireland, before 1730; m. 1. Nancy ——; Children: Hugh, James; m. 2. Agnes ——; Children: John, William, Elizabeth, Joseph, Benjamin.—*Documentary History of Maine, pp. 20, 24; Vital Records of Londonderry, p. 70.*

GREGG, Samuel, of Groton, Mass.; from Londonderry, Ireland, 1712; son of John Gregg; name changed to Gragg; Child: Jacob.—*Morrison's Windham, p. 544; Butler's Groton, p. 404; Documentary History of Maine, p. 24.*

GREGG, Thomas, Londonderry, N. H.; from Ireland, before 1730.—*Documentary History of Maine, p. 24.*

GREGG, William, of Londonderry, N. H.; from Ireland, before 1730; m. Jenat ——; Children: James, Jenat, and another daughter. — *Documentary History of Maine, p. 24; Vital Records of Londonderry, p. 71.*

GREGORY, Patrick, of Rutland, Mass.; from Ireland; b. Ireland 1693; m. Hannah Sever, Nov. 26, 1724, in Boston; d. July 5, 1756, aged 63.—*Rutland Vital Records, p. 229; Boston Rec. Com., Vol. 28, p. 120.*

GREIN, George, of Lancaster, Mass.; from Ireland; b. Ireland cir. 1689; ran away from Lancaster; "hath an Irish Frize coat, Jacket and breeches, a pair of gray yarn stockings, not very long above the knees."

GRENLAW, see Greenlaw.

GREVES, James, Boston, Mass.; a tobacconist, late from London, 1730; admitted an inhabitant, and liberty to keep a shop, Jan. 1731.—*Boston Record Com., Vol.* 13, *p.* 204.

GROOZ, John Mertin, of Waldoboro, Maine; from Germany; b. Feb. 1, 1679; d. Feb. 11, 1768, tablet.—*Miller's Waldoboro, p.* 211.

GROSS, Jans Peter, of Broad Bay, Waldoboro, Maine; from Germany before 1760; a blacksmith.—*Miller's Waldoboro, p.* 51.

GROVE, William, Newbury, Mass.; from Plymouth, England, before 1763; m. Mercy Hunt Sept. 4, 1763.—*Newbury Vital Records, Vol.* 2, *p.* 210.

GROVER, James, of Boston, Mass., from Great Britain, before 1708; m. Susana Knot Dec. 2, 1708.—*Boston Rec. Com., Vol.* 28, *p.* 31.

GROW, Thomas, of Andover, Mass.; from Ireland, before 1712; m. Rebecca Holt; Children: Ruth, Hannah, James, Joseph, Thomas, and one other; illegit. son John, by Elizabeth Nichols, to be provided for by the town, when he was bapt. 1728; signed the petition to Shute.—*Andover Vital Records, p.* 185.

GRYNER, Martin, of Braintree, Mass., (or Graynor); "Germantown," 1753.—*Pattee's Braintree, p.* 481; *Mass. Archives, Vol.* 15A, *pp.* 240-2.

GUILLOW, Francis Lorenzo, of Norton, Mass.; from Italy before 1756; m. Polly Derby, Feb. 7, 1784; Children: Maturin, John, Daniel, Nancy, Salee, Tyler. —*Hayward's Gilsum, p.* 317; *Norton Vital Records, pp.* 67, 244.

GYLES, William, of Portland, Me.; from Ireland in 1718. —*Smith's & Dean's Journal, p.* 60.

HACKNEY, Samuel, of Boston, Mass.; "marriner who came from Barbadoes," sickly, Oct. 1719; warned out Nov. 22, 1719.—*Boston Rec. Com., Vol.* 13, *p.* 64.

HAGGARD, John, of Boston, Mass.; "from anopilus Royal," 1726; warned out June 13, 1726.—*Boston Rec. Com., Vol.* 13, *p.* 154.

HAHN, Hans George, of Broad Bay, Maine; from Germany; m. —— ——; Children: George, Philip, John, Frederick, and Barbara an adopted daughter. —*Miller's Waldoboro, p.* 61.

HAINES, William, Boston, Mass.; from Great Britain before 1715; int. m. Bethiah Peggee, Nov. 21, 1715; forbid by Capt. Benj. Cowell.—*Boston Rec. Com., Vol.* 28, *p.* 95.

HALL, [Isaac?], of Boston, Mass.; from England, cir. 1722; Children: Isaac, Joseph, Nathaniel.—*Eaton's Thomaston, p.* 247; *Boston Rec. Com., Vol.* 24, *p.* 182.

HAMBLETON, Armour, of Hopkinton, Mass.; from Ireland before 1728; m. Agnis Montgomery, July 9, 1728; Children: Ephraim, Mary, Patrick.—*Hopkinton Vital Records, pp.* 96, 288.

HAMBLETON, Patrick, of Hopkinton, Mass.; from Ireland before 1721; m. Anne ——; Children: Mary, John, Ann, Sarah.—*Hopkinton Vital Records, p.* 96.

HAMILETON, Thomas, of Worcester, Mass.; from Ireland, before 1733; perhaps son of James.—*Perry's Scotch-Irish, p.* 14.

HAMILTON, Hugh, of Rutland and Hopkinton, Mass., and Blandford, Conn.; from Ireland, about 1716 or 1718; inspector of swine, Rutland, 1722.—*Reed's Rutland, p.* 27.

HAMILTON, James, of Worcester, Mass.; from Ireland in 1718 (Miss Patten says 1716); m. 1, Margaret ——; d. Feb. 14, 1761, aet. 35; Children: Thomas, Michael, John, Frances; m. 2, Rebecca ——; brother of John Hamilton, and "cuzen" of Samuel Calhoun; d. before May, 1735, in Pelham (will).—*Lincoln's Worcester, p.* 49; *Perry's Scotch-Irish, p.* 114; *Wall's Reminiscences of Worcester, pp.* 128, 204; *Worcester Inscriptions, p.* 38; *Worcester Vital Records, p.* 355; *Worcester Probate, Series A.,* 26681; *Additional Notes to Genealogy of the Hamilton Family; Pelham Vital Records, p.* 167.

HAMILTON, John; see Henderson, Hugh.

HAMILTON, John, of Pelham, Mass., and Shutesbury, Conn.; from Scotland, 1717; son ? of Alexander, of Ayrshire, and brother of James of the West Indies; Child: James.—*Temple's Palmer, p.* 476.

HAMILTON, John, of Rutland, Mass.; from Londonderry, 1717; m. Eleanor ——; she afterwards m. John Savage at Rutland, Jan. 15, 1733; Children: John, Eleanor, Martha?, Mary?.—*Parmenter's Pelham, p.* 446; *Vital Records of Rutland, p.* 148; *Reed's Rutland, p.* 82.

HAMILTON, John, Newbury, Mass.; "a foreigner"; m. Mehitable Duty, of Byfield Rowley, Dec. 25, 1778, at Newbury.—*Newbury Vital Records, Vol.* 2, *p.* 157.

HAMILTON, Samuel, of Brookfield, Mass., and Chesterfield, N. H.; came from Ireland, 1772, with linen goods; b. Ireland, 1752; m. Molly Tyler, May 9, 1775, in Brookfield; d. Dec. 16, 1842, aet. 90; Children: John, Hannah, Hance, Loammi, James, Samuel, Asa, Fanny, Amadella; d. Feb. 12, 1812.—*Randall's Chesterfield, pp.* 327-8; *Brookfield Vital Records, p.* 331.

HAMITT, Thomas, of Portsmouth, N. H.; from Shadwell, Middlesex, before 1717; m. Elizabeth Deneford of Kittery, Me., in Portsmouth, Jan. 1, 1717.—*N. E. Hist. Gen. Reg., Vol.* 23, *p.* 393.

HANCKLETON, John, of Boston, Mass.; from South Carolina, Feb. 1719, plater; warned out Feb. 24, 1719.—*Boston Rec. Com., Vol.* 13, *p.* 52.

HANDLEY, John, of Thomaston, Maine; from Holland, before 1756; m. Lucy Lewis, of Wales, Great Britain; Children: Henry, Joseph, Hannah, William, Samuel, Nancy, Lucy, Jane, John; d. in Canton, Mass. ?.—*Eaton's Thomaston, p.* 251.

HANFORD, Richard, of Boston, Mass.; from South Carolina, Feb. 1719; plater; warned out Feb. 24, 1719.—*Boston Rec. Com., Vol.* 13, *p.* 52.

HANKIN, Edward, of Salem, Mass.; from London, mariner, before 1712; son of Roger, deceased; m. Hope

Borden, late of Barbadoes, daughter of Joseph Borden, merchant, deceased, March 26, 1712.—*Salem Vital Records, Vol. 3, p. 463.*

HANLEY, Henry, of Amherst, N. H.; captured from Burgoyne's Army; m. Mrs. Elizabeth (Eaton) Goodman; d. 1819, aged cir. 90.—*Secomb's Amherst, p. 611.*

HANNAH, James, of Boston, Mass.; from Northern Ireland, 1718, in ship "Friends' Goodwill."—*Court of Sessions of the Peace of Suffolk County.*

HANNAN, John, of Milton, Mass.; from Ireland, in 1764; m. Elizabeth Gove; first chocolate maker in the United States.—*Cullen's Irish in Boston, p. 187.*

HARDWIG, Adam, of Braintree, Mass.; from Germany, cir. 1752; "Germantown."—*Mass. State Archives, Vol. 15-A, pp. 240-242; Pattee's Braintree, p. 480.*

HARDWIG, Frederick Philip, of Braintree, Mass.; from Germany, cir. 1752; "Germantown."—*Mass. State Archives, Vol. 15-A, pp. 240-242; Pattee's Braintree, p. 480.*

HARDWIG, Henry, of Braintree, Mass.; from Germany, cir. 1752; "Germantown."—*Mass. State Archives, Vol. 15-A, pp. 240-242; Pattee's Braintree, p. 480.*

HARDWIG, John, of Braintree, Mass.; from Germany, cir. 1752; "Germantown."—*Mass. Archives, Vol. 15-A, pp. 240-242; Pattee's Braintree, p. 480.*

HARDWIG (afterwards Hardwick), John Peter, of Braintree, Mass.; from Germany, cir. 1752; "Germantown."—*Mass. Archives, Vol. 15-A, pp. 240-242; Pattee's Braintree, p. 480.*

HARE, William, of Boston, Mass.; from Ireland, with Captain Dennis, Nov. 1719; farmer.—*Boston Rec. Com., Vol. 13, p. 64.*

HARKNESS, Adam, of Smithfield, R. I.; from near Belfast, Ireland; in Boston in 1730; b. 1710; m. Mary Gaskill, in Lunenburg, Mass.; Child: Nathan; d. Oct. 25, 1793, aet. 83.—*Bassett's Richmond, N. H., p. 402.*

HARKNESS, Thomas, of Lunenberg, Mass.; from Ireland, before 1733; m. Mary Mickleroy, in Boston, Oct. 30, 1733; Children: Mary, Elizabeth, Jane, John, Robert, and perhaps Adam, who does not appear on the records; d. before April, 1753.—*Lunenburg Records, pp. 225, 238, 258; Worcester Probate Records, Series A-27086; Boston Rec. Com., Vol. 28, p. 184.*

HARKNESS, William, of Pelham, Mass.; from Scotland, 1710; m. Anne Gray, July 28, 1748; Children: John, William, David, James, Daniel, Jonathan, Nancy.—*Parmenter's Pelham, p. 420; Pelham Vital Records, p. 116.*

HARPER, James, of Ellerton, Conn.; from County Derry, Ireland, Oct. 1720; settled at Casco Bay; Indians forced him to leave and he came to Boston; Children: Joseph, Moses, John, and perhaps William and James.—*Stiles's Ancient Windsor, Vol. 2, p. 365; Hist. Delaware Co., N. Y.; Wheeler's Brunswick, p. 875; Lyford's Canterbury, N. H., p. 183.*

HARPER, John, of Boston, Mass.; from Great Britain, cir. 1712; int. m. Mary Millar, Nov. 20, 1712.—*Boston Rec. Com., Vol. 28, p. 92.*

HARRISON, Anne, of Boston, Mass.; from Northern Ireland, 1718, in ship "Friends' Goodwill," Edward Goodin, captain.—*Court of Sessions of the Peace, Suffolk County.*

HARRISON, Mary, of Boston, widow; from England in the "Johnson," galley, Nov. 1709; warned out, Dec. 1709.—*Boston Rec. Com., Vol. 11, p. 99.*

HART, Barshaba, of Boston; from Surinam in Ship "Neptune," 1716; m. William Foster, July 18, 1715 q. v.—*Boston Rec. Com., Vol. 29, p. 230; Vol. 28, p. 94.*

HARTLEY, Jonathan, to New England; from Martown, Yorkshire, 1699, in the "Virginia"; eighteen years old, with seven years to serve. — *N. E. Hist Gen. Reg., Vol. 64, p. 260.*

HARVEY, James, of Derry, N. H.; sailed from Port Rush, Ireland, to Boston, arriving Oct. 8, 1727; m. ———; Children: Robert, Rachel, Thomas, Margaret, Grizel, Rose, Mary L., Elizabeth; d. May 4, 1742.—*Cogswell's Nottingham, N. H., p. 212.*

HARVEY, Rev. John, of Palmer, Mass.; "a gentleman from Ireland"; b. in the North of Ireland; "Grad. of the University"; schoolmaster at Londonderry, N. H.; began to preach at Palmer (The Elbows), May 11, 1731; convicted of drunkenness and accused of immorality; resigned about Nov. 1, 1747; Child: Dorothy; d. at Blandford, Mass.—*Temple's Palmer, pp.* 85, 123.

HARWOOD, Phebe, of Boston, Mass.; from Maryland; "last from Salem Ten Days" with four children; warned out, April 3, 1725.—*Boston Record Com., Vol.* 13, *p.* 137.

HARWOOD, Rev. Thomas, from England, 1730; "lecturer."—*Emigrant Ministers to America, p.* 32.

HARWOOD, Thomas, of Portsmouth, N. H.; from Chatham, Kent, before 1735; m. Elizabeth Hull, April 18, 1735.—*N. E. Hist. Gen. Reg., Vol.* 25, *p.* 122.

HASARD, William, of Boston, Mass.; from Ireland, before 1720; int. m. Sarah Bridge, Jan. 25, 1721.—*Boston Rec. Com., Vol.* 28, *p.* 99.

HASTY, Daniel, of Scarborough, Me.; from Ireland, before 1731; Children: Martha, William, Robert, Mary; d. 1756.—*Saco Valley Families, p.* 725.

HATHORNE, Mrs. Hamilton, of Boston, Mass.; lately from Scotland, 1741; with Mr. Vicar will sell goods at Captain Tyng's warehouse, Milk St.—*Boston News Letter, 3 August,* 1741.

HAWK, John B., of Warren, Me.; from Germany, cir. 1773; m. Sarah ——, of New Brunswick; Children: Martha, John, Sarah, Mary; d. 1824, in Warren, Me.—*Eaton's Warren, p.* 397; *Eaton's Thomaston, p.* 259.

HAWKINS, Francis, of Boston, Mass.; from Munster, Ireland, June, 1727; stole in Malden and Dorchester. —*Court of Sessions of the Peace of Suffolk County,* 1725-32, *p.* 87.

HAWKINS, Henry, of Boston, Mass.; from Great Britain, before 1716; int. m. Mary Girton, June 16, 1716.— *Boston Rec. Com., Vol.* 28, *p.* 95.

HAWKINS, John, of Boston, Mass.; from New York; warned out May 9, 1727.—*Boston Rec. Com., Vol. 13, p. 68.*

HAYNES, Mr. Peter, of Boston, Mass.; from London, before 1727; dancing master, school on Hanover Street 1727.—*Boston News Letter, May 18, 1727.*

HAYTON, Captain William, of Portsmouth, N. H.; from "Sandwitch," Kent, before 1738; m. Mrs. Ann Harvey, Feb. 15, 1738.—*N. E. Hist. Gen. Reg., Vol. 26, p. 378.*

HAZLEY, Richard, Boston, Mass.; from Great Britain cir. 1712; int. m. Tamozine Mills, Sept. 15, 1712. —*Boston Rec. Com., Vol. 28, p. 92.*

HEALY, William, Boston, Mass.; from Ireland, before 1718; int. m. Sarah Clark, June 2, 1718.—*Boston Rec. Com., Vol. 28, p. 97.*

HEDEN, Richard, Boston, Mass.; from Great Britain, Oct., 1714; warned out, June 14, 1715. — *Boston Rec. Com., Vol. 11, p. 229.*

HEDMAN, Joseph, of Boston, Mass.; from Ireland, before 1721; int. m. Sarah Miller, Jan. 24, 1721, forbid by her father; m. Mary Smith Nov. 5, 1728, in Newbury, Mass. (she was also from Ireland).—*Newbury Vital Records, Vol. II, p. 227; Boston Rec. Com., Vol. 28, p. 159.*

HEDMAN, Philip, of Boston, Mass.; in Boston before 1718; m. Elizabeth ———; Children: Eliza, Benjamin.—*Boston Rec. Com., Vol. 24, pp. 129, 145.*

HEIDENHEIM, Frederick, of Broad Bay, Waldoboro, Maine; from Germany, before 1760. — *Miller's Waldoboro, p. 51.*

HELTON, Ann. See John Lobden.

HEMPHILL, David, of Newburyport, Mass.; from Ireland, before 1769; yeoman. — *Deed of Belfast, Maine, 1769.*

HEMPHILL, Nathaniel, of Windham, N. H.; from County Antrim, Ireland, 1728; b. 1700; m. the Widow Isabella Robinson; Children: Jane, Robert, Isabella, Nathaniel; m. 2. Mrs. Mary Dunlap; d. 1780.— *Morrison's Windham, p. 575; Merrill's Ackworth, p. 227.*

HENDERSON, Hugh, of R. I. (alias John Hamilton); from Ireland, in 1729; b. Armagh, Ireland, about 1710; executed Nov. 24, 1737.

HENDERSON, John, of Boston, Mass.; from Ireland, 1719; m. ————; Children: five.—*Cullen's Irish in Boston, p. 5.*

HENDERSON, John, of Portsmouth, N. H.; from Colraine, Ireland, before 1721; m. Sarah Keel, Jan. 1, 1722. —*N. E. Hist. Gen. Reg., Vol. 24, p. 15.*

HENDERY, Malkem, of Rutland, Mass.; from Ireland, Parish of Ardstraw, before 1720; he brought a letter from the Rev. Mr. Halyday there; m. Margaret McCarter, in Rutland, June, 1720; Child: Andrew; d. about 1730.—*Reed's Rutland, pp. 82, 153, 154; Rutland Vital Rec., pp. 50, 151.*

HENDLEY, Matthew, of ————, R. I.; from Limerick, Ireland, cir. 1775.—*Murray's Irish Rhode Islanders, p. 34.*

HENRY, Hugh, of Colraine, Mass.; from Ireland? before 1750; married and had five children; d. 1754. — *McClellan's Colraine, p. 74.*

HENRY, John, of Colraine, Mass.; from Ireland? before 1750; brother of Hugh Henry, q. v.; m. Mary McCrellis from Ireland; m. 1. ——— Foster, 2. ——— Workman, 3. John Henry, 4. Richard Ellis, d. May 11, 1802, aet. 96; Children: William, James, John, Andrew; d. cir. 1750.—*McClellan's Colraine, p. 74.*

HENRY, Robert, of Boston, Mass.; from Ireland, 1741; blacksmith.—*Cullen's Irish in Boston, p. 32.*

HERBERT, John, of Deerfield, Mass., and Bangor, Me.; from England in the "Old French War," as Chaplin and surgeon of a British Regiment; before 1760; m. ————; Child: George; d. 1785.—*Sheldon's Deerfield, Mass., p. 199.*

HERR, Samuel, of Broad Bay, Waldobore, Maine; from Germany, 1760.—*Miller's Waldoboro, p. 61.*

HEWES, Robert, Boston, Mass.; from Ireland, cir. 1714; int. m. Sarah Dunnel, Sept. 30, 1714.—*Boston Rec. Com., Vol. 28, p. 94.*

HEWEY, Samuel, Portsmouth, N. H.; from Colraine, County Derry, Ireland, before 1718; m. Elizabeth Denett, widow, Dec. 23, 1718.—*N. E. Hist. Gen. Reg., Vol. 23, p. 395.*

HEYCE, Martin, of Broad Bay, Waldoboro, Maine; from Germany, 1760; m. ————; Child: Conrad; d. before his son was born.—*Miller's Waldoboro, pp. 25, 26.*

HICKEY, John, of Boston, Mass.; from Dublin, before 1759; linen printer and dyer; m. Elinor Mann, March 8, 1759.—*Boston Gazette, May 7, 1759; Old-Time New England, Vol. 18, p. 39.*

HIGGINS, Alexander, of Newport, R. I.; from Ireland, before 1724; Irish servant of Major Nathaniel Sheffield, aged 18 in 1724; run-away.—*Boston News Letter, Feb. 27, 1724.*

HIGGINS, Fergus, of Scarborough, Me.; from Ireland; Child: Edmund; d. 1777.—*Saco Valley Families, p. 727; History of Scarborough, p. 212.*

HIGGINS, Tully, of Berwick, Me.; from Ireland.—*Saco Valley Families, p. 727; History of Scarborough, p. 212.*

HILDRETH, Mr. ————, of Rutland, Mass.; from England, one of Burgoyne's army, 1775; m. Hannah ————, d. May 12, 1827, aet. 66; d. Dec. 22, 1830, aet. 86. —*Rutland Vital Records, p. 231.*

HILDRETH, Jacob, of Litchfield; from England, cir. 1720; probably son of Ephraim Hildreth; m. Abigail ————; Children: Jacob, Ephraim, William, Abigail, Lucy, John, David.—*Secomb's Amherst, p. 626; Hodgman's Westford, p. 453.*

HILL, Roger, of Boston, Mass.; from Great Britain, before 1717; int. m. Lydia Strong, July 4, 1717.—*Boston Rec. Com., Vol. 28, p. 96.*

HILL, Thomas, of Boston, Mass.; from Ireland, November, 1719; with Captain Dennis; m. perhaps Hannah Cushing, July 13, 1727.—*Boston Record Com., Vol. 13, p. 64; Vol. 28, p. 138.*

HILLIAR, Nicholas, of Boston, Mass.; from Great Britain, before 1712; int. m. Mary Drumer, May 17, 1712.—*Boston Rec. Com., Vol. 28, p. 92.*

HILT, John, of Braintree, Mass.; "Germantown," 1761. —*Mass. State Archives, Vol.* 15A, *pp.* 240-242.

HILT, Captain Peter, of Waldoboro, Maine; from Germany, in 1760; m. Polly Klaus; Children: Mary, John, Philip, Elizabeth, Catherine, Peter, Henry, Anne; d. at sea 1785, aet. 37.—*Eaton's Warren, p.* 398; *New Edition, p.* 551; *Waldoboro grave yard.*

HILTON, Mathias, Portsmouth, N. H.; from Monkweymouth, County Durham, before 1738; m. Margaret King, Aug. 13, 1738.—*N. E. Hist. Gen. Reg., Vol.* 26, *p.* 378.

HINDS, Corliss, of Barre, Mass.; from England, before 1764; m. ————, d. Feb. 13, 1806, aet. 83; Child: Jesse Corlis; d. Nov., 1811, aet. 90.—*Barre Vital Records, p.* 247; *Randall's Chesterfield, p.* 355.

HINES, John, Portsmouth, N. H.; from Kent, before 1724; m. Elizabeth Ray, Aug. 11, 1724. —*N. E. Hist. Gen. Reg., Vol.* 24, *p.* 18.

HINKS, William, of Boston, Mass.; from Northern Ireland, 1718, in ship "Friends Goodwill," Edward Goodin, Captain.—*Court of Sessions of the Peace of Suffolk County.*

HIPSLEY, Peter, of Boston, Mass.; from Virginia, cir. Oct. 1703; warned out, 1703.—*Boston Rec. Com., Vol.* 11, *p.* 28.

HOCH, George, Martin, and C————, of Broad Bay, Waldoboro, Me.; from Germany, before 1760 (see also Conrad Koch).—*Miller's Waldoboro, p.* 51.

HODGES, Sabastian, of Boston, Mass.; from the Barbadoes, with Captain Huntington, 1715; warned out May 3, 1715.—*Boston Rec. Com., Vol.* 11, *p.* 227.

HODGKINS, John, of Warren, Maine; from Scotland, 1753; removed to Boston.—*Eaton's Warren, p.* 85, *p.* 121.

HODGSON, John, of Boston, Mass.; from Scotland, cir. 1762; m. ? Cecilia ————; Children: William, Christian, Elizabeth, Nancy, Cecilia; d. 1781.—*Thomas's History of Printing, Vol.* 2, *p.* 228; *Boston Rec. Com., Vol.* 24, *pp.* 308, 310, 318, 322, 327.

HOFFSES, Anthony, of Broad Bay, Waldoboro, Me.; from Germany, before 1760.—*Miller's Waldoboro, p.* 51.

HOGAN, Dennis, of ———, R. I.; from Limerick, Ireland, before 1775; b. cir. 1751.—*Murray's Irish Rhode Islanders, p.* 28.

HOGG, George, of Salem, Mass.; from Ireland, before 1732; dug a well for Judge Benjamin Lynde.—*Benjamin Lynde's Journal, p.* 33.

HOGG, Joseph, of Londonderry, N. H.; from Ireland, cir. 1754; son of James Hogg; m. Mary Moor, daughter of James and Elizabeth (Gregg) Moor; Children: Thomas, William, Hugh, James, Agnes N., Mary, Sarah; the four sons changed their name to Moor in 1803. — *Cochran's Francestown, p.* 757; *Woodbury's Bedford, N. H., p.* 947.

HOGG, Robert, of New Boston, N. H.; from Ireland, cir. 1754; b. 1732; son of James Hogg; m. Margaret Gregg, of Londonderry, N. H:; Children: Mary, Susan, James, Robert, Margaret, Samuel, Joseph, Thomas, John, Nancy; d. 1795. — *Cogswell's New Boston, p.* 423; *Woodbury's Bedford, N. H.; p.* 311; *Cochran's Francestown, p.* 756.

HOGG, Robert, of Boothbay, Me.; from Great Britain in May, 1764, with John Leishman, who was born in Falkirk, Scotland.—*Greene's Boothbay, p.* 478.

HOLBROOK, John, Boston, Mass.; from Great Britain, before 1710; int. m. Mary Gross, Sept. 13, 1710.— *Boston Rec. Com., Vol.* 28, *p.* 32.

HOLDEN, William, from Dublin, Ireland, husbandman; b. cir. 1710; volunteer against the West Indies, 1740. —*Colonial Wars,* 1899.

HOLE, Henry, of Ashburnham, Mass., (afterwards Hall); from Germany, cir. 1750; b. 1711; m. Anna Mary Saunders, in Germany, d. 1802, aet. 76, (will, she signs as Mary Hall); Children: Mary, John, Henry, Katherine; d. Oct. 14, 1794, aet. 83.—*Stearns Ashburnham, p.* 727; *Worcester Probate, Series A,* 26489.

HOLGRAVE, John, to New England; from Haslingdon, Lancashire, 1699, in the "Virginia," Edmund Ball, Master; twenty-eight years old, with seven years to serve.—*N. E. Hist. Gen. Reg., Vol.* 64, *p.* 259.

HOLLAND, Col. Stephen, of Londonderry, N. H.; from Ireland, before 1775.—*Parker's Londonderry, p.* 107.

HOLMAN, Solomon, of Newbury, Mass.; from England, before 1703; b. cir. 1672; m. Mary ———, b. cir. 1683, d. Oct. 18, 1736, aet. 63; Children: Elizabeth, John, James, Sarah, Ruth, Rachel, Sarah, Anna, Thomas; d. May 7, 1753, aet. 81.—*Newbury Vital Records, Vol.* 1, *pp.* 226, 227; *Vol.* 2, *pp.* 236, 237, 617.

HOLMES, Abraham, of Londonderry, N. H.; from Ireland, in ship "Elizabeth"; warned out Nov. 3, 1719; m. 1. ———; m. 2. Mary Morrison; Child: John; d. 1753, aged 70.—*Parker's Londonderry, p.* 277; *Secomb's Amherst, p.* 634; *Boston Rec. Com., Vol.* 13, *p.* 63; *Documentary History of Maine, p.* 20.

HOLMES, Rebecca, of Boston, Mass.; from New York, 1723; warned out, Feb. 19, 1723.—*Boston Rec. Com., Vol.* 13, *p.* 110.

HOLT, Simon, of Boston, Mass.; from Philadelphia with his wife, 1710; gardner; warned out, Jan. 1710.—*Boston Rec. Com., Vol.* 11, *pp.* 99, 100.

HOLTON, Rowland, of Boston, Mass.; "from London in Demerra, merchant," 1720 (Demerara?); warned out Oct. 28, 1720.—*Boston Rec. Com., Vol.* 13, *p.* 76.

HOLTZAPPLE, David, of Broad Bay, Waldoboro, Me.; from Germany, cir. 1760; went to North Carolina after 1770.—*Miller's Waldoboro, p.* 67.

HOMES, Rev. William, of Chilmark, Mass.; from Strabane, Ireland, 1715; b. 1662; m. Katharine Craighead; Children: Robert, John, Margaret, Jane, Agnes, Elizabeth, Margery, Katherine, William, Hannah; d. 1747.—*Rev. Wm. Homes' Diary, Ms.* owned by the N. E. Hist. Gen. Soc.

HONEYMAN, James, of R. I.; from New York, 1702-3; "clerk"; "formerly chaplain at New York, and is now going chaplain to Rhode Island," 1708.—*Emigrant Ministers to America, p.* 34.

Hood, David, of Marblehead, Mass.; from Ireland, before 1723; m. Elenor McFarland, also from Ireland, at Marblehead, Nov. 27, 1723; Children: Margaret, Breed(?).—*Marblehead Vital Records, Vol. I, p.* 269; *Vol. II, pp.* 219, 582.

Hood, James, of Pelham, Mass.; from Great Britain, before 1738; m. Easter Gray, 1747, d. 1811; Children: 2 sons and 2 daughters (Jennet? Jonathan? Nancy?) record torn.—*Parmenter's Pelham, p.* 17; *Pelham Vital Records, p.* 47.

Hooper, Henry, from Bristol, England, 1716; Chirurgeon.—*Boston Rec. Com., Vol.* 29, *p.* 233.

Hooper, John, of Portsmouth, N. H.; from Apsum, Great Britain, before 1716; m. Mary Waldin Dec. 13, 1716.—*N. E. Hist. Gen. Reg., Vol.* 23, *p.* 393.

Hooton, John, Boston, Mass.; from Great Britain, before 1719; int. m. Sarah Wye (see John Currill) June 5, 1719; Children: John, John, Thomas, Sarah, Richard, William, Joan.—*Boston Rec. Com., Vol.* 28, *p.* 98; *Vol.* 24, *pp.* 144, 151, 160, 171, 182, 193, 203.

Hope, James, of Portland, Me.; from Stoke Damerell, Devonshire, cir. 1762; m. ———, and had one daughter.—*Smith's and Dean's Journal, p.* 210.

Hopkins, ———, of ———, Me. (see William); m. Jenny Morison of Sheepscott, Me.—*Morrison's Windham, p.* 595.

Hopkins, Christopher, of Newcastle, Me.; from Devonshire, England, before 1778; m. 1. Mary ———; m. 2. Abigail Newbit, 1778; Child: William.—*Cushman's Ancient Sheepscot and Newcastle, pp.* 391-2.

Hopkins, Edward, of Portsmouth, N. H.; from Appledore, Devonshire, before 1720; m. Joanna Ball of Berwick, Me., May 3, 1720.—*N. E. Hist. Gen. Reg., Vol.* 24, *p.* 14.

Hopkins, James, of Londonderry, N. H.; from Ireland, 1720; m. Mary ———; Children: John, James, Robert.—*Morrison's Windham, p.* 595; *Cochran's Antrim, p.* 542.

Hopkins, John, of Windham, N. H.; from Ireland, 1730; m. Elizabeth Dinsmoor; Children: James, Margaret,

John, Robert, Nancy or Molly, Ruth; died after February, 1779.—*Morrison's Windham, p.* 589; *Cochran's Francestown. p.* 762; *Cochran's Antrim, p.* 542.

HOPKINS, Robert, of Windham, N. H.; from Ireland, 1720; m. 1. Elenor Wilson; m. 2. Martha ———; Children: Elizabeth, Sarah, James, Robert, Boyd, Elenor.—*Morrison's Windham, p.* 595; *Cochran's Francestown, p.* 762; *Cochran's Antrim, p.* 542.

HOPKINS, Solomon, of Boston, Mass.; wife and one child from "Pencilvania," 1722; warned out May 26, 1722. —*Boston Rec. Com., Vol.* 13, *p.* 101.

HOPKINS, Thomas, of Portland, Me.; from Axminster, England, 1784; Children: James D., Thomas, and three daughters.—*Smith's and Dean's Journal, p.* 252.

HOPKINS, William, of Newcastle, Maine (see Hopkins, ———), from Ireland, before 1735; Children: Jenny, Patty, Solomon; d. in Canada, where he had been carried by the Indians.—*Cushing's Ancient Sheepscot and Newcastle, p.* 319.

HORNE, Robert, of Marlborough and Framingham, Mass.; from Flanders, before 1723; m. Elizabeth Maynard, daughter of Simon Maynard, Aug. 7, 1723; Child: Robert.—*Temple's Framingham, pp.* 596, 597; *Marlborough Vital Records, pp.* 94, 266.

HORNEY, David, of Portsmouth, N. H.; from Gallway, Ireland, before 1720; m. Elizabeth Broughton, Nov. 1720.—*N. E. Hist. Gen. Reg., Vol.* 24, *p.* 14.

HOUDELETTE, Charles Stephen, of Dresden and Frankfort, Me.; from France cir. 1752; lace weaver; b. 1707; Child: Louis; d. 1784, at Pownalboro, Me., aet. 77.—*Maine Hist. Soc. Coll., 2d Series, vol.* 3, *p.* 351; *Allen's Huguenots in Dresden, pp.* 6, 7.

HOUDELETTE, Louis, of Dresden, Maine; Huguenot from France, cir. 1752; b. Sept. 8, 1746, son of Charles Stephen Houdelette; m. Mary Cavalear, Jan. 31, 1770, b. Nov. 15, 1748; d. 1835.—*Allen's Huguenots in Dresden, pp.* 1, 6, 7, 8.

HOUDEN, William, of Petersborough, N. H.; from England, cir. 1775; m. Sarah Barnard, of Lynn, Mass., and settled in Salem; Children: William, John, Sally, Polly, Thomas, Betsy, Betsy; d. 1829, in Bristol, Vt.—*Smith's Peterborough, part* 2, *p.* 122; *Salem Vital Records, Vol.* I, *p.* 454.

HOUSTON, Robert, of Andover, Mass.; from the North of Ireland, in the ship "Elizabeth," at Boston, 1719; warned out, Nov. 3, 1719.—*Boston Rec. Com., Vol.* 13, *p.* 60.

HOW, Richard, of Boston, Mass.; from Ireland, in 1716; glover.—*Boston Rec. Com., Vol.* 29, *p.* 232.

HOWARD, James, of Augusta, Me.; from Ireland, before 1736; b. 1702; m. 1. Mary ——, d. 1778; Children: John, Samuel, Margaret, William; m. 2, Susanna (——) Cony, 1781, who m. 3d, William Brooks; Children: Isabella, James; d. May 14, 1787.—*North's Augusta, p.* 882.

HOWARD, Mary, of Boston, Mass.; from London, 1727; warned out April 15, 1727, warned out July 11, 1727.—*Suffolk Court Files,* 20510; *Boston Rec. Com., Vol.* 13, *p.* 167.

HOWEL, John, of Boston, Mass.; from Great Britain, before 1716; int. m. Eliza Player, March 19, 1716; forbid by Stephen Perks.—*Boston Rec. Com., Vol.* 28, *p.* 95.

HUGHES [alias Freeman], Henry, of East Haven, Conn.; from Wales, 1748; b. 1723; m. Lydia Tuttle, 1749; Child: Henry.—*Amer. Ances., Vol.* 3, *p.* 189.

HUGHES, Hugh, to New England; from Anglesey, Wales, 1699, in the "Virginia"; nineteen years old, with seven years to serve.—*N. E. Hist. Gen. Reg., Vol.* 64, *p.* 260.

HUGHES, John, of Windham, N. H.; from Great Britain, during the Revolution; m. Mehitable Buzwell, of Kingston, N. H.; Children: William, Elizabeth, Sarah, Anna, Polly, Barnet, John, Hannah, Mehitable, Margaret; d. 1819, aged 75.—*Morrison's Windham, p.* 596.

HUGHES, William, of Boston, Mass.; runaway from Boston; "born in Ireland, about 28 years old, a brick layer, of short stature, brown complexion, his hair of a blackish brown colour, with the ring finger on his left hand bent inwards."—*Boston News Letter, Nov. 25-Dec. 2, 1717 [advertisement]*.

HUMPHRIES, Edward, of Scituate, Mass.; from Ireland, before 1740; m. Anna Sandlin, int. Oct. 3, 1739; Children: Margaret, Edward, Richard, Mary, John. —*Dean's Scituate, p. 290; Scituate Vital Records, Vol. I, p. 187, Vol. II, pp. 155, 398.*

HUMPHREY, Lawrence, of Georgetown and Topsham, Me.; from "the Cove of Cork," Ireland, by way of the West Indies, cir. 1780; b. 1757; m. Elizabeth Campbell, daughter of John Campbell, 1788; Children: Mary, Sally, Nancy, John Campbell, Daniel, Eliza, William, Margaret; d. 1835, in Topsham, Maine.— *Wheeler's Brunswick, pp. 839, 840.*

HUMPHREY, William, of Windham, N. H.; from Londonderry, Ireland, 1719; Child: William.—*Morrison's Windham, p. 603.*

HUNT, Thomas, of Salem, Mass.; from Waterford, Ireland, before 1770; m. Susanna Jefferds [widow], April 3, 1770.—*Salem Vital Records, Vol. 3, p. 529.*

HUNTER, Daniel, of Boston, Mass.; with his wife, "Irish people from small point" [Small Point, Maine], warned out Apr. 26, 1723.—*Suffolk Court Files, 16816.*

HUNTER, George, of New England; from Morn, near Newry in County Down, Ireland, in 1707.—*Boston News Letter, June 10, 1717.*

HUNTER, James, of Cornish, N. H.; from Scotland, before 1770; Children: James Sumner, Lucy, Hannah, and perhaps others.—*Child's Cornish, Vol. II, p. 217.*

HUNTER, Jane, of Boston, Mass., spinster; from Dublin, 1721, in the brigantine "Anne and Rebecca"; m. Edward Dixson, Dec. 18, 1722.—*Mass. Archives, Vol. 105; Court of Sessions of the Peace, 1715-18, Vol. 1, p. 117; Boston Rec. Com., Vol. 28, p. 106.*

HURD, Nicholas, to New England; from Pousonby, Cumberland, 1699, in the "Virginia"; nineteen years old, with seven years to serve.—*N. E. Hist. Gen. Reg., Vol. 64, p. 260.*

HURST, John, of Boston, Mass.; from Great Britain, before 1720; int. m. Margaret Pope, Aug. 26, 1720.—*Boston Rec. Com., Vol. 28, p. 98.*

HUTCHIN, Zachary, of Boston, Mass.; from New York by land, with his wife and two children, Oct.-Nov. 1717; butcher; warned out, Dec. 23, 1717.—*Boston Rec. Com., Vol. 13, p. 32.*

HUTCHINS, Anne, of Boston, Mass.; from Newcastle, Great Britain, 1721.—*Court of Sessions of the Peace of Suffolk County, 1719-25, Vol. II, p. 124.*

HUTCHINS, Parley, of Stratford, N. H.; from Edinburgh, Scotland, in the British Army, 1774; settled in Connecticut; Child: Parley.—*Thompson's Stratford, p. 395.*

HUTCHINSON, Henry, Boston, Mass.; from Great Britain, before 1710; int. m. Margaret Syle, July 20, 1710. —*Boston Rec. Com., Vol. 28, p. 32.*

HUTCHINSON, Henry, Boston, Mass.; from Great Britain, before 1710; int. m. Mary Ranger, Sept. 14, 1710.—*Boston Rec. Com., Vol. 28, p. 32.*

HUZZEY, John, of ——, R. I.; from Armagh, Ireland, before 1777; b. cir. 1727.—*Murray's Irish Rhode Islanders, p. 34.*

HYER, Conrad, of Broad Bay, Waldoboro, Me.; from Germany, cir. 1760; b. April 10, 1749; d. Feb. 19, 1856. —*Portrait in the Church, Waldoboro, Maine.*

HYSLOP, William, of Boston, Mass.; from Scotland, cir. 1740; b. Humley Parish, East Lowden, Scotland, cir. 1714; m. Mehitable Stoddard; Children: James, William, David, Elizabeth; pedlar; "In 1746 he lodged at the house of Mr. John Williams at the sign of the Three Sugar Loaves, King Street; d. 1796.— *Bolton's Brookline, p. 28; Ancient and Honorable Artillery Co., p. 74; Boston Rec. Com., Vol. 24, pp. 277, 282, 287, 291; Boston News Letter, May 29, 1746.*

INGRAM, John, of Boston, Mass.; from Lisbon, before 1752; mustard-maker, near Oliver's Dock, Boston.—

Boston Gazette, Sept. 19, 1752; *Old-Time New England, Vol.* 18, *p.* 39.

IRISH, James, of Falmouth, Maine; from England, 1711; m. Elizabeth ——; Children: John, Miriam, Joseph, Elizabeth, Thomas, James, Thomas, William; d. in Gorham, Me., aged 53.—*McLellan's Gorham, p.* 583.

JACKSON, John, of Boston, Mass.; from England, Aug. 1716; "Joyner."—*Boston Rec. Com., Vol.* 13, *p.* 10.

JACKSON, Stephen, of Providence, R. I.; from Kilkenny, Ireland, cir. 1724; b. 1700.—*Murray's Rhode Islanders, p.* 29.

JACKSON, Thomas; from Ireland, cordwainer; b. cir. 1716; volunteer against the West Indies, 1740.—*Colonial Wars, p.* 1899.

JACOB, Daniel, of Dresden, Me.; from France.—*Allen's Huguenots in Dresden, p.* 18.

JACOE, Denis, of Dresden, Maine; from France.—*Allen's Huguenots in Dresden, p.* 18.

JARVIS, Freeman, Portsmouth, N. H.; from Great Britain, before 1736; m. Mehitable Hatch, of Charlestown, in Portsmouth, Dec. 23, 1736.—*N. E. Hist. Gen. Reg., Vol.* 26, *p.* 377.

JAMES, William, of Warren, Maine; from Ireland, cir. 1735; b. 1689; m. Catherine Cunningham; Children: William, Patrick, Phebe, Fanny, Catherine, Anna, Joseph; d. Oct. 29, 1770, aged 81.—*Eaton's Warren, p.* 401; *New Ed., p.* 559.

JAMESON, Hugh, of Dunbarton, N. H.; from the Isle of Man, or from Colraine, Ireland, on the sloop "Molly," cir. 1740; son of William Jameson of Belfast, Ireland; m. 1st, Chrystal or Christine Whitehead, of the Isle of Man, d. cir. 1788; m. 2d, Jane McHenry, widow of John Barr, of Londonderry, N. H.; Children: Jane, Elizabeth, Rosina, Esther, Martha, son, d. e., son, d. e., Molly, Alexander, Daniel, Hugh, Peggy, Sarah, Thomas; d. 1790.—*American Ancestry, Vol.* 3, *p.* 29; *Hadley's Goffstown, pp.* 233-4.

JEROULD, see Gerould.

JEWEL, Philip, of Portsmouth, N. H.; from "the Parish

of Yanton in ye County of Biddeford," before 1739;
m. Elizabeth Wilkinson, Nov. 8, 1739.—*N. E. Hist.
Gen. Reg., Vol.* 26, *p.* 380.

JIRAULD, Reuben, of Cornish, N. H.; from France, "at the time of the Huguenot wars"; b. 1734; settled first at Plainfield, Conn.; m. Joanna Spaulding, b. 1733, d. 1807; Children: Martha, Polly, Hannah, Sally; d. May 8, 1800.—*Childs' Cornish, Vol. II, p.* 231.

JOHNSON, Abraham, of Cornish, Portsmouth and Greenland, N. H.; from England, before 1760; m. Mercy Huggins, cir. 1760, b. 1739, d. 1815; Children: Sarah, Joshua, Hannah, John, Margaret, Rebecca, Elizabeth, Mercy, Mary, Abraham; d. October 24, 1893. —*Childs' Cornish, Vol. II, pp.* 231-2.

JOHNSON, Adam, of Pelham, Mass.; from Great Britain, before 1738.—*Parmenter's Pelham, p.* 17.

JOHNSON, James, of Scarborough, Maine; from Auckley, Scotland, cir. 1732; Children: John, James.—*McLellan's Gorham, p.* 593.

JOHNSON, John, of Boston, Mass.; from London, 1737; gunsmith; granted liberty to follow his calling.—*Boston Rec. Com., Vol.* 15, *p.* 57.

JOHNSON, John, of Shrewsbury, Mass.; from Great Britain, before 1738.—*Parmenter's Pelham, p.* 17.

JOHNSON, Michael, of Londonderry, N. H., Haverhill, Mass., and Hampstead, N. H.; from Londonderry, Ireland, 1727 or 1728; m. Mary Hancock before 1728; Children: Miriam, John, Michael, Sarah, Charles, Robert.—*Whitcher's Haverhill, N. H., p.* 552; *Haverhill Vital Records, Vol.* 2, *p.* 183.

JOHNSTON, Thomas, of Warren, Me.; from Scotland, 1735; removed to Bristol, Me.; d. 1811.—*Eaton's Warren, p.* 85, 121.

JOHNSTON, Rev. William, of Windham, N. H.; from Mullow Male, County Tyrone, Ireland, before 1736; b. 1710; educated at Edinburgh University; m. Annie Cummings; Children: William, Anna, Nancy, Lois, Elizabeth, Witter, Hugh C.; d. Florida, N. Y.,

1782.—*Morrison's Windham, p.* 607; *First Settlers in Northern Worcester, p.* 50.

JAMESON, James; called on Rev. Wm. Homes at Chilmark, Nov. 3, 1717, with John McClellam.

JAMESON, Thomas, of Dumbarton, N. H.; from Belfast, Ireland, cir. 1740; b. 1710; m. Margaret Dickey; Children: Mary, Alexander John, Margaret, Hugh, Thomas, and one other; [see his brother Hugh Jameson].—*Cochran's Antrim, p.* 555.

JAMIESON, William, of Portland, Me.; from Ireland, in 1718.—*Smith's and Dean's Journal, p.* 60.

JAQUIN, George, of Dresden, Me.; from France.—*Allen's Huguenots in Dresden, p.* 18.

JAQUIN, James Frederick, of Frankfort and Dresden, Me.; from France, via Halifax, 1702.—*Allen's Huguenots in Dresden, p.* 14.

JECKYLL, John, of Boston, Mass.; from England, before 1733; born in England, the son of Thomas Jeckyll, D.D.; d. before January 4, 1733 ("died last Friday").—*Boston News Letter, Jan.* 4, 1733.

JEFFERS, John; convict assigned to Apthorp and Hancock, July 18, 1747, from Wm. Cookson of Hull.—*Suffolk Court Files.*

JEFFRIES, Charles, Boston, Mass.; sailor from South Yarmouth, Isle of Wight, to Philadelphia; from Philadelphia on sloop "Humbird," 1737; ill.—*Boston Rec. Com., Vol.* 15, *p.* 48.

JENKINS, Richard, Boston, Mass.; from Great Britain, cir. 1713; int. m. Bethia Hughs, July 27, 1713; bans forbidden by Nathaniel Dew.—*Boston Rec. Com., Vol.* 28, *p.* 93.

JENNESS, Job, of Rye, N. H.; from England, cir. 1750; Children: Samuel, Benjamin; drowned.—*Carter's Pembroke, Vol.* 2, *p.* 163.

JEPSON, William, of Wells, Me.; from Magwater?, Ireland (Moy-water?).—*Browne's Wells and Kennebunk, p.* 313.

JEREE, Peter, of Boston, Mass.; from "Jersie," before 1716; int. m. Anna Foosheron, May 8, 1716, "from

London with Capt. Thomas."—*Boston Rec. Com.,
Vol.* 28, *p.* 95.
JOHONNOT, Daniel, of Boston, Mass.; Huguenot, from
France, before 1700; m. Susannah Johnson, April
18, 1700; Children: Zachariah, Daniel, Andrew, Marianna.—*Temple's Framingham, p.* 610; *Boston Vital
Records, Vol.* 28, *p.* 1; *Vol.* 24, *pp.* 3, 25, 35, 42.
JOINER, Edward, of Sudbury, Charlestown, Leominster
and Deerfield, Mass.; from Wales or Isle of Jersey,
cir. 1740; m. —— ——, d. June 8, 1803, aet. 93;
Children: Edward, Elizabeth, William; d. May,
1796, in Deerfield.—*Sheldon's Deerfield, p.* 221.
JONES, David, of Boston, Mass.; shipwright, from London, April 27, 1727; warned out July 11 (return),
1727; m. Elizabeth Alcott, Feb. 24, 1731.—*Suffolk
Court Files,* 20510; *Boston Rec. Com., Vol.* 13, *p.*
167, *Vol.* 28, *p.* 172.
JONES, Edward, of Boston, Mass.; from Great Britain,
cir. 1713; int. m. Sarah Wayman, June 19, 1714.—
Boston Rec. Com., Vol. 28, *p.* 93.
JONES, Eldridge, of Boston, Mass.; from London, 1741;
corkcutter.—*Boston News Letter, May* 28, 1741.
JONES, John, of Boston, Mass.; from Parish of St. Nicholas, Glamorganshire, Wales, in 1725; he brought
a letter to the Parish in Boston, 1725, when he came
to settle the estate of his brother, Captain Thomas
Jones of Boston, captain of the "Blessing." Other
heirs: brothers William and Richard, sisters Elizabeth, Cicile.—*Suffolk Probate, Vol.* 24, *pp.* 86, 250,
285, 617.
JONES, John, of Newbury, Mass.; from Rochester, Kent,
England, before 1744; m. Martha Mitchell, March
25, 1744, in Newbury.—*Newbury Vital Records,
Vol.* 2, *p.* 330.
JONES, John, to New England; from Clanderry, Denbyshire, Wales, 1699, in the "Virginia." Edmund Ball,
Master; seventeen years old, with seven years to
serve.—*N. E. Hist. Gen. Reg., Vol.* 64, *p.* 259.
JONES, Margaret, to New England; from Ritchen, in

Denbyshire, 1699, in the "Virginia," Edmund Ball, Master; thirty-two years old, with seven years to serve.—*N. E. Hist. Gen. Reg., Vol.* 64, *p.* 259.

JONES, Richard, of Boston, Mass.; bricklayer, from Bristol, April, 1717; warned out June 19, 1717.—*Boston Rec. Com., Vol.* 13, *p.* 21.

JONES, Thomas, of Warren, Me.; from England, before 1782; Children: Hannah, Sarah, Lucy, Williams, William, Thomas, John, Mary, Elija, Rebecca.—*Eaton's Warren, pp.* 561-2.

JONES, Thomas, of Hanover, Mass.; perhaps from Wales; m. ——— ———; Child, Noah.—*Amer. Ances, Vol.* 3, *p.* 165.

JONES, William, of Portsmouth, N. H.; from Rythyn, Wales, before 1720; m. Anna Mason, of Nechowanuck, Sept. 13, 1720.—*N. E. Hist. Gen. Reg., Vol.* 24, *p.* 14.

JONG, Michael, of Broad Bay, Me. (see also Jung); from Germany, before 1764.—*Miller's Waldoboro, p.* 64.

JORDEN, Patrick, of Boston; from Virginia, April 27, warned out July 11 (return), 1727; a hatter from Maryland; admitted a citizen, May 3, 1727, on £100 security.—*Suffolk Court Files,* 20,510; *Boston Rec. Com., Vol.* 13, *pp.* 163, 167.

JUNG, Valentine, of Broad Bay, Waldoboro, Me. (see also Jong); from Germany, before 1782.—*Mass. Archives, Vol.* 15-A, *pp.* 240-2.

JUPP, John, of Shirley, Mass.; from England, a deserter from the British army; m. Mary Simonds, int. Nov. 12, 1774, m. 2. Nathan Smith; Child: Mary; "John Jupp, Englishman," d. Dec. 17, 1780.—*Shirley Vital Records, pp.* 56, 141, 196; *Bolton's Shirley Uplands and Intervales, p.* 356.

KALLOCK, ———, of Portsmouth, N. H. [or Kellock]; from Ireland, before 1725; Children: David, Finley; removed to Philadelphia; d. in Philadelphia.—*Eaton's Thomaston, p.* 294; *New Ed., p.* 563.

KALLOCK, Finley, of Warren, Me. (Kellock); from Ireland, before 1725, son of above, q. v.; m. Mary

Young; Children: David, John, Mary, Matthew, Alexander, Margaret.—*Warren's Eaton, p.* 563.

KARR, James, of Bow, N. H.; from Ireland, 1722; brother of John Karr of Merrimack, N. H.; killed by the Indians, 1748.—*Whiton's Antrim, p.* 59.

KARR, John, of Merrimac, N. H.; from Ireland, 1722; m. Isabella Walker.—*Whiton's Antrim, p.* 59.

KARR, John, of Chester, N. H.; from Bally Wollon, Ireland, cir. 1736; m. Elizabeth Wilson, in Ireland; Children: John, Mark, Joseph; d. 1792, aged 75.—*Chase's Chester, p.* 483.

KARRICK, Bryan, of Boston, Mass.; from Ireland in ship "Catherine," Robert Waters, master, before June 24, 1737; accepted as an inhabitant.—*Boston Rec. Com., Vol.* 15, *p.* 54.

KASSON, Adam, of Voluntown, Conn.; perhaps from near Carrickfergus, Ireland, in 1722; b. 1682; m. Jane Hall; Child: James; d. 1752.—*American Ancestry, Vol.* 3, *p.* 205.

KAVANAUGH, James, of Newcastle, Me.; from Ireland, 1781; b. at New Ross, County Wexford, Ireland; m. Sarah Jackson, of Boston, d. Jan. 16, 1813; owned land and mills at Damariscotta Falls, Me.; Children: Edward, Sally, John, Margaret, Francis M., James, Winniefred; d. June 30, 1828, aet. 72.—*Ancient Sheepscott and Newcastle, pp.* 395-6.

KAY, Brian, of Haverhill, N. H.; from Yorkshire, England, to Fort Cumberland, 1774, and later to Haverhill; m. 1. Dorothy ——, b. 1782, d. cir. 1800; m. 2. Mrs. Elsie McCormack, d. before 1810; m. 3. Mrs. Mary Smith, widow of David Smith; Children: Elizabeth, Hannah, Sarah, Anne, Jane, Bryan, Robert, Hannah; d. 1813.—*Whitcher's Haverhill, p.* 556.

KEAIS, H^m, of Portsmouth, N. H.; from Exeter, England, before 1721; m. Elizabeth Perry, Sept. 14, 1721.— *N. E. Hist. Gen. Reg., Vol.* 24, *p.* 14.

KEESE, Henry, of Portsmouth, N. H.; from Exeter, England, before 1720; m. Sarah White, of Topsum, England, in Portsmouth, N. H., May 19, 1720.—*N. E. Hist. Gen. Reg., Vol. 24, p. 14.*

KELAH, John, of Boston, Mass.; arrived in ship "William," with wife and four children, from Ireland, 1718.—*Court of Sessions of the Peace of Suffolk County, 1718.*

KELLEY, see also Kelly.

KELLEY, John; from England, deserter; matross in Captain Lillie's Co., 1777.—*Soldiers and Sailors of the Revolution.*

KELLOCK, see Kallock.

KELSEY, Alexander, of Londonderry, N. H.; from Ireland before 1720, with three brothers; m. Ann [Kelso?]; Children: Margaret, Jonathan, William. —*Londonderry Vital Records, p. 77; E. S. Bolton, Mss. History of the Kelsey Family; Cogswell's New Boston, p. 383.*

KELSEY, John, of Harvard and Shirley, Mass.; from Ireland, before 1721; m. Martha McFarland, of Lunenburg, Jan. 10, 1740, d. 1774; Children: John, Martha, Betsy; d. March 1, 1780, aet. 85.—*Chandler's Shirley, p. 487; E. S. Bolton, Mss. History of the Kelsey Family; Lunenburg Records, p. 253; Shirley Vital Records, pp. 56, 196.*

KELSO, Hugh, of Worcester; from Londonderry, Ireland, in 1718; wheelwright; m. Sarah ———; Children: Matthew Gray, Jean, John, Sarah, "Shusanah," "Marey," (Matthew Gray married his daughter Jean); will probated 14 June 1737.—*Worcester Probate; Lincoln's Worcester, p. 49; Wall's Reminiscences of Worcester, p. 128; Worcester Probate, Series A, 34,458.*

KELLY, see also Kelley.

KELLY, Daniel, of Portsmouth, N. H.; from Limerick, Ireland before 1741; m. Joan Rijan, of Limerick, in Portsmouth, Jan. 15, 1741.—*N. E. Hist. Gen. Reg., Vol. 27, p. 9.*

KELLY, James, of Boston, Mass.; from Ireland, 1716; joiner.—*Boston Rec. Com., Vol. 29, p. 232.*

KELLY, Michael, of Newport, R. I., from Limerick, Ireland, cir. 1775.—*Murray's Irish Rhode Islanders, p. 34.*

KELLY, Robert, of Newcastle, Me.; from England, 1793-5, with Captain David Otis; b. Liverpool; m. Mary Holmes, daughter of John Holmes, cir. 1809; Children: Robert, James, William, Daniel D.—*Ancient Sheepscott and Newcastle.*

KELLYGRUE, Henry, of Boston, Mass.; in Boston before 1722; m. Mary Worthylak, Sept. 12, 1722.—*Boston Rec. Com., Vol. 28, p. 107.*

KENDALL, [Mrs.] Sarah, of Salem, Mass.; from Staffordshire, England, before 1713; daughter of James Kendall, glover, of Staffordshire; m. Thomas Maule, merchant, Oct. 6, 1713.—*Salem Vital Records, Vol. 4, p. 76.*

KENNEDY, Hugh, Boston, Mass.; in Boston before 1720; m. Mary Wyer, Dec. 28, 1720.—*Boston Rec. Com., Vol. 28, p. 88.*

KENNEDY, Hugh, Boston, Mass.; in Boston before 1738 (see above); m. Susanna Pico, Nov. 2, 1738; Children: Hugh, Margaret, Elizabeth, Abigail.—*Boston Rec. Com., Vol. 28, p. 207; Vol. 24, pp. 237, 240, 246, 267.*

KENNEDY, John, Boston, Mass.; in Boston before 1743; m. Joanna Daniels, Jan. 12, 1743; Child: Mary.—*Boston Rec. Com., Vol. 28, p. 251; Vol. 24, p. 257.*

KENNEDY, Matthew, Boston, Mass.; in Boston before 1747; m. Jane Vibert, May 21, 1747; Child: Mary. —*Boston Rec. Com., Vol. 28, p. 251; Vol. 24, p. 274.*

KENNEDY, Samuel, of Sheepscott, Me.; from Ireland, cir. 1731; Children: Jane, James, William, Agnes, Sarah, Samuel, Robert.—*Ancient Sheepscott and Newcastle, p. 396.*

KENNEDY, William, Boston, Mass.; in Boston before 1750; m. Margaret Dalrymple, Nov. 1, 1700.—*Boston Rec. Com., Vol. 28, p. 341.*

KENNISTON, John, of Nottingham, N. H.; from Scotland, 1746, after battle of Culloden Moor; b. Scotland;

m. —— ——; Children: David, Joseph, Isaac, Joshua, Samuel, Thomas.—*Greene's Boothbay, p.* 554.

KENNY, James, Portsmouth, N. H.; from Cadteen, County Tyrone, Ireland, before 1726; m. Lydia Linsley, Nov. 17, 1726.—*N. E. Hist. Gen. Reg., Vol.* 24, *p.* 358.

KEPPLE, James, of Salem, Mass.; from Roddingham, County Suffolk, before 1771; m. Ruth Williams, of Danvers, late of Lynn, int. Sept. 25, 1771.—*Salem Vital Records, Vol. B, p.* 564.

KERBEL, David, of Broad Bay, Waldoboro, Me.; from Germany, before 1764; m. Margaret ——.—*Miller's Waldoboro, p.* 64.

KERWIN, Robert, of Portsmouth, N. H. and Salem, Mass.; from Newfoundland, before 1770; int. m. Mary Marrow, June 25, 1770.—*Salem Vital Records, Vol.* 4, *pp.* 62, 564.

KERKWOOD, William, of Boston, Mass.; from Glasgow in Snow "Amity," in 1716, with 13 men servants; a pedlar.—*Boston Rec. Com., Vol.* 29, *p.* 232.

KIBLING, or Kiblinger, John, of Ashburnham, Mass.; from Germany, before 1758; b. Germany, 1722; m. Catherine Wolfe, d. 1821, aet. 91; Children: Jacob, John, Catherine, Jane, Elizabeth, Sarah, Margaret, Hannah, Henry; d. 1771.—*Stearn's Ashburnham, p.* 778; *Worcester Probate, Series A,* 26,489.

KID, Matthew, of Londonderry, N. H.; from Ireland, before 1730.—*Documentary History of Maine, p.* 24.

KILBORNE, John, of Boston, Mass.; from Antigua, 1721; a question whether he was a passenger or a sailor.—*Court of Sessions of the Peace of Suffolk County,* 1715-18, *Vol.* 1, *p.* 118.

KILGORE, John, of Kittery, Fryeburg, and Bethel, Me.; from Scotland, before 1764; m. Elizabeth Brickett, of Berwick, Me.; Children: Joseph, John, Benjamin, Samuel, Mary, Sally, Elizabeth, Mehitable, Alice.—*Lapham's Bethel, p.* 571.

KILLICUTT, Thomas, of Dunstable, N. H.; from Ireland, before 1744; m. Mary ——; Children: Submit, Reuben, Jonathan, Thomas, Charity, Othniel.—*Bolton's Shirley Uplands and Intervales, p.* 344.

KILPATRICK, Thomas, of Wells, Maine; from Coleraine, Ireland, 1718-19; m. Margaret ——; Children: John, James, Joseph, William, Thomas, Christopher, Jeremiah, Isaac, Joshua, Mary, Sarah; d. 1762, aet 88.—*Saco Valley Families, p.* 767.

KINCAID, see also Kinkhead.

KINCAID, John, Portsmouth, N. H.; from Waterford, Ireland, before 1718; m. Martha Churchill, Nov. 13, 1718.—*N. E. Hist. Gen. Reg., Vol.* 23, *p.* 395.

KINCAID, John, Boothbay, Maine; came in May, 1764, with John Leishman, who was b. in Falkirk, Scotland.—*Greene's Boothbay, p.* 478.

KINCAID, Patrick, of Brunswick, Maine; from Scotland, cir. 1760; b. cir. 1748; m. Mary Stanwood, daughter of David and Mary (Hunt) Stanwood; d. Dec. 25, 1821; Children: James, David, Patrick, Jeanette, Nellie, Mary; d. Dec. 27, 1817, aet 74.—*Patrick Kincaid and his descendants, MS by Rev. Chas. N. Sinnett, in the N. E. Hist. Gen. Soc., Bolton's Stanwood Family, p.* 73.

KING, James, of Providence, R. I.; from Dublin, Ireland, cir. 1775. — *Murray's Irish Rhode Islanders, p.* 34.

KING, William, Boston, Mass.; from Great Britain, before 1721; int. m. Mary Howard, Feb. 22, 1721. —*Boston Rec. Com., Vol.* 28, *p.* 99.

KINGSTON, Elias, Boston, Mass.; from Great Britain, before 1711; int. m. Martha Brown of Charlestown, May 2, 1711; Children: Elias, Martha, William, Mary, Mary, William, John. — *Boston Rec. Com., Vol.* 28, *p.* 91, *Vol.* 24, *pp.* 84, 114, 137, 145, 161, 176, 187.

KINKHEAD, see also Kincaid.
KINKEAD, Rev. John, of Windham, N. H.; from Ireland, where he was born; perhaps related to Samuel Kinkead of Windham, N. H. — *Morrison's Windham, p.* 613.
KINSEL, Bernhard, of Waldoboro, Maine; from Germany; he went to North Carolina, after 1770. — *Miller's Waldoboro, p.* 67.
KIRKPATRICK, John, of Stirling, Maine; from Scotland, 1753; b. 1734; m. Anne Bradbury; Children: Elizabeth, Ann, William, Roland, Thomas, Mary, Daniel, John, Jabez, Abigail, James; d. 1817, aged 82.— *Eaton's Warren, pp.* 85, 122, 405.
KIRLEY, Nathan, Boston, Mass.; from Great Britain, before 1711; mariner; int. m. Elizabeth Nicholson, April 7, 1711.—*Boston Rec. Com., Vol.* 28, *p.* 91.
KNOX, Adam, of Blandford, Mass.; from the north of Ireland, before 1730; son of William Knox; m. 1. Eleanor ——, d. Dec. 21, 1760; Children: Oliver, Elizabeth, David; m. 2. Mollie Campbell; Children: Jane, Eleanor, Mary, William, John.—*Knox Genealogy, Foote, pp.* 6, 7.
KNOX, Adam, Boston, Mass.; from Ulster, Ireland, 1737; b. 1719; m. Martha King, in Boston, March 12, 1740; Children: Thomas, Adam, Adam, Robert.— *Boston Rec. Com., p.* 246, 249, 270, 282, *Vol.* 28, *p.* 235.
KNOX, John, of Blandford, Mass.; from Ireland, before 1730; son of William Knox; b. cir. 1720; m. Rachel Freeland, Sept. 28, 1741; Children: William, Jane, John, Elizabeth, Rachel, Mary, Sarah, James, Hannah, Eleanor, Elijah; d. cir. 1800, will.—*Knox Genealogy, Foote, p.* 4; *Hopkinton Vital Records, p.* 314.
KNOX, Timothy, of Lancaster, Mass., and Pembroke, N. H.; from Ireland, before 1730; Children: John, William, Margaret, Timothy, David, Mary; d. 1748. —*Lancaster Vital Records, pp.* 57, 279, 280, 282.
KNOX, William, of Hopkinton, Mass.; from the north of Ireland, before 1730; m. Elizabeth ——, alive 1774; Children: John, William, Adam, Griswold (a daughter), Agnes, Elizabeth; d. cir. 1774 (will).—*Knox*

Genealogy, Foote, pp. 1-3, Hopkinton Vital Records, p. 123.

KNOX, William, of Blandford, Mass.; from Ireland, cir. 1730; son of William Knox; b. cir. 1721; m. Isabel Ferguson, Dec. 21, 1749, d. Aug. 25, 1808, aet 76; Children: William, Eleanor, Samuel, Elizabeth, John, Nathan, Mary, David, James, Eunice; d. March 9, 1802.—*Knox Genealogy, Foote, pp.* 5, 6.

KNOX, William, of Boston, Mass.; parents of General Henry Knox.—*Eaton's Thomaston, p.* 303.

KOCH, Conrad, of Braintree, Mass.; "Germantown," from Germany, before 1753 (see also Hoch).—*State Archives, Vol.* 15A, *pp.* 240-242, *Pattee's Braintree, p.* 480.

KOCH, John Walter, of Braintree, Mass. (or Roach?); "Germantown," from Germany, before 1761.—*State Archives, Vol.* 15A, *pp.* 240-242, *Pattee's Braintree, p.* 481.

KROEHN, Peter, of Broad Bay, Maine; from Germany, before 1764; m. Elizabeth ———; three children; they moved North Carolina in 1769. — *Miller's Waldoboro, p.* 64.

KUHN, George, of Broad Bay, Maine; from Germany, before 1760.—*Miller's Waldoboro, p.* 51.

KYE, Robert, of Warren, Maine; from Scotland, 1753; killed at Mill River by Indians.—*Eaton's Warren, pp.* 85, 122.

LACORE, John, of Rutland, Mass.; from Ireland, before 1727; m. Margaret Crawford, May 20, 1731; Children: Sarah, Rosanna. — *Reed's Rutland, pp.* 82, 155, *Rutland Vital Records, pp.* 61, 62, 161.

LA CROIX, Frederick, of Medway, Mass.; from Guadaloupe, in 1775; m. Elizabeth Cobb, of Wrentham; Children: William, Millie, Frederick. — *Jameson's Medway, p.* 166.

LAKE, Dr. Lancelot, of Boston, Mass.; graduate physician from Cambridge, England; d. Sept. 17, 1715, aet 63 years.—*King's Chapel Burying Ground.*

LAMB, Elizabeth, wife of William Lamb; Sally, a daughter; Betty, Nancy, Nellie, Beckie, sisters of William Lamb; from Ireland, with Captain John Carrell,

1736; admitted inhabitants Sept. 18, 1736.—*Boston Rec. Com., Vol.* 15, *p.* 3.

LAMMONT, see Lemon.

LANE, Henry, Boston, Mass.; from Barbadoes, 1706, with Capt. Flint; warned out of Boston, 1706.—*Boston Rec. Com., Vol.* 11, *p.* 50.

LANG, William, of Boston, Mass.; from Scotland, cir. 1760; m. Margaret ———; Children: William, James; d. 1775.—*Thomas's History of Printing, Vol.* 2, *p.* 228, *Boston Rec. Com., Vol.* 24, *pp.* 302, 304.

LANGDELL, Livermore, of New Boston, N. H.; from England, before 1746; m. Mary Whitridge, of Beverly, Mass., Nov. 10, 1746; Children: Joseph, Livermore, John, Thomas, William; d. 1799.—*Cogswell's New Boston, p.* 435, *Secomb's Amherst, p.* 666, *Beverly Vital Records, Vol. I, p.* 197, *Vol. II, p.* 182.

LANGLASERIE, Mr. Louis, of Boston, Mass.; from France, before 1730; admitted an inhabitant, with liberty to keep a school to teach French, Oct. 21, 1730.—*Boston Rec. Com., Vol.* 13, 201.

LANMAN, James, Boston, Mass.; from London, England, 1692-1714; son of Thomas and Mary (Elton) Lanman; m. Joanna Boyleston, July 5, 1716; Children: Peter, James, Mary, Samuel.—*Morrison's Windham, p.* 619, *Boston Rec. Com., Vol.* 28, *p.* 65, *Vol.* 24, *pp.* 127, 134, 151.

LARMAN, Robert, Boston, Mass.; from the Canary Islands, with several others, in the sloop "William," Oct., 1720; held up at Spectacle Island with small pox on board; allowed to land, Oct. 28, 1720; a Robert Larman m. Sarah Tyley, Oct. 24, 1715, in Boston. —*Boston Rec. Com., Vol.* 13, *p.* 76, *Vol.* 28, *p.* 59.

LARRY, Dennis, of Gorham, Maine; from Ireland, during the Indian Wars; m. 1. Margaret Brown; Children: John, James; m. 2. Patience Wooster; Child: Stephen; d. Dec., 1796, aged 102.—*McLellan's Gorham, p.* 610.

LARYE, John, Portsmouth, N. H.; from County Cork, Ireland, before 1723; m. Sarah Tout, June 16, 1723. —*N. E. Hist. Gen. Reg., Vol.* 24, *p.* 16.

LATALE, Thomas, Boston, Mass.; [Lataile]; from the Barbadoes, cir. 1714; int. m. Katherine Beauchamp, Oct. 16, 1714; Child: Margaret.—*Boston Rec. Com., Vol.* 28, *p.* 94, *Vol.* 24, *p.* 126.

LATHOG, Robert, of Worcester, Mass.; from Londonderry, Ireland, 1718.—*Wall's Reminiscences of Worcester, p.* 128.

LATTANIRE, Lazurus, Boston, Mass.; from New York, with Captain DeWose, cir. July, 1708, with wife and children; warned out, 1708.—*Boston Rec. Com., Vol.* 11, *p.* 80.

LAUCHLEN, Thomas, Boston, Mass.; in Boston, before 1723; m. Ann Albee, June 5, 1723.—*Boston Rec. Com., Vol.* 28, *p.* 114.

LAUR, Jacob, of Broad Bay, Waldoboro, Maine; from Germany, before 1752.—*Mass. Archives, Vol.* 15A, *pp.* 240-2.

LAUSSON, John, Boston, Mass.; from Ireland, with Captain Dennis, Nov., 1719; a farmer. — *Boston Rec. Com., Vol.* 13, *p.* 64.

LAWRENCE, John, Boston, Mass.; from "Jersie," before 1713; int. m. Marian Beauchamp, Aug. 28, 1713; Children: Marian, John; m. 2. perhaps Dorothy Sastero, Oct. 1, 1720; Children: Mary, Benjamin. — *Boston Rec. Com., Vol.* 28, *pp.* 93, 127, *Vol.* 24, *pp.* 122, 137, 177, 187.

LAYDON, John, Boston, Mass.; from New York, 1723; warned out of Boston, Feb. 19, 1723.—*Boston Rec. Com., Vol.* 13, *p.* 110.

LAYOR, John Henry, of Dresden, Maine; from France.— *Allin's Huguenots in Dresden, p.* 18.

LECHMERE, Thomas, of Boston, Mass.; son of —— Lechmere, and brother of Lord Lechmere; m. Anne Winthrop, Nov. 17, 1709; Children: Lucy, Thomas, Nicholas Winthrop, Anne, Anne, Margaret, Nicholas, Anthony; d. July 4, 1766 —*Mass. Hist. Soc., Winthrop Ms., Boston Rec. Com., Vol.* 28, *p.* 24, *pp.* 69, 84, 99, 122, 130, 141, 156, 166.

LEDYARD, John, of Groton, Conn.; from Bristol, England; b. 1700; m. 1. Deborah Young; m. 2. Mrs.

Mary Ellery: Children: Young, William; d. Sept. 3, 1771.—*Amer. Ances., Vol.* 3, *p.* 33.

LEE, George, Boston, Mass.; from Great Britain, before 1710; int. m. Marg Soyle, Nov. 9, 1710; "forbid by Mr. Hancock by Soyles order." — *Boston Rec. Com., Vol.* 28, *p.* 33.

LEEKY, Matthew, Boston, Mass.; from London in the "New England Galley," Capt. Stephen Hall, 1737; wool comber; he had liberty to open a shop in Boston.—*Boston Rec. Com., Vol.* 15, *p.* 59.

LEGG, John, Boston, Mass.; from London, May 6, 1727; warned out July 11, 1727; m. perhaps Sarah Prindle, May 1, 1728; admitted a citizen on £100 security; a house-wright.—*Suffolk Court File* 20510, *Boston Rec. Com., Vol.* 13, *p.* 163-167, *Vol.* 24, *p.* 144.

LEIGHT, Peter, of Broad Bay, Maine; from Germany, before 1760; a wheelwright.—*Miller's Waldoboro, p.* 51.

LEISHMAN, John, of Boothbay, Me.; from Scotland, 1764; b. Falkirk, Scotland, 1739; m. Sarah McCulloch, widow of Henry Reed, in 1760. d. 1780; Children: Thomas, John, Jennett; d. 1814.—*Greene's Boothbay, p.* 478.

LA FRANCE, Peter, of Marblehead, Mass.; from France, before 1753; m. Alice Meek, in Marblehead, Mary 10, 1753. — *Marblehead Vital Records, Vol. II, p.* 261.

LE GALLAIS, David, Marblehead, Mass.; from France, before 1727; m. Hannah Browne, in Marblehead, July 30, 1727, d. 7:12:1750-1; Children: John, Hannah, and probably David and Sarah; d. March 1, 1755. —*Marblehead Vital Records, Vol. I, p.* 316, *Vol. II, p.* 261, 603.

LE LEFLEURIE, Charles, of Marblehead, Mass.; (afterward Flowers, Florence &c), from France, before 1725; m. Mary Handcock, in Marblehead, Jan. 25, 1725; Children: John, Charles, Jane, and a nameless daughter, and probably Henry and David.— —*Marblehead Vital Records, Vol. I, pp.* 177, 178, *Vol. II, pp.* 147, 261, 546, 547.

LEITCH or Litch, James, of Lunenburg, Mass.; from Ireland, before 1746; m. Janet ——; Children: Thomas, Manasses, John?—*Lunenburg Vital Records, p.* 310.

LE MERCIER, The Rev. André, of Boston, Mass.; from Caen, Normandy, in 1715; Minister of the French Church in Boston; m. Margaret ——; Children: Andrew, James, Andrew, Margaret, Peter, Zachariah, Jane, Stephen Bartholomew; d. March 31, 1764, in Roxbury (will).—*Boston Gazette, April 2, 1764, Boston Rec. Com., Vol. 24, pp.* 138, 145, 151, 161, 166, 177, 182, *N. E. Hist. Gen. Soc., Vol. 13, pp.* 315-324, *Colonial Society of Mass., Feb.,* 1926, *pp.* 343-348.

LEMON, James, of Palmer and Ware, Mass.; from Ireland, in 1727; son of James and Polly Lemon; m. Mary ——; Children: James, Francis, Jane, William, Mary.—*Temple's Palmer, p.* 502, *Chase's Ware, p.* 265.

LEMON, Samuel, of Palmer and Ware, Mass.; from Ireland, in 1727; son of James and Polly Lemon; m. Jane ——; Children: Mary, Samuel, Margaret.— *Temple's Palmer, p.* 502, *Chase's Ware, p.* 265.

LEMONT, John, of Bath, Me.; from Ireland, in 1722; b. County Londonderry, 1704; settled in "Dromore," part of Phipsburg, anciently Georgetown, Maine, between Dromore and the New Meadows River; Child: John; d. at Bath, 1827, aet 86.—*Reed's Bath, p.* 314.

LEND, Martyn, Boston, Mass.; from Newfoundland, Oct., 1716; a sailmaker; he came with a wife and children, intending to settle in Arrowsic, Maine, in the spring.—*Boston Rec. Com., Vol.* 13, *p.* 14.

LENDSEY, Margaret, see Adam Templeton.

LENNOX, Patrick, of Newcastle, Maine; from Scotland, before 1785; a sea captain; b. at Port Patrick, Scotland, April, 1750; m. Margaret McNear at Newcastle, 1785, d. May 17, 1844; Children: Robert, Thomas, Patrick; d. April 17, 1831.—*Cushman's Ancient Sheepscott and Newcastle, p.* 399.

LE REGLE, John, of Boston; from the Parish of Toin, Jersey, before 1752; a mariner.—*Goldthwaite Record ms., Boston Athenaeum.*

LERMOND, ——, of Milton, Mass.; from Ireland, cir. 1719; Children: Ann, John, William, Alexander.— *Eaton's Warren, p. 74, 407, New Ed., p. 571.*

LERMOND, Alexander, of Warren, Maine; from Londonderry, cir. 1719; b. cir. 1707; m. Mary Harkness, in Warren, in 1735, d. April 1, 1790; Children: John, Margaret, Alexander, William, Mary, James, Elizabeth; d. December, 1790. — *Eaton's Warren, Me., 571.*

LESLIE, The Rev. George, of Ipswich, Mass.; from Ireland, with his father, who d. May 12, 1763; b. cir. 1728; educated at Harvard; m. Hepsibah Burpee, Oct. 26, 1756, d. 1814; Children: George, David, James, William, Hepsibah, Joseph, Jonathan, Mehitable, Elizabeth; d. Sept. 11, 1800.—*Childs' Cornish, Vol. 2, pp. 256-7, Ipswich Vital Records, Vol. 1, p. 238, Vol. 2, pp. 276, 615.*

LESLIE, James, of Londonderry, N. H.; from Ireland, before 1722; m. Mary ——, d. April 8, 1722.—*Parker's Londonderry, p. 90.*

LESLIE, James, of Londonderry, N. H.; from Ireland, before March 17, 1730; m. Mary ——; Children: Janet, Sarah, Barber, Daniel, James.—*Documentary History of Maine, p. 20, Londonderry Vital Records, p. 78.*

LEVERIT, Simon, Portsmouth, N. H.; from the Parish of Santua, Jersey, before 174—; m. Elizabeth Hepworth, April 27, 174—.—*N. E. Hist. Gen. Reg., Vol. 27, p. 8.*

LEVIT, George, Boston, Mass.; from Great Britain, before 1720; int. m. Anie Paden, Dec. 3, 1720.—*Boston Rec. Com., Vol. 28, p. 99.*

LEWIN, William, Boston, Mass.; from Great Britain, before 1712; int. m. Sarah Simons, Jan. 7, 1712.— *Boston Rec. Com., Vol. 28, p. 92.*

LEWIS, Jacob, of Braintree, Mass.; "Germantown," from Germany, before 1743. — *State Archives, Vol. 15A, pp. 240-242, Pattee's Braintree, p. 481.*

LEWIS, Lucy, see John Handley.
LEWIS, Mr. Nathaniel, of Boston, Mass.; from Great Yarmouth, County Norfolk, England; merchant; d. May 12, 1778, aet. 42.—*Copp's Hill Burying Ground.*
LEWIS, Maudlin, to New England; from Carmarthen, Wales, 1699, in the "Virginia"; fifteen years old, with seven years to serve.—*N. E. Hist. Gen. Reg., Vol. 64, p. 260.*
LINCH, Eugin, Boston, Mass.; from Virginia to Beverly, Mass., and then to Boston, Nov. 20, 1714; m. Martha Eliott, int. Oct. 17, 1714, in Beverly, Mass.; warned out of Boston, Jan. 25, 1715; Children: Elizabeth, Eugene.—*Boston Rec. Com., Vol. 11, p. 221, Beverly Vital Records, Vol. 1, p. 207.*
LINDSEY, Alexander, Portsmouth, N. H.; from "fforfaine," County Aungus, Scotland, before 1719; m. Lydia Cross, Dec. 3, 1719.—*N. E. Hist. Gen. Reg., Vol. 24, p. 13.*
LINDSEY, Margaret, see Templeton, Adam.
LINSY, Martha, Boston, Mass.; from Ireland, on the ship "Elizabeth"; warned out of Boston, Nov. 3, 1719. —*Boston Record Com., Vol. 13, p. 63.*
LITCH, see also Leitch.
LITCH, Thomas, of Londonderry, N. H., and Winchendon, Mass.; from Ireland, before 1750; b. 1720, the son of James and Janet Litch; m. Jane Kennedy, Sept. 19, 1750, in Lunenburg, Mass.; Children: John, Samuel, Sarah? Jane? Elizabeth?; d. Feb. 28, 1792, in Winchendon, Mass.—*Stearns' Ashburnham, p. 799; Winchendon Vital Records, pp. 49, 139, 202, Lunenburg Records, p. 254.*
LITHGOW, Robert, of Topsham, Maine; from Glendermoth, County Derry, Ireland, 1719; in ship "Olive"; m. Jane McCurdy; Children: Martha, Margaret, Mary, Janet, William, [Susan]; Robert Lithgow, with Susan, William, Jean, and Susan were warned from Boston August 12, 1722, having come from the "East ward."—*Ms. of the Lithgow Family in the N. E. Hist. Gen. Soc.*
LITTLE, Alexander, of Boston, Mass.; from Ireland, before 1769.—*Deed of Belfast, Maine, 1769.*

LITTLE, Archibald, Newcastle, Maine; from Ireland, cir. 1731; Children: James, John, Henry, Alexander, Samuel, and two daughters.—*Cushman's Ancient Sheepscot and Newcastle, p.* 401.

LITTLE, Edward, Newbury, Mass.; from Jamaica, before 1727; b. cir. 1705; m. Elizabeth Gurney, of New York (b. 1708), September 21, 1727, in New Hampshire.—*Newbury Vital Records, Vol.* 2, *p.* 189.

LITTLE, Thomas, of Shirley, Mass.; from Ireland, cir. 1737; b. 1688; m. Jean, d. Sept. 29, 1783, aet 81; Children: William, Peggy, Thomas, Jean, Elizabeth, Martha, Mary; d. Jan. 2, 1767, "supposed to be in the 79th year of his age."—*Chandler's Shirley, p.* 501, *Shirley Vital Records, p.* 198, *Cochran's Antrim, p.* 573, *Smith's Peterborough, pt.* 2, *p.* 133.

LITTLE, Thomas, of Shirley, Mass.; from Ireland, cir. 1737; b. 1727; son of Thomas and Jean Little; m. Susanna Wallace, of Peterborough, d. Mar. 6, 1822; Children: William, Esther, Elizabeth, Susanna, Joseph, Thomas, John, Walter; d. June 6, 1808. — *Chandler's Shirley, p.* 507 *et seq., Shirley Vital Records, pp.* 61, 62, 198.

LITTLE, William, of Shirley, Mass.; from Ireland, cir. 1737; b. July 19, 1730; son of Thomas and Jean Little; m. Elizabeth Wallis, daughter of Matthias Wallis of Worcester, Dec. 1, 1748, d. August 3, 1802, aet 84; Children: Wallis, William, Elizabeth, Rebecca, Thomas; d. July 20, 1797, aet 77.—*Chandler's Shirley, p.* 502 *et seq., Shirley Vital Records, pp.* 61, 62, 198, *Lunenburg Records, p.* 261.

LIVENSTON, Elizabeth, of Boston, Mass.; from North Carolina, 1725, on the sloop "Adventure."—*Court of Sessions of the Peace,* 1725-32, *p.* 10.

LLOYD, Andrew, from Ireland; m. Mary Lawless; Child: Frances Maria, mother of William Lloyd Garrison, editor of the *Liberator.*—*Amer. Ances., Vol.* 3, *p.* 83.

LLOYD, Thomas, Boston, Mass.; in Boston, before 1724; m. Isabella Ayres, Aug. 16, 1724.—*Boston Rec. Com., Vol.* 28, *p.* 121.

LOBDEN, John, Portsmouth, N. H.; from "ye parish of Harly," Devonshire, before 1716; m. Ann Hetton of

London, England, in Portsmouth, N. H., Nov. 8, 1716.—*N. E. Hist. Gen. Reg., Vol.* 23, *p.* 393.

LOCHENER, George and Frederick, of Waldoboro, Maine; from Germany; they moved to North Carolina, after 1770.—*Miller's Waldoboro, p.* 67.

LOCK, see also Overlock.

LOCK, Richard, Boston, Mass.; from England with Captain Bond, June 13, 1715; warned out of Boston. —*Suffolk Court Files* 12413.

LOCKYER, John, from England, to "Rhode Island near New York," 1751; "clerk."—*Emigrant Ministers to America, p.* 41.

LOGAN, James, from London to Boston on the "Adventurer," 1774; a gentleman's servant, aged 27, "go to his master."—*N. E. Hist. Gen. Reg., Vol.* 63, *p.* 343.

LORTHERIDGE, Robert, of Worcester, Mass.; from Ireland, in 1718.—*Lincoln's Worcester, p.* 49, *Parmenter's Pelham, p.* 17.

LOSCH, Casimer, of Broad Bay, Waldoboro, Maine; from Germany, before 1752.—*Mass. Archives, Vol.* 15A, *pp.* 240-2.

LOVERIDGE, Benjamin, Boston, Mass.; from Newfoundland, Oct. 1716; butcher; warned out Oct. 31, 1716; m. Mary Mugeridge, Aug. 27, 1720, in Boston.— *Boston Rec. Com., Vol.* 13, *p.* 13, *Vol.* 28, *p.* 88.

LOWDEN, Thomas, of Leicester, Mass.; from Ireland, before 1738; he had a family and was alive as late as 1764.—*Parmenter's Pelham, pp.* 17, 99, 102, 118.

LOWTHAIN, Dr. Thomas, of Medfield, Mass.; from Pereth, Cumberlandshire, England; b. in Cumberlandshire; d. Medfield, 1749.—*Tilden's Medfield, p.* 427; *Medfield Vital Records, p.* 221.

LOWTHER, John, of "New Falmouth in Casco Bay," Maine; from England, before 1768; he was a brother of Dr. George Lowther of Savana La Marr, Jamaica; a surgeon.—*Misc. Mss. in the Boston Athenaeum.*

LUCAS, George, Boston, Mass.; from Ireland, with Captain Carrell, 1736; he brought a wife and child; they lodged with Mr. James Wimble in 1736. — *Boston*

Rec. Com., Vol. 15, *p.* 3, *Cullen's Irish in Boston,* p. 56.

LUCAS, William, Boston, Mass.; from Great Britain, before 1713; int. m. Ruth Pitman, Feb. 23, 1714.—*Boston Rec. Com., Vol.* 28, *p.* 93.

LUCY, John, of Cornish, N. H.; from France, before 1750; m. Eleanor Yuran, cir. 1750, bapt. 1726; Children: William, John, George, Polly, Samuel, Hosmer, Betsy, Sarah.—*Childs' Cornish, Vol.* 2, *pp.* 262-3.

LUDWIG, Jacob, of Waldoboro, Maine; from Wendemalhae, Nassau-Dillenburg, 1753; b. 1730; son of John Joseph Ludwig; m. Margaret Hilt, 1755; Children: Catherine Elizabeth, Eliza, Eve Catherine, Joseph Henry, Catherine, Jane, Katy, Jacob; d. January 1 1826, aged 91 years.—*Eaton's Warren, p.* 82, *Eaton's Thomaston, p.* 314, *Miller's Waldoboro, p.* 236.

LUDWIG, Joseph, of Warren, Maine; from Wendemalhae, Nassau-Dillenberg, 1753; son of John Joseph Ludwig; m. Catherine Elizabeth Kaler; Children: Jacob, Joseph Henry. — *Eaton's Warren, p.* 82, 143, *Eaton's Thomaston, p.* 314, *Miller's Waldoboro, pp.* 51, 236.

LUNT, John, of Newbury, Mass.; from Poolton, Parish of Wallasy, Cheshire, before 1747; m. Mrs. Hannah Moodey, Aug. 17, 1747, in Newbury, Mass.—*Newbury Vital Records, Vol.* 2, *p.* 333.

LUSK, John, Thomas, William, of Newington, Conn.; from Ireland early in the 18th century.—*Ancient Wethersfield, p.* 490.

LYLE, John, of Boston, Mass.; from Belfast, Ireland, before 1731; m. Mrs. Hannah Newton, of Boston, in Newbury, June 29, 1731.—*Newbury Vital Records, Vol.* 2, *p.* 352.

LYNCH, Maurice, of New Boston, N. H.; from Ireland; b. 1738; m. Catherine Sheehan; Children: John, a child, Mary Ann; d. 1779, aged 40.—*Cochran's Antrim, p.* 579.

LYNDLEY, Thomas, Portsmouth, N. H.; from Stoke Newington, Middlesex, before 1722; m. Sarah Whiden,

March 17, 1723.—*N. E. Hist. Gen. Reg., Vol.* 24, p. 16.
LYON, The Rev. John, from England to New England, 1764; son of Matthew Lyon of Warrington, Lancashire; matriculated, 1743. — *Emigrant Ministers to America*, p. 41.
LYONS, James, from England to New England, 1743.— *Emigrant Ministers to America*, p. 41.
MCADAMS, Samuel, of Windham, N. H.; from Londonderry, Ireland, cir. 1740; b. cir. 1716; m. Mary ——, d. Feb. 21, 1791, aet 58; Children: Jane, John, Margaret, James, Samuel, Robert, Gawin, Mary, Sarah; d. Jan., 1790, aged 74.—*Morrison's Windham*, pp. 625, 626.
MCADAMS, William, of Pelham, Mass., Windham and Londonderry, N. H.; from Londonderry, Ireland, cir. 1740; Children: Samuel, William.—*Morrison's Windham*, p. 625.
MACANNIS, John, of Boston, Mass.; from Ireland, 1719; m. ——; Children: four.—*Cullen's Irish in Boston*, p. 51.
MCAFFERTY, Charles, of Bristol, R. I.; from Londonderry, Ireland, cir. 1777; b. cir. 1748.—*Murray's Irish Rhode Islanders*, p. 51.
MCALISTER, Randall, of Peterborough, N. H.; British soldier and deserter, 1775; b. 1744, in Scotland; m. Mary Blair, b. 1749, d. 1833; Child: Mary; d. 1819, aged 75.—*Smith's Peterborough*, pt. 2, p. 140.
MCALLISTER, Angus, of Lancaster, Mass., and Londonderry, N. H.; from Ireland, in 1718; m. Margaret Boyle; Children: William, David, John, Mary Ann and four others.—*Cochran's Antrim*, p. 581; *N. H. Genealogies*, p. 473, *Hadley's Goffstown, Vol.* 2, p. 294, *Londonderry Vital Records*, p. 85.
MCALLISTER, Archibald, of Wiscasset, Maine; from Ireland, 1738/9; son of Richard and Anne (Miller) McAllister.—*Woodbury's Bedford*, p. 971.
MCALLISTER, David, of Londonderry, N. H.; son of Angus and Margaret (Boyle) McAllister; m. Eleanor Wilson, of Charlestown, Mass., daughter of Alexander Wilson; Children: Alexander, John, Archi-

bald, George, Janette, Margaret; d. 1750, aet 46.—
N. H. Genealogies, p. 473, *Londonderry Vital Records, p.* 83.

McAllister, John, of New Boston, N. H.; from Ireland, in 1748; Children: Archibald, Angus, Daniel, Mary; d. in Francestown.—*Cogswell's New Boston, p.* 386.

McAllister, Richard, of Bedford, N. H.; from Ireland, 1738-9; m. Anne Miller, in Ireland, d. March 12, 1776, in her 67th year; Children: "Archy," John, William, Mary, Ann, Susannah, Richard, James, Benjamin.—*Cochran's Antrim, p.* 582, *Woodbury's Bedford, p.* 97.

McAllister, William, of Lancaster, Mass., and Londonderry, N. H.; from Ireland, 1718; son of Angus and Margaret (Boyle) McAllister; m. Janette Cameron; Children: Margaret, John, David, William, Peter, Hugh, Thomas; d. 1755, aet 55.—*Lancaster Vital Records, pp.* 279, 281.

McAlpine, Walter, of Boston, Mass.; from Scotland, cir. 1743; removed to Connecticut. — *Thomas's History of Printing, Vol.* 2, *p.* 226.

McAlpine, William, of Boston, Mass.; from Scotland, cir. 1753; d. 1788, in Glasgow, Scotland.—*Thomas's History of Printing, Vol.* 1, *p.* 150.

McAlvin, see McIlvaine.

McAphee, Martha, of Rutland, Mass.; m. William Gordin, October 12, 1745.—*Rutland Vital Records, p.* 163.

McArthur, John, of Limington, Me.; from Perth, Scotland; m. Mary Miller; Children: John, Peter, Arthur, James, Margaret, Eleanor, Catherine?; d. 1816, aet 71.—*Saco Valley Families, p.* 897.

McBride, Alexander, of Concord, Mass.; from Ireland, before 1725; m. Mary ——; Children: William, John, James, Mary. — *Lancaster Vital Records, p.* 284, *Concord Vital Records, pp.* 122, 123, 130.

McBride, Edmund, Portsmouth, N. H.; from Danfenihana, County Donegal, before 1731; m. Sarah Devett, widow, Oct. 28, 1731.—*N. E. Hist. Gen. Reg., Vol.* 25, *p.* 118.

McBride, James, of Brunswick, Maine; from Ireland, before 1723; soldier, 1723-4, under Capt. John Giles.—*Wheeler's Brunswick, p.* 875.

McCallum, John, of Warren, Maine; from Scotland; b. 1767; m. Mary Miller; Children: John, Rebecca, Archibald, Andrew, Mary, Rebecca, Alexander, Duncan, William and Elizabeth, twins; d. September 23, 1837, aet 80.—*Eaton's Warren, p.* 578.

McCarter, Sarah, of Rutland, Vt.; from Ireland, before 1729; m. Jonas Buckingham, Dec. 10, 1729; she was probably a sister of Mrs. Malcam Hendery, and William McCarter.—*Reed's Rutland, pp.* 82, 154, *Rutland Vital Records, p.* 163.

McCarter, William, of Rutland, Mass.; from Ireland, before June, 1720; m. Elizabeth ———; he and wife were church members in Rutland; Children: Andrew, Sarah, William. — *Rutland Vital Records, p.* 62, *Reed's Rutland, p.* 82.

McCarthy, William, of Newbury, Mass.; from Kinsale, Ireland, before 1729; m. Margaret Pulsafer, of Boston, in Newbury, June 25, 1729.—*Newbury Vital Records, Vol. 2, pp.* 311, 412.

McCase, James, of Newport, R. I.; from "Ireland," in ———.—*Murray's Irish Rhode Islanders, p.* 42.

McCauley, Alexander, of Hillsborough, N. H.; from Ireland, cir. 1741; b. 1707; m. Mary Pinkerton, b. Ireland, 1712, d. Jan. 20, 1791; Children: James, Robert, Sarah; d. Oct. 11, 1788, in Merrimac, N. H.—*Cochran's Antrim, p.* 589, 590.

McCauley, James, of Hillsborough, N. H.; from Ulster, Ireland, cir. 1741.—*Cochran's Antrim, p.* 590.

Maclain, John, Boston, Mass.; in Boston, before 1721; m. Patience Norcott, April 12, 1721.—*Boston Rec. Com., Vol. 28, p.* 102.

McClanathan, John, of Rutland, Mass.; from Ireland, with Edward Savage, cir. 1720; m. Martha Shaw; Children: Mary, Martha, Elizabeth, John, Sarah, Eleanor, Thomas, William; he was probably son of Thomas McClanathan (C. K. Bolton); bondsman, 1746, for Duncan McFarland.—*Reed's Rutland, pp.* 155, 156, *Rutland Vital Records, p.* 62.

McClanathan, Deacon Thomas, of Palmer, Mass.; from ——, brother of William; grantee, 1733; b. 1685; Children: Thomas, William; d. Jan. 30, 1764, aet 78. — *Temple's Palmer, p. 510, Palmer Vital Records, p. 223.*

McClanathan, Thomas, of Rutland, Mass.; from Ireland, before 1729; m. ——; Children: William, Anne, Eleanor, and perhaps John and Thomas.— *Reed's Rutland, p. 82, Rutland Vital Records, p. 62.*

McClanathan, William, of Palmer, Mass.; from ——; brother of Thomas; he lived on the east side of Pottoquattuck Mountain; m. Jane ——, d. July 22, 1783; Children: Samuel, Robert, Thomas, William. —*Temple's Palmer, p. 510, Palmer Vital Records, p. 223, 224.*

McClenachan, The Rev. William; from Ireland, in 1734; minister at Georgetown and Cape Elizabeth, Maine, and Chelsea, Mass.; was a convert to the Church of England, and was a missionary of the "Society for Propagating the Gospel in Foreign Parts"; 1758 moved to Pennsylvania. — *Chamberlain's History of Chelsea, Vol. 2, pp. 254-257, notes, Greene's Boothbay, p. 176, Emigrant Ministers to New England, p. 42.*

Maclannon, John, Boston, Mass.; in Boston, before 1721; m. Susanna Norton, March 22, 1721.—*Boston Rec. Com., Vol. 28, p. 101.*

McClary, Andrew, of Nottingham and Epsom, N. H.; from Londonderry, Ireland, sailing from Port Rush to Boston, arriving Oct. 8, 1727; m. Ele ——; Children: John, Andrew, Margaret, Jane, Ann; a selectman of Nottingham, N. H., 1733/4.—*Curtis's Epsom, N. H., Cogswell's Nottingham, pp. 212, 217, Lyford's Canterbury, N. H., p. 236, The McClary Family, pp. 11-13.*

McClary, David, of Boston, Mass.; from Ireland, 1751; m. Rachel Strathearn; Children: David, Thomas, John, Molly, Sally, Betty, William; d. in Bedford, N. H.—*Cochran's Antrim, p. 591, Brown's Hillsborough, N. H., p. 379.*

McCLARY, Thomas, of Windham, N. H.; from Londonderry, Ireland; b. 1706; perhaps brother of Daniel McCleary; Children: David, Samuel, Sarah, Thomas, John.—*Morrison's Windham, p.* 627.

McCLEARY, Daniel, of Methuen, Mass.; from Ireland, cir. 1718, with his father, whose name is unknown; b. 1708, in Maghera, Londonderry, Ireland; m. Mary Mullican, Feb. 19 [1739?]; Children: Daniel, Martha, John, Mary, Jeane, Samuel, David, William, Thomas, Elizabeth; d. Dec. 23, 1788, in Methuen.— *Methuen Vital Records, pp.* 78, 225.

MACLEHN, John, Boston, Mass.; in Boston, before 1723; m. Elizabeth Wardwell, April 11, 1723. — *Boston Rec. Com., Vol.* 28, *p.* 108.

McCLELLAN, Bryce, of Portland, Maine; from Ballymoney, County Antrim, before 1720; m. ——, d. 1771, aged 78; Children: Joseph, William, Alexander, James.—*Lewis's Gorham, pp.* 658, 662, *Bourne's Wells and Kennebunk, p.* 313.

McCLELLAN, Collan, Worcester, Mass.; "a highlander, prisoner of war in this place," 1776; m. Elizabeth ——, of the County of Inverness, in Scotland; Child: Elizabeth.—*Worcester Vital Records, p.* 172.

McCLELLAN, Hugh, of Gorham, Maine; from Ireland, 1733; m. Elizabeth McClellan, daughter of Cary McClellan, in Ireland, d. July 16, 1804; Children: William, Cary, Abigail, Mary, Alexander, Cary, Jane, Martha, Thomas, Martha; d. Jan. 2, 1787, aet 77.—*Lewis's Gorham, pp.* 658-660.

McCLELLAN, James, of Worcester, Mass.; from Ireland, in 1718; m. Margaret —— ("alias Thorne"); Children: William, James; d. Oct., 1729. — *Lincoln's Worcester, p.* 49, *Wall's Reminiscences of Worcester, p.* 127, *Perry's Scotch Irish, p.* 17.

McCLELLAN, James, of Worcester, Mass.; from Ireland, in 1718; son of James and Margaret McClellan; m.

Elizabeth Hall, of Sutton, Dec. 26, 1722, the daughter of Percival Hall; Children: John, James, Moses, David, Rebekah, Mary; will probated March 12, 1736.—*Worcester Probate Records, Series* A39770, *Worcester Vital Records, pp.* 171, 172, 383, *Benedict's Sutton, p.* 693, *Sutton Vital Records, p.* 271.

McClellan, John, called upon Rev. William Homes at Chilmark, Mass., Nov. 3, 1717. — Contributed by *C. K. Bolton.*

McClellan, Michael, of Colrain, Mass.; from Currin, Londonderry, Ireland, in 1749; m. Jane Henry; Children: Jeanette, Ann, Margaret, Hugh and six others.—*McClellan's Colrain, p.* 83, *Amer. Ances., Vol.* 3, *p.* 35.

McClellan, William, of Gorham, Maine; from Ireland, 1733; b. cir. 1724; son of Hugh and Elizabeth McClellan; m. Rebecca Haston, of Falmouth, d. Oct. 13, 1823, aet 81; d. Nov. 19, 1812, aet 83.—*Lewis's Gorham, pp.* 660-662.

McClery, John, Boston, Mass.; in Boston, before 1743; m. Mary Wire, Dec. 15, 1743; m. 2? Sarah Campbell, Jan. 1, 1750.—*Boston Rec. Com., Vol.* 28, *p.* 340.

McClery, Samuel, Boston, Mass.; in Boston, before 1744; m. Elizabeth Foster, Sept. 25, 1744.—*Boston Rec. Com., Vol.* 28, *p.* 240.

Macclewain, ——, of Rutland, Mass.; from ——; m. —— Blair.—*Reed's Rutland, p.* 120.

Macclewain, Jane, of Rutland, Mass.; from Leicester, Mass.; m. George Smith, June 9, 1752, and had issue; her "parents and four of their children drowned in the passage."—*Reed's Rutland, p.* 120, *Rutland Vital Records, p.* 164.

McClintock, James, of Marblehead, Mass.; m. Margaret ——; Child: William, b. Marblehead, Aug. 30, 1724.—*Marblehead Vital Records, Vol.* 1, *p.* 328.

McClintock, John, of Worcester, Mass.; from Londonderry, Ireland, in 1718; laborer; d. insolvent and intestate, 1746.—*Lincoln's Worcester, p.* 49, *Wall's Reminiscences of Worcester, p.* 128.

McClintock, Thomas, of Palmer, Mass.; from Blandford; Children: William, Thomas, Sarah, James, Joseph, Margaret, John, Homer, Margaret, David. —*Temple's Palmer, p.* 511, *Palmer Vital Records, p.* 53.

McClintock, William, of Medford, Mass. (also McClintin); from Ireland, 1730; b. in Scotland; m. 1. ——, m. 2. ——, m. 3. ——, m. 4. ——; Children: William, Samuel, and 17 others, of these two were perhaps Aaron and Rachel; d. May 28, 1770.— *Rambles in Portsmouth, Vol.* 2, *p.* 160, *Hill's Rambles about Greenland, p.* 215, *N. H. Genealogies, p.* 45, *Medford Vital Records, p.* 406.

McClure, David, of Chester and Candia, N. H.; from Edinburgh, Scotland, cir. 1720, and from Londonderry, Ireland, 1740; m. Martha Glyn or Martha Glenn, d. in a snowstorm, 1770; Children: David, James, Martha, Mary, Elizabeth; d. cir. 1762 in a snowstorm.—*Chase's Chester, p.* 559, *Hadley's Goffstown, p.* 296, *Cochran's Antrim, p.* 592, *Eaton's Candia, p.* 89, *McClure Family, p.* 164.

McClure, Richard, Hillsborough, N. H.?; from Ireland, 1727; Child: Robert, q. v.—*Brown's Hillsborough, p.* 383.

McClure, Robert, of Hillsborough, N. H.; from Ireland, 1727; b. 1718, son of Richard McClure above; m. Martha Rogers; Children: James, Robert, Thomas, Peggy, Martha, Mary, John; d. cir. 1817, aged 99. —*Brown's Hillsborough, N. H., p.* 383, *Drummond's James Rogers of Londonderry, Merrill's Ackworth, p.* 242.

McClure, Samuel, of Boston, Mass.; from Ireland, 1728-9; son of John McClure; b. near Londonderry; said to have come over with William McClintock; Children: Jane, David, Anna, Samuel, Margaret, John. — *Stiles Ancient Windsor, Vol.* 2, *p.* 475, *Diary of David McClure, The McClure Family, p.* 160.

Maccane, George, Boston, Mass.; in Boston, before 1727; m. Jane Callwell, Jan. 25, 1727. — *Boston Rec. Com., Vol.* 28, *p.* 139.

McCobb, James, of Phipsburg (then Georgetown), Me.; from Ireland, before 1737; b. 1710 in Londonderry, Ireland; m. 1. Beatrice Rogers, dau. George Rogers, Dec. 1, 1737, d. 1772; Children: John, Isabella, George, Samuel, James, Beatrice, Thomas, Margaret, Frances, Anna; m. 2. Mrs. Hannah Nickels Miller, 1774; Children: Molly, Jeney, Thomas; m. 3. Mrs. Mary Langdon Storer Hill. — *Drum-Rogers Family of Georgetown, Georgetown Vital Records, p. 20.*

McCobb, Samuel, of Boothbay, Me.; from Ireland, 1730; b. Ireland, 1707; m. Mary ———, about 1738-9, d. Dec. 25, 1801, aet 81; Children: William, John, James, Jean, Frances, Mary, Samuel; d. Feb. 8, 1791.—*Greene's Boothbay, p. 570.*

McCollester, Archibald, of Rutland, Mass.; from Ireland, before 1734; m. Mary Hamilton, March 26, 1734, in Rutland.—*Rutland Vital Records, p. 164.*

McColley, Alexander, from Ireland, laborer, before 1740; b. cir. 1705; volunteer against the West Indies, 1740.—*Colonial Wars 1899.*

McColley, James, of Hillsborough, N. H.; from Ireland, cir. 1737; b. 1709; brother of Alexander McColley; m. Margaret Moore; Children: Margaret, John, James, John and James (twins), William, John, Hugh, Alexander, Nathaniel; d. May 4, 1749. —*Brown's Hillsborough, N. H., p. 384.*

McColloch, James, of Pelham, Mass.; from Ireland, before 1738, probably son of Alexander McColloch; d. July 10, 1759.—*Parmenter's Pelham, p. 17, Pelham Vital Records, p. 170.*

MacCollock, Thomas, Boston, Mass.; in Boston, before 1727; m. Abigail Neland, Jan. 25, 1727.—*Boston Rec. Com., Vol. 28, p. 139.*

McCollum, Alexander, of Londonderry, N. H.; from Londonderry, Ireland, cir. 1730; m. Janet ———; Children: Alexander, Thomas, Jean, Robert, Archibald, John, Janet.—*Parker's Londonderry, p. 283, Merrill's Ackworth, p. 244.*

McConkey, Alexander, of Worcester, Mass.; from Ireland, in 1718; in Dec. 1722 bought 57 acres; m. Margaret ——; Children: Alexander, William. —*Parmenter's Pelham, p.* 17, *Worcester Vital Records, p.* 172.

McConkey, John, of Worcester, Mass.; from Londonderry, Ireland, in 1718; m. Mary ——; Children: Alexander, William.—*Lincoln's Worcester, p.* 49; *Parmenter's Pelham, p.* 17, *Wall's Reminiscences of Worcester, p.* 128, *Worcester Vital Records, p.* 172.

McCoy, Alexander, of Windham, N. H.; from the Highlands of Scotland, cir. 1721; Children: John, Jane. —*Morrison's Windham, p.* 629, *Hadley's Goffstown, p.* 297.

McCraken, Samuel, of Worcester, Mass.; m. Lettice Carlisle, of Lunenburg, Dec. 8, 1762; Children: David, Samuel, David, Sarah, John, Joseph, David, Luke.—*Lunenburg Records, pp.* 235, 255, *Worcester Vital Records, pp.* 172, 173, *Worcester Inscriptions, p.* 49.

McCrie, see Crie.

McCrillis, Daniel, of Nottingham, N. H., and Lebanon, Me.; from Ireland, Oct., 1726; b. cir. 1710, near Agadowey, Ulster; son of John and Margaret McCrillis; m. Elizabeth Tomson, April 8, 1740, in Portsmouth, N. H.; she was born in Ballywoolin, County Antrim; m. 2. Col. John Kenney, d. aet. 96; Children: John, Jean, Robert, Elizabeth, Mary, Anna; d. 1763.—*McCrillis Family, pp.* 38-44, *MS. in the N. E. Hist. Gen. Soc.*

McCrillis, John, of Nottingham, N. H.; from near Agadowey, Ireland; he and his family sailed from Port Rush, Ireland, August 7, 1726, arriving in Boston, Oct. 8, 1726; went to Haverhill, Mass., and Londonderry, N. H.; m. Margaret Burnside, cir. 1700, d. at Agadowey; Children: Jean, Mary, Martha, John, William, Daniel, David; d. cir. 1762. —*Lyford's Canterbury, pp.* 237, 238, *Records of the McCrillis Family, pp.* 22, 24, *MS. in the N. E. Hist. Gen. Soc.*

McCrillis, John, of Boxford, Mass., Deerfield, and Nottingham, N. H.; from Port Rush, Ireland, in 1726; b. 1700, near Agadowey, Ireland; son of John and Margaret McCrillis; m. probably, Margaret Harvey, cir. 1732, the daughter of James and Ann (Maxwill) Harvey; Children: William, John, David, James, Henry, Elizabeth.—*Records of the McCrillis Family, pp. 28 et seq. MS.*

McCrillis, Martha, of Nottingham, N. H.; from Ireland, in 1726; b. 1702, near Agadowey, Ireland; daughter of John and Margaret McCrillis; m. Captain Hugh Morrison of Colraine, Mass.; she d. June 13, 1772.—*Records of the McCrillis Family, p. 33, MS.*

McCrillis, Mary, of Colraine, Mass.; from Ireland, in 1726; b. 1706, near Agadowey, Ireland; daughter of John and Margaret McCrillis; m. 1. —— Foster; m. 2. —— Foster; m. 3. John Henry; m. 4. Richard Ellis; she d. May 11, 1802, aet. 96.—*Records of the McCrillis Family, p. 34 MS.*

McCrillis, William, of Nottingham, N. H.; from Ireland, in 1726; b. near Agadowey, Ireland; son of John and Margaret McCrillis; m. Jean Kelsey, daughter of William and Margaret (Hay) Kelsey; Children: John, William, Mary, Jane; d. 1767 or 1768.—*Records of the McCrillis Family, pp. 36, 37 MS.*

McCulloch, Adam, of Kennebunk Port, Me.; from Dornach, Scotland, cir. 1766; b. 1742; m. Louisa Brown, 1769; Children: Hugh, Alexander, Margaret, Elizabeth, Isabella, and two others. — *Bradbury's Kennebunk Port, p. 262.*

McCulloch, Hugh, of Kennebunk, Me.; from Scotland, before 1768; a merchant; son of Adam McCulloch; m. Abiel Perkins, daughter of Thomas Perkins, of Kennebunk, April 10, 1790; Children: Adam, Thomas, Louisa. — *Bourne's Wells and Kennebunk, p. 769.*

McCullock, Alexander, of Pelham, Mass.; from Ireland, about 1730; he was a wheelwright; m. 1. Ann

——, d. before 1755; m. 2. Sarah Pebbels, Feb. 10, 1755, d. Dec. 10, 1784; Children: John, Janet, Margaret, Alexander, James, Henry, Sarah; d. Feb. 21, 1781.—*Parmenter's Pelham, pp.* 33 *et seq., Pelham Vital Records, pp.* 57, 128, 170.

McCULLOCH, Sarah, of Boothbay, Me., m. Henry Reed of Antrim, Ireland, and, a widow, came to Boothbay; William, Janet, and Mary McCulloch were members of the Boothbay church in 1766.—*Greene's Boothbay, p.* 611.

McCULLY, John, of Middleboro, Mass.; from Ireland; bought land 1735.—*Weston's Middleboro, p.* 434.

McCUNE, Isaac, of Palmer, Mass.; from the North of Ireland, petitioner, 1732; Children: Isaac, William and Margaret.—*Temple's Palmer, p.* 511.

MACURDIN, Mr., of Chelsea, Mass.; from Ireland, before 1727; "who brought a letter from Ireland," 1728, to the Church at Chelsea; Child: Abraham.—*Chelsea Vital Records, p.* 193, *Chelsea MS. Church Records, p.* 41.

McCURDY, Archibald, of ——, N. H.; from Ballymoney, Ireland, 1737; b. 1684; m. 1. —— ——; Children: Robert, Daniel, John; m. 2. —— ——; Children: James, Sarah, and a child who died on the voyage over.—*N. H. Genealogies, p.* 1838.

McCURDY, John, of Lyme, Conn.; from Belfast, Ireland, in 1745; m. Ann ——, d. Sept. 31, 1802, aet. 73; Children: John, Lynde, Mary; d. Nov. 10, 1785, aet. 61. — *Inscriptions at Old Lyme, Conn., N. E. Hist. Gen. Reg., July,* 1923.

McCURDY, John, of New York and Lyme, Conn.; from Belfast, Ireland, in 1745; from the Isle of Arran, Ballintoy, Ireland. — *Salisbury Family Histories, Vol. I, pp.* 1-170.

McCURDY, John, of Gilsum, Surry, N. H., and West Concord, Vt.; from Larne, Ireland, 1771; son of Samuel McCurdy; m. Sarah Watts, of Alstead, in Keene, 1788; Children: Mary, Sarah, Elizabeth, John, Samuel, Thomas, Nancy, Richard, Lynde.— *Kingsbury's Surry, p.* 757.

McCurdy, James, of Surry, N. H., and Northfield, Vt.; from Ireland, 1772; son of Samuel McCurdy; m. Margaret Gilmore, cir. 1780/1 (she was probably born in Ireland, cir. 1755); Children: John, Margaret, Mary, Thomas, Peggy, Betsy, Jenny, Lynde. —*Kingsbury's Surry, pp. 755, 756.*

McCurdy, Samuel, of Surry, N. H.; from Ireland, 1772; innkeeper; b. Ulster, Antrim, 1721; m. Elizabeth Gray (or Elizabeth Mooty?), d. Dec. 22, 1808; Children: Anan, James, John, Jane, Samuel, Jeannette; d. Jan. 5, 1808.—*Kingsbury's Surry, p. 755, Haywood's Gilsum, p. 365.*

McCutcheon, Phedris, of Barrington, R. I.; from Londonderry, Ireland, cir. 1719; m. Judith ———; Child: Phedris.

McDaniel, Timothy, Captain, of Boston, Mass.; from County Wicklow, Ireland, before 1732; m. Mrs. Elizabeth Foster of Charlestown, in Newbury, August 11, 1732.—*Newbury Vital Records, Vol. 2, p. 311.*

McDaniels, James, of Brookline, N. H., and Groton, Mass.; a James McDaniel m. Elizabeth Fisher in Boston, March 15, 1741; Children: Roxanna, Randall, Susanna, Lucy, Mary, Elizabeth, James, John. —*Parker's Brookline, N. H., 491, Boston Rec. Com., Vol. 28, p. 271.*

McDennil, Timothy, of Portland, Me.; from the Highlands of Scotland; m. Mary Winslow; Child: Washington Shirley.—*Morrison's Windham, p. 632.*

McDonald, Donald, of Lynn, Mass.; from Scotland, b. cir. 1722; "he was at the taking of Quebec when Wolf fell"; d. Oct. 3, 1830, aet. 108 years.—*Lynn Vital Records, Vol. 2, p. 530.*

McDonald, John, of Wells and Gorham, Me.; from Glencoe, Scotland, before 1726; m. Susanna ———; Children: John, Robert, Mary, Joseph, Peletiah, Abner; d. May 9, 1768.—*Lewis's Gorham, p. 653.*

McDonald, Patrick, of Salem, Mass.; from Ireland, before 1749; m. Mrs. Abigail Gilpin, int. Feb. 18, 1749.—*Salem Vital Records, Vol. 3, p. 418.*

McDonald, Randal, of Falmouth, Me.; from Ireland, 1718.—*Willis's Portland,* 326.
McDougall, James, of Stroudwater, Me.; from Scotland; m. Mary Patrick; Children: David, James, and perhaps others; d. in Stroudwater.—*McLellan's Gorham, p.* 655.
McDuffee, Daniel, of Londonderry, N. H., and Bradford, Vt.; from Ireland, 1720; spring of 1721 in Andover, Mass.; of Ireland, pastor the Rev. James McGregor; m. Ruth Britton of Coleraine, Ireland; Children: Hugh, Mansfield, Archibald, Daniel, Mary, two more sons and two daughters; d. 1768. — *McKeen's Bradford, Vt.,* 236, *Chase's Chester, p.* 560.
McDuffee, John, of Rochester, N. H.; from Ireland, 1729; m. Martha ———; Children: Mansfield, Archibald, John, Daniel.—*N. H. Genealogies, p.* 609.
Mace, Thomas, of Londonderry, N. H.; from Ireland, 1730.—*Documentary History of Maine, p.* 24.
McElwaine, Andrew, of Bolton, Mass.; d. intestate and insolvent, 1756; widow Harediah, Hajadiah, or Hasadiah, m. 2. Andrew Haskell, April 18, 1764 in Bolton, Mass.; Children: Mary, Jane, John, Andrew, James, William, David, Lydia. — *Bolton Vital Records, pp.* 53, 149, *Suffolk Probate, Worcester Probate, Series A,* 39784.
McElwane, James, of Palmer, Mass.; from Ireland, before 1727; m. Elenor ———; Children: James, Timothy; d. 1730-1.—*Temple's Palmer, p.* 520.
McElwaine, Robert, of Wenham, Mass.; from Ireland, before 1769; yeoman.—*Deed of Belfast, Me.*
McFadden, Andrew, of Bowdoinham, Me.; from Summerset, Garvagh, Ireland, 1718; m. Jane ———, b. 1684; Children: Andrew, a daughter born on the Kennebec, Daniel, James; with his wife and six children, warned from Boston, July 13, 1722; d. before 1767.—*Boston Rec. Com., Vol.* 13, *p.* 101, *Bolton's Scotch-Irish, p.* 331, *Huguenots in Dresden, Me., pp.* 27, 28.
McFadden, James, of Bowdoinham, Me.; from Ireland, 1718-20; son of Andrew; m. Rebecca Pierce;

Children: John, Mary, James, Hannah, Thomas, Andrew, Jane.—*Georgetown, Me., Records, p. 19.*

McFarland, Andrew, of Concord, Mass., and Chester, N. H.; from Londonderry, Ireland, cir. 1718; m. Margaret Christie, Dec. 8, 1725, in Billerica, Mass.; Children: Janet, Margaret, Elizabeth, Mary, Andrew, Daniel, David, Jesse, John, Moses, James, Andrew; d. after 1778.—*Concord Vital Records, p. 129, Worcester Vital Records, p. 174, Carter's Pembroke, p. 334, Billerica Vital Records, p. 290.*

McFarland, Andrew, of Marblehead and Worcester, Mass.; from Ireland, in 1718; son of Daniel McFarland; m. Rebecca Gray, d. March 20, 1762, aet. 62; Children: Andrew, William, John, Janes, Margaret, Daniel, Rebecca, Eliner; d. June 4, 1761, aet. 71.— *Wall's Reminiscences of Worcester, pp. 128, 204, McFarland Genealogy, p. 7; Worcester Vital Records, Worcester Epitaphs, p. 11.*

McFarland, Daniel, of Worcester, Mass.; from Ulster, Ireland, 1718, husbandman; arrived in Boston, August 4; he and Andrew, laborers of Marblehead, buy 185 acres in south part of Worcester near Prospect Meadow, 26 Oct. 1727; will probated May 12, 1738 "being very aged and infirm in body"; Children: James of Brunswick, Me., Margery McKolney of South Carolina, Margaret Campbell of Tyrone, Ireland, Andrew, Daniel and John of Worcester, Elinour Gray of Worcester, Patience, Elizabeth Samuel; (Andrew McFarland & Matthew Gray exrs.).— *Some Worcester McFarlands and Descendants, pp. 3-6, Worcester Probate Series A, 39918, Worcester Inscriptions, p. 49.*

McFarland, Daniel, of Worcester, Mass.; from Ireland, in 1718; son of Daniel McFarland; d. s. p.—*McFarland Genealogy, p. 7.*

McFarland, Daniel, Boston, Mass.; in Boston, before 1723; m. Elizabeth Thompson, May 19, 1723. — *Boston Rec. Com., Vol. 28, p. 114.*

McFarland, Duncan, of Rutland, Mass.; from Ireland, with his brother, Daniel McFarland, in 1718; m.

Christian ——; his wife a church member in Rutland; Children: Elizabeth, Janet, Nancy, Nancy, Daniel, Alexander, Christian; d. Windsor, Conn., 4 Sept. 1747, aet. 57.—*Reed's Rutland, p.* 82, *Rutland Vital Records, p.* 63, *Stiles' Ancient Windsor, Vol.* 2, *p.* 475, *Worcester Probate Series A* 3992.

McFARLAND, Elenor, see David Hood.

McFARLAND, James, of Brunswick, Me.; from Ulster, Ireland, in 1718; son of Daniel McFarland; m. Mary ——, before 1722; Child: Margaret. — *McFarland Genealogy.*

McFARLAND, James, of Chester, N. H.; from Scotland. —*Chase's Chester, p.* 562.

McFARLAND, John, of Worcester, Mass.; from Ulster, Ireland, in 1718; son of Daniel McFarland; m. Margaret ——; alive in 1748 in Pemaquid, Maine; Children: Sarah, Elmer, Andrew, Mary.—*Perry's Scotch-Irish, p.* 14, *McFarland Genealogy, p.* 6, *Worcester Vital Records, pp.* 174, 175.

McFARLAND, John, of Boothbay, Maine, and Boston, Mass.; from Ireland, with Captain Dennis, Nov. 1719; probably from Ardstraw, Donegal, with John and Andrew McFarland; perhaps at Arrowsic and Georgetown first; Children: Ephraim, Andrew Thomas, Sarah; warned out of Boston, Jan. 1720; d. 1773.—*Greene's Boothbay, p.* 575, *Boston Record Com., Vol.* 13, *p.* 64.

McFARLAND, Robert, Boston, Mass.; from Ireland in the ship "Elizabeth"; warned out of Boston Nov. 3, 1719.—*Boston Record Com., Vol.* 13, *p.* 63.

McFERLIN, George, of Lunenburg, Mass. [McFarland]; from Ireland, before 1752; m. Margaret Terrance, of Lancaster, Mass., m. April 16, 1752; a brick maker, d. 1758 (will). — *Lancaster Vital Records, pp.* 21, 32, *Lunenburg Records, p.* 234, *Worcester Probate Records, Series A.*

McFRADRICK, Aspel, Boston; from Ireland, in ship "Elizabeth"; warned out of Boston, Nov. 3, 1719. —*Boston Record Com., Vol.* 13, *p.* 63.

McGaw, Jacob, of Bedford, N. H.; from Lineygloss, Ireland; b. 1737; m. Margaret Orr, 1772; Children: John, Margaret, Jacob, Robert, Rebecca, Isaac, Martha; d. 1810.—*Morrison's Londonderry, p. 632.*

McGee, Thomas, of Chester, N. H.; from Ireland, before 1735; m. Anna Stewart, of Concord, Mass., Nov. 26, 1741; removed to Colraine, Mass.—*Chase's Chester, p. 563, Concord Vital Records, p. 152.*

McGlathery, Robert, of Bristol, Maine; from Belfast, Ireland, before 1752; m. Polly Dobbin; Children: Jane, William, Alexander, John, Sally, Peggy; d. 1768 (will).—*Bangor Hist. Mag., Vol. 9, p. 145, Maine Hist. Magazine, 1844.*

McGlathery, William, of Bristol, Camden, and Frankfort, Maine; from Ireland, cir. 1750; b. 1748, in Ireland; son of Robert McGathery; m. Elizabeth Stinson, of Rutherford's Island, d. July 21, 1819, aet. 67; Children: John, Charles, Betsy, Alexander, Martha; d. 1834, aet. 85.—*Bangor Hist. Mag., Vol. 9, pp. 145, 146, Lock's Camden, pp. 211-213.*

McGrah, John, of Lancaster, Mass.; from Ireland; died December 27, 1717.—*Lancaster Vital Records, p. 327.*

McGraw, ——, of Dublin, N. H., and Bellingham, Vt.; from Scotland, before 1772; Child: Samuel.—*McGraw Family Record.*

McGraw, John, of Salem, Mass.; from Waterford, Ireland, before 1765; m. Elizabeth Cloutman, int. March 30, 1765.—*Salem Vital Records, Vol. 4, p. 43.*

MacGregor, Alexander, Londonderry, N. H.; from Ireland, 1718, with Rev. James MacGregor, his father. —*Documentary History of Maine, p. 24.*

MacGregor, Rev. David; from Ireland, 1718; b. Nov. 6, 1710; son of Rev. James MacGregor; m. Mary Boyd of Londonderry, N. H.; Children: Robert, Nancy, Isabella, Alexander and five others.—*Hadley's Goffstown, p. 306, Londonderry Vital Records, p. 86.*

MacGregor, Rev. James, of Londonderry, N. H.; "Gent."; from Agadowey, Ireland, 1718; admitted student of theology, Jan. 18, 1697, at the University of Glasgow; m. Marion (Maryann) Cargil, Aug. 29, 1706; Children: Robert, Daniel, David, Jane, Alexander, Mary, Elizabeth, Margaret, John, James, Susannah; first minister of Londonderry; d. March 5, 1729, aged 52. —*Parker's Londonderry, p.* 280, *Boston News Letter,* 1729, *No.* 117, *Lincoln's Worcester, pp.* 49, 201, *Monumenti Alumni Univ. Glas., Vol. III, p.* 245, *Deed of Belfast, Me.,* 1769, *Wall's Reminiscences of Worcester, p.* 128.

McGregory, Alexander, Boston, Mass.; from Ireland, before April 1719; with his family, warned out of Boston, April 17, 1719.—*Cullen's Irish in Boston, p.* 51, *Boston Rec. Com., Vol.* 13, *p.* 52.

McHaan, Duncan, of Middleboro, Mass.; from ———; m. Patience, who as widow joined the church March 17, 1728; Child: Christiana.—*Weston's Middleboro, p.* 654, 658.

Machan, David, Boston, Mass.; in Boston, before 1727; m. Margaret Lithcoo, April 4, 1727. — *Boston Rec. Com., Vol.* 28, *p.* 139.

McHan, William, of Worcester, Mass.; from Ireland, in 1718.—*Lincoln's Worcester, p.* 49.

McIlvaine, Daniel, of Windham, N. H.; from Sisson, County Donegal, Ireland; brother of John and William McIlvaine; m. Mary Smith, in Boston, Mass.; Children: Robert, Daniel, John, William, Mary, Ebenezer, James; d. July, 1785.—*Morrison's Windham, p.* 635, *Cochran's Francestown, p.* 824.

McIlvaine, William, of Portland, Me.; from Sisson County Donegal, Ireland; brother of Daniel McIlvaine; m. ———; Child: Margaret; d. 1812.—*Morrison's Windham, p.* 634.

McIntire, John, of Rutland, Mass.; from Ireland, before 1719; b. in the Parish of Kilmoore, County of Tyrone, Ireland, 1678; m. Grace ———; Children: Agnes, Christian, perhaps also Elizabeth, Jane, Janet, Mary, Ann; d. May 26, 1769, aged 91. —

Rutland Vital Records, pp. 63, 235, *Monumental Inscriptions of Rutland, p.* 20.

McINTYRE, William, of Warren, Me.; from the north of Ireland, about 1720; lived for a time in Boston; and at St. George's River, upper Town (Warren), about 1735; Children: William, Robert, Martha, Esther, John, Mary; d. about 1758.—*Eaton's Warren, p.* 579, *F. P. McIntyre MS.*

MACK, John, of Londonderry, N. H.; from Londonderry, Ireland, 1732; blacksmith; m. Isabella Brown [Sybella], daughter of Sir John Brown of Londonderry, Ireland, d. cir. 1770; Children: William, Jeannette, John, Robert, Martha, Elizabeth, Andrew, Daniel; d. 1753, aged 55.—*Parker's Londonderry, p.* 278, *100th Anniversary of Bedford, N. H., p.* 313, *Secomb's Amherst, p.* 680, *History of Bedford, N. H., p.* 961, *Livermore and Putnam's Wilton, p.* 443.

McKALAPS, David, of Salem, N. H.; from Ireland, before 1754; m. Sarah ——; Child: Ann.—*Gilbert's Salem, N. H.*

MACKAHAN, Denis, Boston, Mass.; from Ireland, before 1719.—*Boston Rec. Com., Vol.* 28, *p.* 97.

MACKFEE, Robert, Boston, Mass.; in Boston, before 1725; m. Margaret Watson, March 28, 1725.—*Boston Rec. Com., Vol.* 28, *p.* 127.

McKEAN, William, of Boston, Mass.; tobacconist from Glasgow "at his house opposite the head of Charles' Wharf at the North End." — *Boston Gazette, Oct.* 8, 1764.

McKEE, Robert, of Pelham, Mass.; from Ireland, before 1739; m. Mary Gray, August 21, 1746; Children: four sons (the record is torn); two of them may be John and Josiah; d. Dec. 23, 1780.—*Pelham Vital Records, pp.* 58, 129, 171, *Parmenter's Pelham, p.* 33.

McKEEN, James, of Londonderry, N. H.; from Ballymoney, County Antrim, Ireland, 1718; son of James McKeen; b. 1665; m. 1. Janet Cochran, d. before 1718, in Ireland; m. 2. Annis Cargil, d. Aug. 8, 1782, aet. 94; Children: Elizabeth, Janet, John,

Mary, James, Janet, Martha, David, Margaret, Annis, Samuel; d. Nov. 9, 1756, in Londonderry. — *Merrill's Ackworth, p.* 244, *McKeen Genealogies, pp.* 14, 15, *Parker's Londonderry, p.* 284, *Morrison's Windham, p.* 639, *N. H. Genealogies, p.* 1925, *Documentary History of Maine, p.* 20.

McKEEN, James, of Londonderry, N. H.; from Ireland, in 1718; b. Ballymoney, Ireland, 1714; son of James and Annis McKeen; m. Mary McKeen, daughter of his uncle, John McKeen; Child: Mary.—*McKeen Genealogies, p.* 15.

McKEEN, James, of Hillsborough, N. H.; from Ireland, in 1718; son of John and Janet McKeen.—*McKeen Genealogies, p.* 17.

McKEEN, Janet, of Londonderry, N. H.; from Ballymoney, Ireland, 1718; widow of John McKeen; Children: John, Robert, Samuel, Mary; m. 2. Capt. James Barnett.—*Parker's Londonderry, p.* 284, *McKeen's McKean Genealogies, pp.* 17, 48.

McKEEN, Robert, from Ireland, in 1718; son of John and Janet McKeen.—*McKeen Genealogies, p.* 17.

McKEEN, Samuel, of Amherst, N. H.; from Ireland, in 1718; son of John and Janet McKeen; m. Agnes ———; Children: Hugh, John, Robert, James, Samuel.—*McKeen Genealogies, p.* 17.

McKEEN, William, of Charlestown, Mass.; from Halifax, N. S., 1764; m. Agnes Clement, 1764.—*Wyman's Charlestown, p.* 643.

McKENNEY, William, of Boston, Mass.; from Limerick, Ireland; d. April 6, 1811, aged 43. — *Copp's Hill Burying Ground.*

McKINNAN, James, of Rutland, Mass.; from ———, before 1745; m. Margaret ———; Children: John, Agnes, James, Jean, George, Andrew, Isaac, Daniel, Mary. *Rutland Vital Records, p.* 63.

McKINSTRY, Rev. John, of Sutton, Mass.; from Ireland, 1718; arriving in Boston August 4; b. 1677 in Brode Parish, County Antrim; son of Roger and Mary (Wilson) McKinstry; grad. Univ. of Edinburgh, M. A. 1712; minister of Sutton, Mass.; emigrated to Boston Aug. 1718, to Worcester; in 1719, to Sutton; in 1733, to East Windsor, Conn.; m. Elizabeth Fairfield of Wenham, Oct. 31, 1722, in Boston; Children: John, Mary, Alexander, William, Paul, Elizabeth, Abigail; d. Jan. 20, 1754. — *Benedict's Sutton, p. 691, N. E. Hist. Gen. Reg., Vol. 12, pp. 321, 322, McKinistry Family, Willis, pp. 11, 12, Stiles' Windsor, Vol. I, p. 821, Boston Rec. Com., Vol. 28, p. 108.*

McKinstry, John, of Londonderry, N. H.; from Armagh, Ulster Co., Ireland, cir. 1740; b. 1712, in Armagh; m. Jane (Dickie) Belknap; Children: John, Thomas, David, Charles, Sarah; d. Oct. 6, 1776, aet. 64, in Hinsdale, N. Y.—*McKinstry Family, Willis, pp. 22, 23.*

McKinstry, William, of Southbridge, Mass.; from Carrickfergus, Ireland, cir. 1740; b. 1722; m. Mary Morse; Children: James, Sarah, William, Molly, Amos, John, Experience, Elizabeth, Joseph, Margaret, Alexander, Jane, Nathan; d. 1815, aet. 41.— *McKinstry Family, Willis.*

Macklening, Hugh, servant of John Harrington of Lexington; complained to the court Jan. 18, 1720-1 that Harrington did not furnish clothing and made him sleep in a barn; see Hugh McLellan of Gorham, Maine.—*Middlesex Warnings, Middlesex County, Gen. Sessions of the Peace.*

McKnight, John, of Ellington, Conn.; from Scotland, 1718, New Haven, Hartford; b. abt. 1702?; m. in England Jerusha Crane, abt. 1720, d. Sept. 5, 1783; Child: John(?), although Stiles seems to skip a generation; d. 16 March 1785. — *Stiles's Ancient Windsor, Vol. 2, p. 478.*

MacKollo, Archibald, of Concord, Mass.; m. Margaret ———; (Margaret McCollo and John Parlin of Concord m. 1745 in Concord); Children: John, Eleazer. —*Concord Vital Records, pp. 113, 123, 161.*

McKonkey, see McConkey.

MacKonne, Robert, Boston, Mass.; arrived from Ireland, 1718, in the ship "William" with a wife and six children.—*Court of Sessions of the Peace, Suffolk County.*

Moor, Hugh, of Shirley, Mass.; from Ireland, before 1743; son or grandson of John and Agnes Moor; b. cir. 1714; m. Ruth Mitchell, in Lunenburg, Dec. 28, 1743, m. 2nd, perhaps, William Dunsmoor of Lancaster, 1766; Children: Ruth, Mary, Agnes, Hugh; d. June 22, 1758.—*Bolton's Shirley Uplands and Intervales, p. 348.*

Moor, John, of Londonderry, N. H.; from Ireland, in 1720; son of John Moor, and nephew of Samuel Moor; b. Glencoe, Scotland, Feb. 13, 1692; m. Jean Cochran, April 2, 1723, in Londonderry; Children: Robert, William, Euphemia, Samuel, Mary, Ann, Agnes, John; d. 1741; will prob. Aug. 26, 1741.—*Moor Family, pp. 9, 10 et seq.*

Moor, John, Londonderry, N. H.; from Ireland, 1724; son of Samuel Moore.—*Moor Family, p. 8.*

Moor, John, of Scituate, Mass.; from Ireland, cir. 1731; Children: Mary, John.—*N. E. Hist. Gen. Reg., Vol. 59, p. 136; Scituate Vital Rec., Vol. 1, p. 261.*

Moor, John, of Rutland, Mass.; from Ireland; m. Rose Crawford, Dec. 4, 1735; Children: Oliver, Samuel, William, John, Isabel, Anne.—*Rutland Vital Records, pp. 69, 70, 171; Reed's Rutland, pp. 82, 155.*

Moor, Samuel, of Portsmouth, N. H.; in Portsmouth, 1696, mariner, later innkeeper; m. Mary [Partridge?]; m. 2, Richard Elliott; Children: John, Samuel; d. between 1711-1722.—*Descendants of Ensign John Moore,* 1918.

Moor, Samuel, of Londonderry, N. H.; from Ireland, 1720; Child: John.—*Moor Family, p. 8.*

Moore, Charles, of Chester, N. H.; from Ireland, before 1738; brother of John Moore of Londonderry, N. H.; m. Jane Wilson, daughter of William Wilson, Sen.; Children: William, Joshua.—*Chase's Chester, p. 570.*

Moore, James, of Pembroke or Suncook, N. H.; from Ireland, 1727, landing in Boston; b. 1702; Children: James, William, Hannah, Ephraim, John, Daniel, Robert, two daughters, Eunice.—*Carter's Pembroke, p.* 230.

Moore, Jean, of Palmer, Mass.; from Ireland, 1718; grantee, 1733; Children: John, James [both signed petition to Gov. Shute]; d. 27 Feb. 1748, aet. 86 yrs. 8 mo.—*Temple's Palmer, pp.* 130, 508.

Moore, John, of Londonderry, N. H.; from Ireland; b. 1683, in Ireland; m. Janet ——, d. March 8, 1776; Children: Daniel, William, Elizabeth, [Samuel, Robert, Agnes]; d. January 24, 1774.—*Hadley's Goffstown, p.* 343; *Vital Records of Londonderry, p.* 89.

Moore, John, of Londonderry, N. H.; from Ireland, before 1738; m. Jane Morrison, in Ireland, d. Oct. 5, 1786; Children: James, John, Henry, Charles, Peggy, Molly; d. 1777.—*Chase's Chester, p.* 569.

Moore, John, of Shirley, Mass.; came, probably from Ireland, before 1743; m. Agnes ——, d. July 23, 1757, aet. 89; Child: Hugh; d. May, 1758, aged 96, in Shirley, Mass.—*Chandler's Shirley, p.* 563; *Bolton's Shirley Uplands and Intervales, p.* 348.

Moore, Jonathan, of Londonderry, N. H.; from Ireland, before 1729; m. Mary ——; Children: Agnes, William.—*Londonderry Vital Records, p.* 89.

Moore, Samuel, of Londonderry, N. H.; from Ireland? cir. 1721.—*Morrison's Windham, p.* 649.

Moore, William, of Londonderry, N. H.; from Ireland, cir. 1718; b. 1680, in Derry or Antrim, Ireland; m. Martha Anderson; Children: William and six others; d. January 1, 1739.—*Hadley's Goffstown, pp.* 341, 342.

Moore, William, Boston, Mass.; from Ireland in ship "Elizabeth"; warned Nov. 3, 1719.—*Boston Record Com., Vol.* 13, *p.* 63.

Moore, William, Scituate, Mass.; "a stranger from Ireland," before 1724; Child: Thomas.—*N. E. Hist. Gen. Reg.,* Vol. 57, p. 388; *Scituate Vital Records,* Vol. 1, p. 264.

MOORETON, Matthew, to New England from Presbury, Cheshire, 1699, in the "Virginia," Edmund Ball, master; b. Nov. 22, 1676, in Presbury, the son of Matthew Moreton; twenty years old, with seven years to serve.—*N. E. Hist. Gen. Reg.,* Vol. 64, p. 259.

MORE, Thomas, of Boston, Mass.; from Bristol, England, in 1716; shipwright; perhaps m. Mary Holegate, Oct. 1, 1722.—*Boston Rec. Com.,* Vol. 29, p. 232, Vol. 18, p. 108.

MORE, Thomas, Boston, Mass.; a blind man from Virginia, June-July, 1718; warned out July 14, 1718.— *Suffolk Court Files,* 12463; *Boston Rec. Com.,* Vol. 13, p. 40.

MOREHEAD, Rev. John, of Boston, Mass.; from Ireland, cir. 1726; b. (Miston?) Devonshire, England, 1703; pastor of Federal Street Church; m. Sarah Parsons, June 22, 1730; Children: Parsons, Mary, John; d. 1773, aged 70.—*Sprague's Annals,* Pt. 3, p. 44, *Boston Rec. Com.,* Vol. 24, p. 28, Vol. 28, p. 155.

MORGAN, Luther, of Kingston, Hampton, Kensington, Exeter and Suncook, N. H.; from Wales, before 1731; m. Abigail ———; Children: Nathaniel, b. 1731, Abigail, Rachel, Jeremiah.—*Carter's Pembroke,* Vol. 2, p. 236.

MORISON, see also Morrison.

MORISON, David, of Londonderry, N. H.; from Ireland, before March 17, 1730, in ship "Elizabeth"; warned from Boston, Nov. 3, 1719; m. Martha Ann McAlister and had no issue; d. March 1775, aged 85.— *Documentary History of Maine,* p. 20; *Boston Rec. Com.* Vol. 13, p. 63.

MORISON, Halbert, of Londonderry, N. H.; from Ireland, cir. 1718; son of Samuel Morrison or John Morison, q. v.; m. 1, Stella ———; m. 2, ———, m. 3, Mary ———; Children: Martha and others.—*Smith's Peterborough,* Pt. 2, p. 174; *Londonderry Vital Records,* p. 90.

MORISON, James, of Londonderry, N. H.; from Ireland, cir. 1718; son of Samuel Morison or John Morison, q. v.; m. Jeanette Steele; Children: John, Thomas, daughter; d. Londonderry.—*Smith's Peterborough, Pt. 2, p.* 174; *Londonderry Vital Records, p.* 90.

MORISON, John, of Windham, N. H.; from Aghadowey, Londonderry, Ireland, 1720; b. in Aberdeenshire, Scotland; m. 1, ——; m. 2, Janet Steele; Children: James, John, Halburt, Martha, Samuel, Mary, Joseph, Hannah; d. 1736, reputed to be 108 years old. —*Parker's Londonderry, p.* 289; *Morrison's Windham, p.* 656.

MORISON, Joseph, of Londonderry, N. H.; from Ireland, 1718; son of Samuel or John Morison; m. Mary Holmes.—*Smith's Peterborough, Pt. 2, p.* 174.

MORISON, Samuel, of Windham, N. H.; from Ireland, cir. 1730; b. in Scotland; m. Mary ——; Children: Susanna, Samuel, Mary, John; d. 1752.—*Morrison's Windham, p.* 655.

MORISON, Samuel, of Londonderry, N. H.; from Ireland; son of Samuel or John Morison; m. Catherine Allison; Children: three sons.—*Smith's Peterborough, Pt. 2, p.* 174.

MORISON, Samuel, of Londonderry, N. H.; from Ireland, before 1723; m. 1, Martha ——; m. 2, Margaret Henry; Children: Martha, Samuel, Abraham; d. Sept. 1757, aged 76.—*Morrison's Windham, p.* 655; *Londonderry Vital Records, p.* 90.

MORISON, Thomas, of Londonderry, N. H.; b. 1710, in Ireland; son of John Morison; m. Mary Smith of Lunenburg, Oct. 2, 1739; Children: John, Elizabeth, Robert, Margaret, Jonathan, Thomas, Sally, Samuel, Mary, Ezekiel.—*Lunenburg Rec., p.* 254; *Londonderry Vital Records, p.* 90; *Smith's Peterborough,* 1st 2 pp. 178, 179.

MORISON, Rev. William, of Londonderry, N. H.; from Auchlinnes, Perthshire, Scotland; b. 1748; pastor 2d Church, Londonderry, 1783; m. Jean Fullerton; Children: William Fullerton, Jenny, Daniel, James, Sally; d. Sept. 1829.—*Morrison's Windham, p.* 655; *Londonderry Vital Records, pp.* 90, 91.

MORRICE, Thomas, of Boston, baker; from London.—*Suffolk Court of Common Pleas.*

MORRIS, Charles, of Scarboro, Maine; from Wales, cir. 1768; b. Sept. 29, 1749; m. Rhoda Libby, 1770; Children: Martha, John W., Sally, James H., Rhoda, Elizabeth, Charles, Ann Louisa, Polly, Charles; d. Feb. 6, 1818.—*McLellan's Gorham, p.* 678.

MORRIS, Hannah, at Boston, Mass.; picked up on the ocean by the ship "Industrious Bee," from a schooner bound from North Carolina to Virginia, in distress; a widow with six children; put in the Almshouse at Province charge.—*Boston Record Com., Vol.* 13, *p.* 296.

MORRIS, John, of Boston, Mass.; "a stranger," 1726.—*Court of Sessions of the Peace,* 1725-32, *p.* 56.

MORRIS, Richard, Boston, Mass.; from Great Britain, before 1714; int. m. Sarah Bowdoin, Sept. 1, 1718.—*Boston Rec. Com., Vol.* 28, *p.* 94.

MORRIS, Robert, of Boston, Mass.; from England in the ship "Success," Jonathan Snelling, master, October, 1740; will of Sarah Dolbeare.—*The Dolbeare Family, p.* 29.

MORRIS, Rev. Theophilus; from England to Connecticut, 1740.—*Emigrant Ministers to America, p.* 46.

MORRISON, David, Portsmouth, N. H.; from Waterford, Ireland, before 1730; m. Sarah Macpheden, March 23, 1731.—*N. E. Hist. Gen. Reg., Vol.* 25, *p.* 118.

MORRISON, Hugh, of Colrain, Mass.; from Ireland in 1725 or 1726; m. Martha McCrellis; Children: David, Robert, John, Martha, Samuel, and perhaps others; d. cir. 1765.—*McClellan's Colrain, p.* 71.

MORRISON, James, of Nottingham, N. H.; from Port Rush, Ireland, 7 Aug. 1726; b. 7 May 1725, in Ireland, son of William and Mary (Henry) Morrison; m. (1) Jane Kelsey, of Boston, b. 1727; Children: William, Robert, James; m. (2) Martha White of Pembroke, N. H.; Children: Isaac, Henry, Hugh, John White, ——, Mary, Jane, Martha; d. Nov. 15, 1798.—*Carter's Pembroke, Vol.* 2, *p.* 238.

MORRISON, John, of Londonderry, N. H.; from Ireland,

cir. 1726; m. ——; Children: Samuel, Joseph, Hannah.—*Londonderry Vital Records, p.* 90.

MORRISON, John, of Londonderry, N. H.; from Ireland, 1718; b. 1678; son of Samuel Morrison; m. Margaret Wallace; Children: Thomas, Jonathan, Jane, Elizabeth, Janet, John, Margaret, Hannah, Moses; d. 1776, aged 98.—*Smith's Peterborough, Pt.* 2, *p.* 174; *Parker's Londonderry, p.* 289; *Londonderry Vital Rec. p.* 90.

MORRISON, John, of Boston, Mass.; from Belfast, Ireland, cir. 1747; b. in 1722.—*Goldthwaite Records, Ms. in the Boston Athenaeum.*

MORRISON, Rev. John, of Peterborough, N. H.; from Pathfoot, Scotland; b. 1743; grad. Edinburgh, 1765; first minister of Peterborough, N. H., d. Charleston, S. C., 1782.—*Parker's Londonderry, p.* 187.

MORRISON, Robert, of Londonderry, N. H., from Scotland (prob.), 1719; m. Elizabeth ——; Children: Robert, William.—*Morrison's Windham, p.* 655; *Londonderry Vital Records, p.* 90.

MORRISON, William, of Nottingham, N. H.; from Port Rush, Ireland, 7 Aug. 1726; b. Scotland, cir. 1684; m. Mary Henry, d. 1758; Child: James, q. v.; d. 1758.—*Carter's Pembroke, Vol.* 2, *p.* 238.

MORROO, Peter, Boston, Mass.; from Great Britain, before 1720; int. m. Priscilla Hamberton, July 18, 1720.—*Boston Rec. Com., Vol.* 28, *p.* 98.

MORROW, John, of Windham, N. H.; from Ireland, before 1739; m. Agnes ——; Children: James, Agnes, William, John, Alexander; d. 1767, aged 87.—*Morrison's Windham, p.* 685.

MORY, Hugh, Portsmouth, N. H.; from Tarkum, Devon, before 1736; m. Grace Lee, widow, Aug. 22, 1736.—*N. E. Hist. Gen. Reg., Vol.* 26, *p.* 377.

MOTLEY, John, of Falmouth, Me.; from Belfast, Ireland, before 1738; m. Mary Roberts, 1738; Children: John, Richard, Ann, Thomas; m. Lydia Libby, 1754; Children: Alexander, Samuel, William, Jacob, John, Mary, Thomas.—*Smith's and Deane's*

Journal, p. 118; *N. E. Hist. Gen. Reg., Vol.* 19, *p.* 298, *Vol.* 31, *p.* 364; *Willis's Portland, p.* 823.

MOULTON, Robert, Boston, Mass.; from Great Britain, before 1718; int. m. Silence Critchfeeld, of Weymouth, Sept. 25, 1718.—*Boston Rec. Com., Vol.* 28, *p.* 97.

Mow, Peter, Portsmouth, N. H.; from "Rochel." France, before 1718; m. Sarah Lewis of Kittery, Me., Sept. 10, 1718.—*N. E. Hist. Gen. Reg., Vol.* 23, *p.* 395.

MOWATT, Magnus, of Salem, Mass.; from Shomness, Orkneys, before 1767; m. Anna Pickman, March 22, 1767.—*Salem Vital Records, Vol.* 4, *p.* 105.

MUCLEWEE, John, of Warren, Me.; from Scotland, 1753. —*Eaton's Warren, p.* 85.

MUHLER [Miller], Frank, of Broad Bay, Maine; from Germany, 1753; b. 1725, near Bremen; m. Anna ———, d. October 26, 1820, aet. 90; Children: Henry, Charles; d. Feb. 21, 1805.—*Miller's Waldoboro, pp.* 40, 259-261.

MULLEGAN, John, in Boston, Mass.; lately arrived from London, mariner, guilty of stealing.—*Court of Sessions of the Peace,* 1715-8, *Vol.* 1, *p.* 12.

MUNDAY, William, of Salem, Mass.; from London, England, before 1760; b. cir. 1742; m. Mary Pease, April 27, 1760; Child: William; d. Sept. 1, 1818, aet. 76.—*Salem Vital Records, Vol.* 4, *p.* 107, *Vol.* 2, *p.* 93; *Vol.* 6, *p.* 80.

MUNDEN, Patrick, of Leicester, Mass.; from Ireland; a Scotchman; about 24 years old in 1719; ran away from his master, John Meinzeis, Esq., 11 Sept. 1719. *Boston News Letter, Sept.* 14-21, 1818.

MUNRO, John, of Salem, Mass.; from North Britain, 1769; int. m. Elizabeth Larrabee, April 21, 1770, she objected.—*Salem Vital Records, Vol.* 4, *p.* 108.

MURDOUGH, Thomas, of Litchfield and Hillsborough, N. H.; from Ireland; b. at Londonderry, Ireland; m. Margaret McColley, b. Londonderry, Ireland, August 30, 1734; Children: Sukie, Robert, Nathaniel, Nathan, Pattie, Thomas, Samuel, Eunice, Isaac, Frank; d. Jan. 1814.—*Brown's Hillsborough, N. H., p.* 431.

MURRAY, Captain John, of Rutland, Mass.; from Ireland with Edward Savage, before 1727; b. 1720; m. 1, Elizabeth McClanathan, d. 1760; Children: Alexander, Isabel, Robert, John, Daniel, Elizabeth, Martha, Samuel [there were reputed to be ten children]; m. 2, Lucretia Chandler of Boston, Sept. 1, 1761, in Worcester; Child: Lucretia; m. 3, Deborah Brinley of Boston, Jan. 24, 1770, in Boston; Child: Deborah; removed to Nova Scotia, 1774; d. St Johns, New Brunswick, Aug. 30, 1794.—*Rutland Inscriptions, p.* 22; *Boston Rec. Com., Vol.* 30, *pp.* 40, 315, 363; *Rutland Vital Records, pp.* 71, 173, 238, 239; *Reed's Rutland, pp.* 156, 157, 158.

MURRAY, Rev. John, of Boothbay, Maine; from Ireland, in fall of 1763; b. Antrim, Ireland, May 22, 1742; nephew of Andrew and Jean (Murray) Reed of Boothbay, Me.; graduate of the University of Edinburgh; m. Susanna Lithgow, Dec. 15, 1772, dau. Gen. William Lithgow of Georgetown; Children: John Wentworth, Katherine, Robert L.; d. March 13, 1793, in Newburyport.—*Greene's Boothbay, p.* 178-188; *N. H. Hist. Coll., Vol.* 6, *p.* 157.

MURRAY, John, of Boothbay, Me.; perhaps from Ireland; m. Anne, daughter of Robert Montgomery, 1766, d. 1771, aet. 30; Children: Robert Montgomery, John, James, Samuel, there was a Robert at the same time. —*Greene's Boothbay, p.* 593.

MURRY, William, of Hadley, Mass.; from Scotland, cir. 1720; m. Mary Dickinson; Children: Elijah, William, Dorothy, David, Seth, Hannah.—*Sheldon's Deerfield, p.* 246.

MURRY, William, of Portsmouth, N. H.; from Charleston, S. C., before 1727; m. Hannah Gove, of Ipswich, Mass., in Portsmouth, Nov. 9, 1727.—*N. E. Hist. Gen., Vol.* 24, *p.* 359.

NARDING, Zachariah, of Dresden, Maine; from France.— *Huguenots in Dresden, p.* 18.

NEAL, Mary, Boston; widow from London, admitted as an inhabitant Oct. 23, 1734.—*Boston Record Com., Vol.* 13, *p.* 261.

NEALLY, William, of Nottingham, N. H.; from Ireland, before 1725; m. ———; Children: William, Matthew, John, a son and a daughter.—*Cogswell's Nottingham, pp.* 231-2.

NEIL, John, of Scituate, Mass.; from Ireland before 1730, "an Ireland man and woman"; Children: John, Jane, Martha, George; removed to Maine.—*Dean's Scituate, p.* 314; *Scituate Vital Records (Neal), p.* 268; *N. E. Hist. Gen. Reg., Vol.* 57-77.

NELSON, Jane, of Sudbury, Mass.; from Ireland, cir. 1720; widow of John Nelson.—*Middlesex County Sessions of the Peace.*

NESMITH, James, of Londonderry, N. H.; from valley of the River Bann, Ireland, 1718; b. 1692; m. Elizabeth McKean, 1714, daughter of James and Janet (Cochran) McKean; Children: Arthur, James, Arthur, Jean, Mary, John, Elizabeth, Benjamin, Thomas, d. May 9, 1767.—*Parker's Londonderry, p.* 290; *McKean's McKean Genealogy: Morrison's Windham, p.* 688; *Cochran's Antrim, p.* 613; *Documentary History of Maine, p.* 20; *Kingsbury's Surry, p.* 779; *Hadley's Goffstown, p.* 356; *Londonderry Vital Records, p.* 82.

NEWBERRY, Mary, Boston, Mass., see James Colter.

NEWBERT, Charles, of Waldoboro, Maine; from Germany, 1748, with wife and four children.—*Miller's Waldoboro, p.* 210.

NEWBUT, Christopher, John, and Zachariah, of Broad Bay, Maine, before 1760.—*Miller's Waldoboro, p.* 51.

NEWELL, Joseph, Boston, Mass.; from Dublin; arrived at Boston, 1719.—*Boston News Letter, July* 13-20, 1719.

NEWELL, Martha, of Boston; from Ireland, August, 1719; warned out, Sept. 23.—*Cullen's Irish in Boston, p.* 5; *Boston Rec. Com., Vol.* 13, *p.* 61.

NEWMAN, Richard, Boston, Mass.; from Great Britain, before 1720; int. m. Annie Gileris, ———, 1720.—*Boston Rec. Com., Vol.* 28, *p.* 98.

NEWTON, Rev. Christopher; from England to New England, 1755.—*Emigrant Ministers to America, p.* 47.

NICHOLS, Clement, Boston, Mass.; from "Jersie," cir. 1714; int. m. Sarah Rogers, Nov. 1, 1714.—*Boston Rec. Com., Vol.* 28, *p.* 94.

NICHOLS, Rev. James; from England to Connecticut, 1774.—*Emigrant Ministers to America, p.* 47.

NICHOLS, Samuel, of Francestown, N. H.; from Ireland; Children: John, Samuel, James, Peggy, Jenny, Sally, Mary Ann, Susan, Nancy; moved to Holland Purchase, N. Y.—*Cochran's Francestown, pp.* 21, 854.

NICHOLS, Samuel, of Antrim, N. H.; from Antrim, Ireland; Children: Thomas, Daniel, Adam, John; d. 1804, in Antrim.— *Whiton's Antrim, p.* 56.

NICHOLSON, Henry, Portsmouth, N. H.; from Williamsburg, Virginia, before 1716; m. Sarah Cotton, Dec. 13, 1716.—*N. E. Hist. Gen. Reg., Vol.* 23, *p.* 393.

NICHOLSON, John, to New England from Lancaster, 1699; twenty years old, bound to Mr. Thomas Tyler for seven years.—*N. E. Hist. Gen. Reg., Vol.* 64, *p.* 260.

NISBETT, Thomas, from Ireland, laborer; b. cir. 1693; volunteer against the West Indies, 1740.—*Colonial Wars,* 1899.

NIXON, John, from Ireland, laborer; b. cir. 1720; volunteer against the West Indies, 1740.—*Colonial Wars,* 1899.

NIXON, John, of Dedham, Mass.; from Great Britain, before 1745; m. Katharine Wentworth, of Stoughton, Aug. 6, 1745.—*Canton Vital Records, pp.* 134, 57.

NODES, William, Boston, Mass.; from Great Britain, before 1716; int. m. Elizabeth Egbear, Oct. 29, 1716. —*Boston Rec. Com., Vol.* 28, *p.* 96.

NOLE, Stephen, Portsmouth, N. H.; from Lelant, Cornwall, before 1717; m. Joanna Boarn [Bourn], Feb. 25, 1717.—*N. E. Hist. Gen. Reg., Vol.* 23, *p.* 394.

NORTH, John, of Pemaquid, Maine; from Clooneen, County Kings, Ireland, 1730; m. Lydia ——; Children: John, James, Elizabeth, Mary, Rebecca, Lydia, Sarah, Ann; d. 1740.—*Eaton's Warren, p.* 592.

NORTH, John, of Warren, Maine; from Clooneen, Ireland, 1730; son of John North; m. 1, Elizabeth Lewis; m. 2, Elizabeth Pitson, of Boston; Children: Joseph, Mary, William.—*Eaton's Warren, p.* 593.

NORTON, John, of Westminster, Vt.; from Scotland; Child: Anna.—*Randall's Chesterfield, p.* 240.

NORTY, Peter, Boston, Mass.; from Great Britain, before 1720; int. m. Rose Hicks of Middleberry, May 30, 1720.—*Boston Rec. Com., Vol.* 28, *p.* 98.

NUGEN [Nugel], William, Boston, Mass.; an Irishman from Philadelphia, April 21, 1727; warned out, July 11 (return); warned April 21, 1727.—*Suffolk Court Files,* 20510; *Boston Record Com., Vol.* 13, *p.* 167.

NUTT, David, of Camden, Maine; from Scotland or Ireland; b. 1738; Child: Nancy; d. 1797.—*Eaton's Thomaston, p.* 340.

NUTT, John, of Camden, Maine; from Scotland or Ireland; m. 1, ——; m. 2, ——; Children: David, William, Joanna, Ashley, John, Elizah, Nancy, Susan.—*Easton's Thomaston, p.* 340.

NUTTES, James, to New England, from Blackburn, Lancashire, 1699, in the "Virginia," Edmund Ball, master; eighteen years old, with seven years to serve. —*N. E. Hist. Gen. Reg., Vol.* 64, *p.* 259.

OBERLACK, John Godfrey, of Broad Bay, Maine; from Germany, before 1760.—*Miller's Waldoboro, p.* 51.

OBERLOCK, see Overlock.

O'BRIEN, John, of Castine and Warren, Maine; from Ireland, schoolmaster; b. 1755, Craig, Ireland; m. Mary Starrett, Nov. 14, 1785; Children: Elizabeth, Lewis, Mary, John, Edward, James, Sarah, Rebecca, William, George, Thomas, David; d. June 19, 1828. —*Eaton's Warren, pp.* 593-4.

O'BRIEN, Morris, of Scarborough and Machias, Maine; from Cork, Ireland, cir. 1740; a tailor; m. Mary Keen, of Kittery, d. 1805; Children: Gideon, Jeremiah, John, William, Dennis, Joseph, Martha, Joanna, Mary; d. 1799.—*Southgate's Scarborough, p.* 176; *Drisko's Machias, pp.* 513, 514.

O'HARA, Rev. Joseph, from England to Providence in New England, 1728.—*Emigrant Ministers to America, p.* 48.

OLIPHANT, Andrew, of Providence, R. I.; from Scotland, cir. 1762; removed to South Carolina.—*Thomas's History of Printing, Vol. 2, p. 234.*

OLIVER, George, of Salem, Mass.; from Madeira, before 1764; m. Hannah Manning, int. Oct. 20, 1764.—*Salem Vital Records, Vol. 4, p. 56.*

OLIVER, Lancelot, of Barre, Mass.; from the North of Ireland; b. 1704; "brother" of William Walker; 1741 member of the Church at Georgetown; m. Mary Walker, 1741, who outlived her husband; Children: William, Margaret, James, David, Robert, Alexander, Katherine; d. June 21, 1781, in the 78th year of his age.—*Worcester Probate, Series A, Case 44358; Barre Vital Records, p. 259.*

OLIVER, Robert, Portsmouth, N. H.; from Yeaton, Northumberland, before 1715; m. Pasco Malvern, of Newcastle, N. H., in Portsmouth, Oct. 7, 1715.—*N. E. Hist. Gen. Reg., Vol. 23, p. 272.*

ORPH, Nicholas, of Broad Bay, Maine; from Germany, with Hans George Hahn; m. Margaret ———.—*Miller's Waldoboro, p. 64.*

ORR, Clement, of Orr's Island, Harpswell, Me.; from Ireland, before 1742; brother of Joseph Orr.—*Wheeler's Brunswick, p. 845.*

ORR, John, of Mair Point, Brunswick, Maine; from Ireland, early 18th cen.; m. Susan Skolfield; no issue. —*Wheeler's Brunswick, p. 846.*

ORR, John, of Chester, N. H.; from Ireland in 1736 or 7; m. Martha Templeton, sister of Allen Templeton; Children: James, Molly.—*Chase's Chester, pp. 497, 572.*

ORR, John, of Goffstown, N. H.; from Ireland, before 1754; b. 1721 at Antrim; m. Jane McConnell, of Pembroke, 1735, d. 1817; Children: Samuel, John, Rebecca, Mary Katherine, William; d. March 23, 1809.—*Hadley's Goffstown, p. 362.*

ORR, Joseph, of Orr's Island, Harpswell, Maine; from Ireland, before 1742; m. Mrs. William Wyer; Children: Mary, Lettice.—*Wheeler's Brunswick, p. 845.*

ORR, Mary, of Brunswick, Maine; from Ireland, before 1742; sister of Clement and Joseph.—*Wheeler's Brunswick, pp.* 845-6.

ORROCK, David, Boston, Mass.; in Boston before 1723; m. Sarah Tillet, Oct. 31, 1723; Child: Edward.— *Boston Rec. Com., Vol.* 28, *p.* 115.

ORSBORN, James, Boston, Mass.; from Great Britain, before 1722; int. m. Elizabeth Stevens, Oct. 22, 1722. —*Boston Rec. Com., Vol.* 28, *p.* 159.

OSBORN, Rev. Samuel, of Eastham, Mass.; from Ireland or Scotland, at the end of October, 1707; "bringing letters of commendation subscribed by Rev. Robert Rainey of Newry, County Down"; said to be 22 years old; b. about 1685; m., Edgartown, Mass., Jedidah Smith, Jan. 1, 1710; teacher at Sandwich, Plymouth, etc.; ordained 1718; m. Mrs. Experience Hopkins, b. Chatham, in Boston, Oct. 19, 1743; d. probably at Boston, about 1774.—*Doane Family pp.* 498-515.

OSBORNE, Samuel, of Eastham and Boston, Mass.; from Ireland, 1718; graduate of the University of Dublin; minister of Eastham, 1718-1738; schoolmaster in Boston; died "at a great age."—*History of Barnstable County, pp.* 383, 391[n] (probably the same as the above).

OTT, Peter, of Rockport, Maine; from Germany; Children: Elizabeth, Peter; d. at great age.—*Eaton's Thomaston, p.* 344.

OTTERSON, Andrew, of Hookset, N. H.; from Ireland, before 1760?; brother of William Otterson.—*Chase's Chester, pp.* 572, 573.

OTTERSON, Ann, of Chester, N. H.; from Ireland, before 1760; sister of Andrew and William; m. Dr. Joseph Brown.—*Chase's Chester, pp.* 477, 478, 573.

OTTERSON, William, of Chester, N. H.; from Ireland, before 1760; m. —— Temple; Children: James, Mary; d. 1760.—*Chase's Chester, p.* 572.

OULD, Richard, Boston, Mass.; from Great Britain, cir. 1713; int. m. Mercy Pilkenton, May 24, 1714.— *Boston Rec. Com., Vol.* 28, *p.* 93.

OVERLOCK, John, of Ashburnham, Mass. [also Aberlock];

from Germany, 1758; m. Mary ——; Children: John, Philip, Elizabeth, Jacob; d. Jan. 2, 1783, aet. 80.—*Stearns' Ashburnham, p.* 800; *Ashburnham Vital Records.*

OWEN, Humphrey, of Boston, Mass., alias *Isaac Moore;* from New York, 1730.—*Court of Sessions of the Peace,* 1725-32, *p.* 87.

OXENTON, William, Boston, Mass.; shipwright, from London, April 27, 1727; warned out July 11 (return). —*Suffolk Court Files,* 20510; *Boston Rec. Com., Vol.* 13, *p.* 167.

PACCANET, Michael, Boston, Mass.; seaman; from North Carolina; warned out June 15, 1735; with a wife and blind daughter.—*Boston Selectman's Rec.,* 1701-15, *p.* 230.

PACE, James, Boston, Mass.; from Great Britain, before 1714; int. m. Eliza Ward, July 7, 1714; Child: perhaps Peter.—*Boston Rec. Com., Vol.* 28, *p.* 93.

PAGE, John; from South Carolina; b. cir. 1716; volunteer against the West Indies, 1740.—*Colonial Wars,* 1899.

PAGE, Robert, of Wells, Me.; from Donaghedy, Barony of Strabane, County Tyrone.—*Bourne's Wells, p.* 313.

PAINE, Benjamin, Boston, Mass.; from London, before 1734; int. m. Sarah Godfrey, Oct. 31, 1734.—*Boston Rec. Com., Vol.* 28, *p.* 222.

PAINE, William, of Boston, Mass.; from London to Boston on the "Minerva," 1774, to settle; gentleman, aged 24.

PAINTER, Richard, Boston, Mass.; from England, 1716; warned out July 8, ten weeks residence.—*Boston Rec. Com., Vol.* 13, *p.* 11.

PAKE, Ann, of Rhode Island; from London, on the ship "Charlotte," aged 40; "going to her husband."— *N. E. Hist. Gen. Reg., Vol.* 63, *p.* 21.

PALLET, Joseph, of Canterbury, N. H.; Spanish stowaway; b. Dec. 19, 1723; m. 1, Jane ——, d. Aug. 16, 1794, aged 70 years; Child: Nathaniel; m. 2, Lydia ——, d. Sept. 12, 1822; d. Dec. 1823, aet. 100 years.—*Lyford's Canterbury, p.* 275.

PALMER, Joseph, of Braintree, Mass.; from England,

1746; b. Shaugh, Devonshire, 1716; m. Mary Cranch, of Brood, Devon; d. 1788.—*Pattee's Braintree, pp.* 486-490.

PARIS, Amos, of Dresden, Maine; from France, Huguenot.—*Huguenots in Dresden, Me., p.* 18.

PARK, Alexander, of Windham, N. H.; from County Antrim, Ireland, 1728-9; b. 1688, in Scotland; m. Margaret Waugh, b. cir. 1691, d. May 11, 1750; Children: Robert, Jennet, Thomas, Alexander, Sarah, Mary, Joseph; d. January 26, 1760.—*Morrison's Windham, p.* 713; *Park Family, p.* 178.

PARK, William, of Groton, Mass.; from Scotland, 1756, to Boston; b. in Glasgow, Scotland, Oct. 7, 1704; m. Anna Law in Glasgow, May 6, 1730, d. October 2, 1789; Children: Margaret, Janette; d. June 17, 1788.—*Green's Groton Historical Series; Park Family, pp.* 194-5.

PARKES, John, Portsmouth, N. H.; from Ireland, before 1716; m. Susanna Preston, Oct. 14, 1716.—*N. E. Hist. Gen. Reg., Vol.* 23, *p.* 393.

PARKER, Doctor ——, of Machias, Maine; from Nova Scotia, before 1776; m. Judith Lunt; Children: Samuel P., John, Phillips.—*100th Anniversary of Machias, p.* 158.

PARKER, William, of Rhode Island; from County Waterford, Ireland, before 1775; b. cir. 1734.—*Murray's Irish Rhode Islanders, p.* 28.

PARKINSON, William, of Londonderry, N. H., from Scotland and Ireland, 1744; m. Esther Woods; Children: Henry, Aaron, Jonathan, Reuben, Esther, Elizabeth, Sylvanus, William, Katherine, Mary, Susan.—*Cochran's Francestown, p.* 806.

PARNIS, Andrew, of Boston; from Ireland, 1719; cooper. —*Cullen's Irish in Boston, p.* 51.

PARSONS, Lawrence, of Warren, Maine; from Ireland, 1740; m. Eleanor Young; Children: James, William, Lawrence, Dorothy, Mary, Eleanor, Saraah; d. Cushing, Maine.—*Eaton's Warren, p.* 418, 63.

PATRICK, Christopher, to New England; from Great Musgrove, Westmoreland, 1699, in the "Virginia," Edmund Ball, master; twenty years old, with seven years to serve.—*N. E. Hist. Gen. Reg., Vol.* 64, *p.* 259.

PATRICK, John, of Worcester, Mass.; from Ireland before 1733, of Palmer, 1734.—*Perry's Scotch-Irish, p.* 14.

PATRICK, Matthew, of Warren, Mass.; from the north of Ireland, cir. 1724; b. 1681; m. Mary ——; Children: John, Thomas, Isaac, Matthew; d. Nov. 10, 1767, G. S.—*Lyford's Canterbury, pp.* 277-8.

PATRICK, Robert, of Rutland, Mass.; from Ireland, before 1720; m. Margaret ——, Rutland, June, 1720; Children: Dinai, Elizabeth, Margaret, Mary, Robert. —*Vital Rec. of Rutland, p.* 75; *Reed's Rutland, p.* 82.

PATTEN, Actor, of Kennebunk, Maine; from Colerain, Flying Point in Freeport, and Surry, Maine; from Colerain, Ireland, cir. 1737; Elder of the Presbyterian Church in Ireland; Child: John.—*Wheeler's Brunswick, p.* 846.

PATTEN, Actor, of Kennebunk, Maine; from Colerain, Ireland, cir. 1737; b. in Ireland, Jan. 22, 1737, son of Robert Patten; m. Jane McLellan, daughter of Hugh McLellan, of Gorham, Me., b. 1746, d. 1835; Children: Elizabeth, Robert, Actor, Mary, Abigail, Jane, Rebecca, Hugh, Rachel, William, Margaret; d. 1816.—*Wheeler's Brunswick, p.* 846.

PATTEN, John, Boston, Mass.; arrived from Northern Ireland, 1718, in the ship "William," Robert Montgomery, master; with a wife and one child.—*Court of Sessions of the Peace, Suffolk County.*

PATTEN, John, of Brunswick, Maine; from Colerain, Ireland, cir. 1727; b. 1717; son of Actor Patten; m. Mary Means, daughter of Robert Means, d. 1798; Children: Robert, Sarah Jane, Mary, Hannah, Margaret, John, William, Thomas, Matthew, Dorcas, Actor; d. 1795.—*Wheeler's Brunswick, p.* 846.

PATTEN, John, of Bedford, N. H.; from Ireland, cir. 1728; in Bedford in 1738; m. Mary ——, d. October 21, 1764; Children: Samuel, Matthew; d. April 14, 1746.—*History of Bedford, p.* 1036.

PATTEN, Jonathan, of Hancock, N. H.; from Ireland, 1776; son of Samuel and Priscilla Patten; b. 1700; m. Abigail Blood, daughter of Ebenezer Blood, 1784; Children: David, and 7 others.—*Hayward's Hancock, p. 799.*

PATTEN, Matthew, of Saco, Maine; from Coleraine, Ireland, 1727 or 1737.—*Wheeler's Brunswick, p. 846; Savage's Bedford, p. 11.*

PATTEN, Robert, of Kennebunk, Maine; from Coleraine, Ireland; m. 1, —— McGlauthlin; m. 2, Florence Johnson; Children: Actor, Robert, James, Margaret, Mary, John, Rachel.—*Wheeler's Brunswick, p. 846; Bradbury's Kennibunkport, p. 267; Chase's Chester, p. 578.*

PATTEN, Samuel, of Bedford, N. H.; from Ireland, 1728; b. 1713, son of John Patten; m. Mary Bell of Londonderry, N. H., Dec. 5, 1746, d. May, 1816; Children: Mary, Sarah, Elizabeth, Samuel, Margaret, John, Joseph, Jean, Matthew, Ann; d. April 25, 1792.—*History of Bedford, p. 1036.*

PATTEN, Samuel, of Londonderry, N. H., and Deering, Me.; from Ireland, 1768; m. Priscilla Miltmore, 1759; Child: Jonathan.—*Hayward's Hancock, p. 799.*

PATTEN, William, of Boston, Mass.; from Coleraine, Ireland, 1727 or 1735; m. Mary Lambert, 1735; no births recorded in Boston.—*Wheeler's Brunswick, p. 846; Boston Rec. Com., Vol. 28, p. 223.*

PATTERSON, Abraham, of Leicester, Mass.; before 1738. —*Parmenter's Pelham, p. 17.*

PATTERSON, Alexander, of Londonderry, N. H.; came with his father in 1721; b. Bush Mills, Ireland, 1714; m. Elizabeth Arbuckle.—*Cogswell's Henniker, p. 668.*

PATTERSON, George, Boston, Mass.; from North Britain [Scotland], before 1713; int. m. Susanna Copstick, Nov. 7, 1713.—*Boston Rec. Com., Vol. 28, p. 93.*

PATTERSON, George, Boston; from Ireland, on the ship "Elizabeth," Jan. 22, 1720.—*Boston Record Com., Vol. 13, p. 63.*

PATTERSON, John, of Palmer, Mass.; from North of Ireland, 1718, assignee of Andrew Farrand; brother of William Patterson.—*Temple's Palmer, p. 131.*

PATTERSON, John, Boston, Mass.; from Ireland, with Captain Dennis, Nov. 1719; warned out, Jan. 22, 1720. —*Boston Record Com., Vol. 13, p. 64.*

PATTERSON, Peter, of Londonderry, N. H.; from Priestland, Glenluce, County Antrim, Ireland, cir. 1730; m. Grisey Wilson, 1742; Children: Robert, Thomas, John, Rachel, Margaret, Sarah, Grisey, Elizabeth.— *Parker's Londonderry, p. 292.*

PATTERSON, William, of Palmer, Mass.; from North of Ireland, 1718; brother of John; grantee 1733; m. Mary ——, d. July 23, 1735.—*Temple's Palmer, p.* 131; *Palmer Vital Records, p. 228.*

PATTERSON, William, of Londonderry, N. H.; from Priestland, Glenluce, County Antrim, Ireland, cir. 1724; son of John and Sarah; Children: John, Robert, Peter, Adam, David, and one daughter.— *Parker's Londonderry, p. 294; Hadley's Goffstown, p. 381.*

PAUL, Robert, of Bristol, Maine; from Ireland, in 1740; m. —— Patterson; Children: John, Matthew, Jane, Samuel, Betsy, Hugh, William, James, Nancy, Alexander.—*Eaton's Thomaston, p. 349.*

PAULEY, Thomas, Boston, Mass.; from Great Britain, before 1712; int. m. Sarah Pitman Aug. 29, 1712.— *Boston Rec. Com., Vol. 28, p. 91.*

PAULIN, Alexander, Boston, Mass.; from Great Britain, before 1712; int. m. Elizabeth Spencer, Feb. 6, 1712. —*Boston Rec. Com., Vol. 28, p. 91.*

PEABLES, John, of Worcester, Mass.; from Londonderry, Ireland, in 1718; m. Dorothy, dau. Rev. John Harvey, Nov. 7, 1740; Children: John Harvey, Jean.— *Lincoln's Worcester, p. 49, Temple's Palmer, pp. 131, 524, Wall's Reminiscences of Worcester, p. 128, Palmer Vital Records, pp. 62, 166.*

PEABLES, Patrick, of Worcester, Mass.; from Londonderry, Ireland, in 1718; son of Robert Peables; m. Frances Hamilton; Child: Robert, of New Salem, N. H., and a daughter. — *Parmenter's Pelham, p. 17, Lincoln's Worcester, p. 49, Wall's Reminiscences of Worcester, p. 128, Pelham Vital Records, p. 64.*

PEABLES, Robert, of Worcester, Mass.; from Ireland in 1718, with wife and two children in ship "William"; m. Sarah ——; Child: Patrick, Sarah, Mary Ann; in 1726 purchased 80 acres in Worcester with highway through.—*Lincoln's Worcester, p. 49, Parmenter's Pelham, p. 17, Court of Sessions of the Peace, Transcript, March 20, 1907, Worcester Vital Records, p. 206.*

PECHIN, John George, and Peter, of Dresden, Maine; from France.—*Huguenots in Dresden, p. 18.*

PEDLEY, John, Boston, Mass.; from Great Britain, before 1712; int. m. Joanna Tyler Feb. 19, 1713.—*Boston Rec. Com., Vol. 28, p. 92.*

PEIRSON, Joseph, Boston, Mass.; laborer, from Havana, Sept. 12, 1716; warned out Sept. 24.—*Boston Rec. Com., Vol. 13, p. 10.*

PELHAM, Peter, of Boston, Mass.; from London, 1726; b. cir. 1684; m. 1. Martha ——; Children: Peter, Charles, William; m. 2. Mary (Singleton) Copley, May 22, 1748; d. 1789; Child: Henry; d. December 1751.—*Cullen's Irish in Boston, p. 35, Dictionary of National Biography, Boston Rec. Com., Vol. 24, pp. 194, 267, Vol. 28, p. 343.*

PENNELL, Thomas, of Brunswick, Maine; from the Isle of Jersey, cir. 1740; m. Rachel Riggs; Children: Matthew, Thomas, Jacob, John, Stephen, and daughters; d. at New Meadows, Brunswick, Me., Nov. 12, 1812.—*Wheeler's Brunswick, p. 847.*

PENNOCK, Samuel, Lyme, Conn.; from London, with Capt. Moses Thomas, April, 1714, with a wife and three children; warned from Boston August 17, 1714.—*Boston Rec. Com., Vol. 11, p. 215.*

PEPPER, Robert, of Boston, Mass.; from Ireland, with Captain Dennis, Nov., 1719; warned out January, 1720.—*Boston Rec. Com., Vol. 13, p. 64.*

PERARO, Emanuel, of Boston, Mass.; from Portugal, before 1739; m. Elizabeth Gyles, Nov. 30, 1739; Child: Hannah. — *Mass. Hist. Soc. Proceedings* 1858-60, p. 343, *Boston Rec. Com., Vol.* 28, p. 212, *Vol.* 24, p. 242.

PERHAM, John, of Ackworth and Manchester, N. H.; from Ireland; m. Sarah Moore; Child: John.—*Merrill's Ackworth,* p. 257.

PERKINS, Daniel, Boston, Mass.; a dancing master from New York, April 24, 1727; warned out July 11 (return).—*Suffolk Court Files* 20510, *Boston Rec. Com., Vol.* 13, p. 167.

PERKINS, William, Boston, Mass.; tailor; from Great Britain, before Feb. 15, 1715; to give security (see below).—*Boston Rec. Com., Vol.* 11, p. 222.

PERKINS, William, Boston, Mass.; from Great Britain, before 1719; int. m. Elizabeth Pullen, Dec. 8, 1719 (see above).—*Boston Rec. Com., Vol.* 28, p. 98.

PERKS, Thomas, Boston, Mass.; late of London, admitted to dwell. Oct. 11, 1715.—*Boston Rec. Com., Vol.* 11.

PERREY, George, Newbury, Mass.; from Fenington, England, before 1729; "a seafaring man"; m. Jane Bussell, of Boston (born in Amesbury), Nov. 11, 1729. —*Newbury Vital Records, Vol.* 2, p. 383.

PEVISE, Alexander, Boston, Mass.; from Great Britain, before 1718; int. m. Katherin Tucker, June 21, 1718. —*Boston Rec. Com., Vol.* 28, p. 97.

PHILHOUR, Daniel, of Broad Bay, Maine; from Germany, before 1760.—*Miller's Waldoboro,* p. 51.

PHILLIPS, Neal, of Portsmouth, N. H.; from Weymouth, Dorset, before 1725; m. Elizabeth Snow, widow, Oct. 21, 1725.—*N. E. Hist. Gen. Reg., Vol.* 24, p. 357.

PHONNE, Robert, Boston, Mass.; "an Irishman from Wales," 1727; warned out, July 11, 1727.—*Suffolk Court Files* 20510.

PICKENS, Thomas, of Middleboro, Mass.; from Ireland; bought land, 1732.—*Weston's Middleboro,* p. 434.

PICKLES, William, of Bedford, N. H.; from Wales.— *Parker's Londonderry,* p. 193.

PICKREN, Robert, Portsmouth, N. H.; from Bastable, Devonshire, before 1717; m. Sarah Abott, June 13, 1717.—*N. E. Hist. Gen. Reg., Vol.* 23, *p.* 394.

PIDGEON, Joseph, Newbury, Mass.; from "Southampton, Great Britain," before 1718; m. Sarah Nesbe, April 29, 1718.—*Newbury Vital Records, Vol.* 2, *p.* 391.

PIERCE, Thomas, Portsmouth, N. H.; from Helstone, Cornwall, before 1724; m. Mary Jackson, Nov. 1, 1724.—*N. E. Hist. Gen. Reg., Vol.* 24, *p.* 18.

PIGGOT, Rev. George; from England to Connecticut, 1722. —*Emigrant Ministers to America, p.* 50.

PILLIN, Rev. Thomas, from England, to Rhode Island, 1754.—*Emigrant Ministers to America, p.* 50.

PINKERTON, John, of Londonderry, N. H.; from County Antrim, Ireland, in 1724; Children: David, John, Matthew, Samuel, James, Mary, Elizabeth, Rachel, Jane; d. 1780, aged 80.—*Parker's Londonderry, p.* 295.

PINKERTON, Mary, see Alexander McCauley.

PITSON, James, Boston "cyderman"; from London, retaylor in Marshall's Lane, Nov. 16, 1715; m. Hannah ———; Child: James.—*Boston Rec. Com., Vol.* 11, *p.* 218; *Vol.* 24, *p.* 131; *Vol.* 28, *p.* 216.

PITTS, William, Boston, Mass.; from Great Britain, before 1717; int. m. Grace Hewet, July 26, 1717.— *Boston Rec. Com., Vol.* 28, *p.* 96.

PLAISTRIDGE, Isaac, of ———, Conn.; Child: Caleb, of Cornish, N. H., b. cir. 1752.—*Child's Cornish, Vol. II, p.* 289.

PLANT, Rev. Matthias, of Newbury, Mass.; from Staffordshire, Great Britain, before 1722; minister of the church of England; m. Mrs. Lydia Bartlett, Dec. 27, 1722, d. Oct. 8, 1753, aet. 65; d. April 2, 1753, aet. 62.—*Newbury Vital Records, Vol.* 2, *pp.* 399, 696; *Emigrant Ministers to America, p.* 50.

POCHARD, Jean, of Frankfort and Dresden, Me. [Pushard]; weaver; from Chenebie, Hericourt, dept. of Haute-Saone, France, on ship "Pricilla," from Rotterdam, 1751; son of the Hon. Nicholas Pochard, mayor of Anne-Sur-l'eau; b. Sept. 20, 1706; m.

Jeanne Mounier; Children: Abraham, George, Jacques Christophe, Pierre Emanuel.—*Maine Hist. Coll.*, 2d Series, *Vol.* 3, *p.* 357, *Huguenots in Dresden, Allen, pp.* 9-13, 18.

POLERCZKY, John, of Waldoboro, Maine; from France, in Rochambeau's army; took the 1790 census of Waldoboro.—*Miller's Waldoboro, p.* 264.

POOR, Robert, Boston, Mass.; husbandman, from Newfoundland, Oct., 1716; warned out, Nov. 1, 1716.—*Boston Rec. Com., Vol.* 13, *p.* 15.

POOR, Robert, of Rye, N. H.; from England, served under John Paul Jones; m. Betsy Shapley, 1788; Children: Robert, Judith, Sally, Eliza, Mary, George, Abigail Daniels, Daniel Sheafe, Nancy.—*Parsons' Rye, p.* 498.

PORTERFIELD, Patrick, of Thomaston, Me.; from Ireland, 1749; m. 1. Martha Jamison; m. 2. Mary (Webster) McLellan; Children: William, John, Elizabeth, Catherine, Ruth, Martha, Nancy, Robert; d. 1799, aged 77.—*Eaton's Thomaston, p.* 361.

POSLEY, John, of Boston, Mass.; from Ireland, with Captain Dennis, Nov., 1719; farmer.—*Boston Rec. Com., Vol.* 13, *p.* 64.

PREESON, William, Boston, Mass.; from Great Britain, before 1711; int. m. Rachel Draper, Jan. 14, 1712; Child: William.—*Boston Rec. Com., Vol.* 28, *p.* 91, *Vol.* 24, *p.* 107.

PRESBURY, Nathaniel, Portsmouth, N. H.; from Blackfriars, London, before 1726; m. Parthenia Benson, March 31, 1726.—*N. E. Hist. Gen. Reg., Vol.* 24, *p.* 350.

PRESTON, Jedediah, of Hillsboro, N. H.; from Yorkshire, 1770, in the ship "Constantine"; b. 1749; m. Esther Burt; Child: Samuel. — *Cochran's Francestown, p.* 885.

PRESTON, Samuel, of Hillsboro, N. H.; from Yorkshire, England; brother of Jedediah.—*Cochran's Francestown, p.* 885.

PRICE, Margaret, Boston, Mass.; from New York, 1722; warned out, Sept. 2, 1722; m. perhaps John Davis, Jan. 11, 1728.—*Boston Rec. Com., Vol.* 13, *p.* 107, *Vol.* 28, *p.* 166.

PRICE, Rev. Roger, of Boston, Mass.; from England, to New England, 1729; son of William Price, rector of Whitfield, Northamptonshire; m. Elizabeth Bull, April 14, 1735, in Boston.—*Emigrant Ministers to America, p.* 51, *Boston Rec. Com., Vol.* 28, *p.* 192.

PRICE, Thomas, Boston, Mass.; from Great Britain, before 1721; int. m. Sarah Baker, April 18, 1721.— *Boston Rec. Com., Vol.* 28, *p.* 158.

PRICE, Thomas, of Salem, Mass.; from Cedar Point, Maryland, before 1760; m. Mary Fowler, int. April 12, 1760.—*Salem Vital Records, Vol.* 3, *p.* 381, *Vol.* 4, *p.* 218.

PRIEST, Richard, Portsmouth, N. H.; from Clovelly, Devonshire, before 1731; m. Charity Quick, May 24, 1731.—*N. E. Hist Gen. Reg., Vol.* 25, *p.* 118.

PROCTOR, Agnes, Boston, Mass.; wife of Thomas Proctor; from Ireland, with Capt. John Carrell, 1736; admitted, Sept. 18, 1736.—*Boston Rec. Com., Vol.* 15, *p.* 3.

PRUST, Thomas, Portsmouth, N. H.; from Northam, Devonshire, before 1720; m. Sarah Collins, cir. Dec. 1720.—*N. E. Hist. Gen. Reg., Vol.* 24, *p.* 14.

PUGOL, Joseph, Boston, Mass.; from Monte Real in Canada, via New York, May, 1736; a soldier who deserted; a dyer by trade. — *Boston Record Com., Vol.* 13, *p.* 317.

PULLEY, Mr. John, Boston, Mass.; from London, 1737; brass founder; voted that he may open a shop and hang out a sign.—*Boston Rec. Com., Vol.* 15, *p.* 17.

PULMAN, James, of Boston, Mass.; from Newfoundland; "Taylor"; admitted an inhabitant and liberty to open a shop, etc., Oct. 16, 1729; m. Mary Tippin, March 13, 1729.—*Boston Rec. Com., Vol.* 13, *p.* 191, *Vol.* 28, *p.* 156.

PURFIELD, see Purple.

PURPLE, John, of Amherst, N. H.; from Wales; impressed in British navy and deserted; m. Lydia Lewis, 1785; Children: Robert, John; d. 1842, aged 98.—*Secomb's Amherst, p. 737.*

PUSHARD, see Pochard.

PYM, Charles, Boston, distiller; from Jamaica, 1715; admitted an inhabitant, Jan. 25, 1715. — *Boston Rec. Com., Vol. 11, p. 221.*

QUEEN, Thomas, from Ireland, laborer; b. cir. 1719; volunteer against the West Indies, 1740.—*Colonial Wars,* 1899.

QUIGLEY, Patrick, from Ireland, laborer; b. cir. 1714; volunteer against the West Indies, 1740.—*Colonial Wars,* 1899.

QUIGLEY, Thomas, of Windham and Francestown, N. H.; from Ireland, cir. 1724; b. 1703, in northeastern Ireland; m. 1734; Children: John, Jane, Mary A., William, Margaret, Susanna, Betsy, Thomas, and one other; d. Aug. 22, 1793, aged cir. 90.—*Morrison's Windham, pp. 45, 46, Cochran's Francestown, pp. 889, 892.*

QUINTON, Duncan, of Palmer, Mass.; b. 1694; m. Eunice Little; Children: Elizabeth, Dorcas, Ann, John, Thomas, Jean, Mary, Unis, Sarah; d. March 7, 1776, aet 82. — *Temple's Palmer, p. 527, Palmer Vital Records, pp. 64, 168, 229.*

QUIRCKE, Capt. John, from Bristol, England, before 1725; m. Dorothy Frothingham, of Boston, Feb. 3, 1725, in Newbury.—*Newbury Vital Records, Vol. 2, p. 186.*

RADCLIFF, Jane, to New England; from Rachdale [Rochdale], Lancashire, 1699, in the "Virginia," Edmund Ball, master; a spinster, 20 years old, with seven years to serve.—*N. E. Hist. Gen. Reg., Vol. 64, 65, p. 259.*

RAGGET, Thomas, Boston, Mass.; from Great Britain, with Captain Porter, cir. June 4, 1715, with a wife and four children; joiner; warned out, June 14, 1715.—*Boston Rec. Com., Vol. 11, p. 228.*

RAGLAND, John, Boston, Mass.; from Great Britain, before 1712; int. m. Judith Munden, Feb. 14, 1713. —*Boston Rec. Com., Vol. 28, p. 92.*

RALEIGH, see Riley.

RALSTON, Alexander, of Surry, Keene and Claremont, N. H.; from Scotland, 1773; b. 1755, at Falkirk, Scotland; m. Jane Ballock, d. 1833, in Cornish, N. H.; Children: Mary, Elizabeth, Janette, Hannah, Alexander, Ann, James B., Nancy, Sally; d. 1810, in Keene.—*Kingsbury's Surry, p. 816.*

RAMSAY, John, from the Island of Jersey; cordwainer; b. cir. 1719; volunteer against the West Indies, 1740.—*Coonial Wars, 1899.*

RANCHON, John, Boston, Mass.; from France, before 1713; int. m. Mary Beachamp, April 3, 1713.— *Boston Rec. Com., Vol. 28, p. 92.*

RANKIN, Hugh, of Londonderry, N. H.; from Dungiven, County Londonderry, Ireland, before 1721; b. 1672; m. —— Dunlap; Children: Mary, Martha, Joan, Esther, Janet, Agnes, Anne, Dinah.—*Drummond's Rogers Family of Georgetown, p. 3; Parker's Londonderry, p. 296; Autobiography of the Rev. Samuel Gregg, p. 4, MS. at the N. E. Hist. Gen. Soc.; Morrison's Windham, p. 380.*

RANKIN, James, of Worcester, Mass.; from Ireland, 1718; Child: Anna.—*Wall's Reminiscences of Worcester, p. 128.*

RANKIN, John, of Littleton, Mass.; from Glasgow, Scotland; Child: Andrew.—*Dearborn's Salisbury, N. H., p. 166.*

RANKINS, William, of Boston, Mass.; from Great Britain, before 1719; int. m. Sarah Clark, Sept. 4, 1719. —*Boston Rec. Com., Vol. 28, p. 98.*

RANTOUL, Robert, of Salem, Mass.; from Middletowne, Kinross, 1769; b. 1753; m. Mary Preston, Nov. 3, 1774, d. July 17, 1816, aet 61; Child: Robert; Robert, Sr. d. 1783.—*Amer. Ances., Vol. 3, p. 211; Salem Vital Records, Vol. 4, p. 239, Vol. 6, p. 175.*

RASPIN, Thomas, Boston, Mass.; from Great Britain, with Capt. Walker, Oct. 10, 1717; tailor, works with Mr. George Monks; warned out, Oct. 28, 1717; m. Mary Nexon, Oct. 30, 1717.—*Boston Rec. Com., Vol.* 13, *p.* 30, *Vol.* 28, *p.* 72.

RAY, Isaac, of Portsmouth, N. H.; from Kent, before 1720; m. Elizabeth Wells, Dec. 1, 1720.—*N. E. Hist. Gen. Reg., Vol.* 24, *p.* 14.

READ, Hugh, of Boston, Mass.; from New York, with wife and one boy, April 3, 1720; warned out, April 6, 1720.—*Boston Rec. Com., Vol.* 13, *p.* 69.

READING, Daniel, of Boston, Mass.; tailor, from Newfoundland, Oct., 1716; warned out, Nov. 1, 1716. —*Boston Rec. Com., Vol.* 13, *p.* 15.

RECKETT, Alice, see David Beverland.

REDMOND, William, see Goodwin, William.

REE, Thomas, of Boston, Mass.; from Bristol in Great Britain, 1722; cordwainer; admitted an inhabitant on bonds of himself and Wm. Pain, Esq., March 26, 1722.—*Boston Rec. Com., Vol.* 13, *p.* 95.

REED, Col. Andrew, of Boothbay, Me.; from Antrim, Ireland, 1743; b. 1693, in Antrim; m. Jean Murray (b. 1698), in Ireland, d. 1780; she was an aunt of Rev. John Murray; Children: Andrew, Henry, David, John, William, Paul, Joseph, Thomas, Sarah; d. 1762. — *Greene's Boothbay, p.* 610, *Maine Hist. Soc. Coll.,* 2d *Series, Vol.* 9, *p.* 284, *Amer. Ances., Vol.* 3, *p.* 169.

REED, Mrs. Henry, see McCulloch.

REED, Captain John, of Newbury, Mass.; from England; d. June 7, 1729.—*Newbury Vital Records, Vol.* 2, *p.* 705.

REED, Matthew, of Londonderry, N. H.; from Ireland, before March 17, 1730. — *Documentary History of Maine, p.* 24.

REED, Thomas, Portsmouth, N. H.; from London, before 1716; m. Elizabeth Brooks, Aug. 4, 1716.—*N. E. Hist. Gen. Reg., Vol.* 23, *p.* 392.

REEL, Peter, Boston, Mass.; from Hanover, Germany, before 1715; int. m. Anna Duncan, "her husbd. not dead in Law," Dec. 24, 1715.—*Boston Rec. Com., Vol.* 28, *p.* 95.

REEVES, Richard, Boston, Mass.; with his wife, from England, Sept. 1716; a tailor; warned out, Oct. 23, 1716; m. Anne ———; Child: Robert.—*Boston Rec. Com., Vol. 13, p. 11, Vol. 24, p. 124.*

REID, Alexander, of Londonderry, N. H.; from Scotland, 1730, with James Reid.—*Documentary History of Maine, p. 24.*

REID, James, of Londonderry, N. H.; from Scotland, 1730; b. 1695; graduate of Edinburgh University; m. Mary ———; Children: Matthew, Abraham, Elizabeth, Thomas, John, George; d. 1755, aged 60.— *Parker's Londonderry, p. 297, Morrison's Windham, p. 746, Documentary History of Maine, pp. 24, 26, Vital Records of Londonderry, p. 104.*

REID, Michael, of Broad Bay, Maine; from Germany, before 1760.—*Miller's Waldoboro, p. 51.*

REINER, Phillip, of Broad Bay, Waldoboro, Maine; from Germany, before 1752. *Mass. Archives, Vol. 15A, pp. 240-2.*

REISER, Johana Martin, of Broad Bay, Waldoboro, Me.; from Germany, before 1752.—*Mass. Archives, Vol. 15A, pp. 240-2.*

RENDELL, John, of Thomaston, Me.; from England; m. Jane Clark; Children: James, John, Thomas, William, Margaret, Hannah, Jane, Mary, Sally; d. 1781. —*Eaton's Thomaston, p. 368.*

RENKIN, Alexander, of Londonderry, N. H.; from Ireland, before 1727/8; m. Mary ———; Child: Agnes. —*Londonderry Vital Records, p. 104.*

REYNOLDS, William, Newbury, Mass.; from Ireland, before 1771; m. Anna Godstead, July 28, 1771. — *Newbury Vital Records, Vol. 2, pp. 195, 418.*

RICHARDS, Charles, of Shirley, Mass.; from England, before 1729; m. Janet Mitchell, of Marblehead, Mass., Feb. 23, 1729; Children: John, Margaret, Charles, Mitchell, Edward, Elizabeth, Moses, Eleanor, Lurania; d. in Shirley.—*Chandler's Shirley, p. 607, Shirley Vital Records, pp. 81, 82, 206, Bolton's Shirley Uplands and Intervales, pp. 351-353, Marblehead Vital Records, Vol. 1, p. 431, Vol. 2, p. 359.*

RICHARDS, Edward, of Lunenburg, Mass.; from England, before 1729; brother of Charles; m. Martha Mitchell, sister of his brother's wife, Sept. 7, 1782, d. May 20, 1786, s. p.—*Bolton's Shirley Uplands and Intervales, p.* 351.

RICHARDS, John, Boston, Mass.; from North Britain, before 1720; int. m. Priscilla Bass, Nov. 23, 1720.—*Boston Rec. Com., Vol.* 28, *p.* 99.

RICHARDSON, Francis, Boston, Mass.; from New York, April 23, 1727; warned out, July 11 (return).—*Suffolk Court Files* 20510, *Boston Rec. Com., Vol.* 13, *p.* 167.

RICHARDSON, Rachel, from London, in 1716; a servant. —*Boston Rec. Com., Vol.* 29, *p.* 234.

RICHAY, John, of Londonderry, N. H.; from Ireland, before March 17, 1730. — *Documentary History of Maine, p.* 20.

RICHEY, Alexander, of Windham, N. H.; from Great Britain, cir. 1736; m. Sarah ———; Children: William, James, Mary, Elizabeth, Hannah.—*Morrison's Windham, p.* 751.

RICHEY, Francis, of Windham, N. H.; from Ballymanaugh, County Antrim, Ireland; perhaps son of Alexander; d. 1777, aged 61.—*Morrison's Windham, p.* 751.

RICHMOND, John Montague, of Portland, Me.; from Ireland; schoolmaster. — *Smith's and Dean's Journal, p.* 188.

RIDAL [Rittall], ———, of Dresden, Maine; from France. —*Miller's Waldoboro, p.* 18.

RIDDLE, Gawn or Gann, of Londonderry and Bedford, N. H.; from Balleymeath, County Londonderry, Ireland, 1718; b. May 16, 1688, at Balleymeath, son of John and Janet (Gordon) Riddle; m. Mary Bell, b. 1724, d. Jan. 7, 1813, daughter of John Bell q. v. —*Brown's Bedford, p.* 1046.

RIDDLE, Hugh, of Londonderry, N. H.; from Ballymeath, Ireland, 1718; b. 1692, son of John and Janet (Gordon) Riddle; m. Mrs. Anna Aiken of Concord;

Children: Nancy, Hugh, William, Robert; d. 1775 in Colerain.—*Ancient Ryedales, p.* 245, *Brown's Bedford, p.* 1045, *Vital Records of Londonderry, p.* 106.

RIDDLE, John, of Bedford, N. H.; from Balleymeath, County Londonderry, Ireland, 1718; son of John and Janet (Gordon) Riddle; m. —— ——; Children: Mary, Elizabeth (both died unmarried); d. July 6, 1757.—*Brown's Bedford, p.* 1046.

RIDDLE, Robert, Londonderry, N. H.; from Balleymeath, County Londonderry, Ireland, 1718; son of John and Janet (Gordon) Riddle.—*Brown's Bedford, p.* 345.

RIDLON, Magnus, of York and Saco, Maine; from Orkney Islands, Scotland; b. 1674; m. 1 Susannah Young; m. 2 Massie Townsend; Child: Matthias, [John, Daniel, Jeremiah, Abraham]; d. 1771, aged 78.—*Amer. Ances., Vol.* 3, *p.* 98, *Pepperrellborough Church Records, p.* 118, *N. E. Hist. Gen. Reg., Vol.* 71, *pp.* 218-221.

RIJAN, Joan, see Daniel Kelly.

RILEY, or Raleigh, Philip, of Antrim, N. H., and Sudbury, Mass.; from Ireland, to Boston, 1743; b. 1719, in Ireland; m. Susanna Joiner, Oct. 8, 1731, in Sudbury; Children: Major, Charles, Elizabeth, John, Lois, Sarah; removed to Concord, Mass., for a time; d. cir. 1790.—*Cochran's Antrim, p.* 652, *Whiton's Antrim, pp.* 15, 53, *Sudbury Vital Records, pp.* 116, 117, 255.

RINNELL, Matthew, of Broad Bay, Waldoboro, Maine; from Germany, before 1752.—*Mass. Archives, Vol.* 15*A. pp.* 240-2.

RITTER, Daniel, of Lunenburg, Mass.; weaver; m. Lydia ——; Children: Moses, Thomas, Elizabeth, Ann; will probated, Jan. 31, 1743.—*Worcester Probate.*

RITZ, Rev. Frederick Augustus Rudolphus Benedictus, of Waldoboro, Maine; from Germany, 1784; b. 1752; graduate of the University of Helmstadt; ordained in Pennsylvania, 1793; m. Margaret Hahn, of Waldoboro, after 1794; d. Feb. 21, 1811, aet 59.— *Miller's Waldoboro, pp.* 232-3.

RIVERS, Joseph, of Cushing, Maine; from Ireland; m. Margaret Robinson; Children: Thomas, Mary, Moses, Archibald, Betsy, Sarah, Joseph, Margaret. —*Eaton's Thomaston, p.* 373.

RIVINGTON, James, of Boston, Mass.; from London, cir. 1762; removed to New York.—*Thomas's History of Printing, Vol.* 2, *p.* 229.

RIX, Samuel, Boston, Mass.; from New York, Sept. 25, 1706; dyer; warned out, April 28, 1707.—*Boston Rec. Com., Vol.* 11, *p.* 58.

ROADLEY, John, to New England; from Norwich, Norfolk, 1699, in the "Virginia"; seventeen years old, with seven years to serve.—*N. E. Hist. Gen. Reg., Vol.* 64, *p.* 260.

ROBB, John, of Ackworth, N. H.; from Scotland; m. Mary Alexander; Child: Mary; d. 1799.—*Merrill's Ackworth, p.* 260.

ROBBE, William, of Lunenburg, Mass.; from Ireland, cir. 1726; b. 1692; m. 1 Elizabeth ——; Child: Margaret; m. 2 Agnes or Anne Patterson, b. 1685, d. 1762; Children: John, James, Alexander, Elizabeth, William; d. 1769, aged 77, in Peterborough. — *Smith's Peterborough, Pt.* 2, *p.* 235 *et seq., Lunenburg Records, p.* 321.

ROBERTS, Joseph, Boston, Mass.; from Great Britain, before 1717; int. m. Margrait Ditchfield, Oct. 31, 1717. —*Boston Rec. Com., Vol.* 28, *p.* 96.

ROBERTSON, [Alexander?] of Plymouth, Mass.; from Scotland, with wife Abigail? and seven children; Children: John (Salisbury, N. H.), Alexande, Micah, four others.—*Dearborn's Salisbury, p.* 1717, *Davis's Ancient Landmarks of Plymouth, p.* 221.

ROBERTSON, Alexander, of Norwich, Conn.; from Scotland, before 1773; d. 1784 in Shelburne, Nova Scotia,—*Thomas's History of Printing, Vol.* 1, *p.* 192.

ROBERTSON, Archibald, of Chesterfield, N. H.; from Scotland, 1754; b. 1708; m. Elizabeth ——; d. April 15, 1791, in her 80th year; Children: James, William, John, Anna. — *Randall's Chesterfield, pp.* 417-18.

ROBERTSON, Gain, of Plymouth, Mass.; from Ireland before 1750; m. Margaret Watson; Children: Alexander, Susanna.—*Davis's Ancient Landmarks of Plymouth, p.* 221; *N. E. Hist. Gen. Reg.* 1845, *p.* 13.

ROBERTSON, James, of Norwich, Conn.; from Scotland, before 1773; removed to Edinburgh, Scotland.—*Thomas's History of Printing, Vol.* 1, *p.* 192.

ROBERTSON, William, of Londonderry and Pembroke, N. H.; from Ireland; b. Feb. 8, 1703; m. Margaret Woodend, 1729, b. 1705, d. 1785; Children: Andrew, and seven others; d. March 7, 1790.—*Lapham's Bethel, p.* 605.

ROBBINS, Thomas, Newbury, Mass.; from "Waller Hampton," Staffordshire, England, before 1703; m. Priscilla Mallard, Dec. 1, 1703, in Newbury; Child: Thomas.—*Newbury Vital Records, Vol.* 1, *p.* 441, *Vol.* 2, *p.* 314.

ROBINSON, ———, of Boston, Mass., and South Thomaston, Me.; from England, before 1748; Children: Susanna, George.—*Eaton's Thomaston, p.* 382.

ROBINSON, Andrew, of Thomaston, Me.; from Ireland, before 1742; brother of Dr. Moses Robinson; d. 1742. —*Eaton's Thomaston, p.* 376.

ROBINSON, John, of Exeter, N. H.; from England, 1737; b. 1715; m. Martha Scribner, 1737, d. 1789; Children: Jonathan, Mary, Abigail, David, John, Thomas; d. 1784.—*Fowler's Pembroke, p.* 279 *et seq.*

ROBINSON, Dr. Moses, of Cushing, Maine; from Ireland, before 1742; Children: Joseph, Moses, John, Hanse, Archibald, William, Margaret; d. 1742. — *Eaton's Thomaston, p.* 376, *Eaton's Warren, p.* 605.

ROBINSON, Nathaniel, Portsmouth, N. H.; from New York, before 1716; b. in New York; m. Sarah Broughton, May 29, 1716.—*N. E. Hist. Gen. Reg., Vol.* 23, *p.* 392.

ROBINSON, William, Boston; cabinet maker; from London, with Capt. Beard, Sept., 1714, with his wife; warned out, April 19, 1715. — *Boston Rec. Com., Vol.* 11, *p.* 226.

RODGERS, James, of Dunbarton (then Starkstown), N. H.; from Ireland; m. Mary ——; Children: Daniel, Samuel, James, Robert "the Ranger," Richard, John, Catharine; shot in winter of 1752-3.—*Drummond's James Rogers of Londonderry.*

RODGERS, John, of Boston, Mass.; from Ireland, August 7, 1718; warned from Boston, Oct. 22, 1718.—*Cullen's Irish in Boston, p. 51, Suffolk Court Files 12620, Boston Rec. Com., Vol. 13, p. 46.*

ROGERS, George, of Londonderry, N. H., and Georgetown, Me.; from Dromore, Luce Bay, Antrim, Ireland, about 1720; b. about 1662; m. Isabella, possibly McCobb or Cobb, b. cir. 1678, d. Dec. 5, 1743, aet 65; Children: William, George, Patrick, Frances, Margaret, Beatrice; d. Oct. 30, 1743, aged 81.— *Maine Hist. Soc. Coll., 2d Series, Vol. 8, p. 96, Drummond's Rankin Family of Georgetown, Maine, p. —, Georgetown Vital Records, MS. p. 56 in N. E. Hist. Gen. Soc.*

ROGERS, George, of Georgetown, Maine; from Ireland, 1726; b. 1704, Londonderry, son of George Rogers (above); m. 1. Ann Ferguson or Cochrane? of Pelham, N. H., 1742, d. 1768; Children: John, Mary, George, David, Thomas, Ann, Margaret, Alexander, Beatrice, William, Jennie; m. 2. Sarah Wyman, 1769; Children: George, Francis, Nathaniel, Sarah; d. Jan. 29, 1801. — *Georgetown Vital Records, pp. 37, 38.*

ROGERS, James, of Billerica, Mass., and Londonderry, N. H.; from Ireland, before 1721; m. Jean ——; Children: Thomas, William, John, James, Margaret, Mary, Jean, Esther, Samuel(?), Martha; will dated Sept. 15, 1755; he and his brother Hugh petitioners to Governor Shute.—*Drummond's James Rogers of Londonderry, Documentary History of Maine, p. 24.*

ROGERS, Robert, of Palmer, Mass.; from North of Ireland, 1718; bought a farm, 1740; b. 1707; m. Jane ——, d. May 14, 1749; Children: Elizabeth, James, Robert, Joanna, Lettice, John; d. May 17, 1776.— *Temple's Palmer, p. 131, 530, Palmer Vital Records, pp. 65, 229, 230.*

ROGERS, William, of Georgetown, Maine; from Ireland, before 1746; m. 1. Dinah ——; m. 2. Ruth ——; Children: Margaret, Ann, William, John, Robert, George, Thomas, Hugh. — *Wheeler's Brunswick, p. 850, Georgetown Vital Records, p. 38.*

ROMINGER, David, of Broad Bay, Maine; from Germany, before 1752; b. Wurtemburg, 1716; m. Catherine ——; removed with his wife to North Carolina, 1769; d. Bethabara, N. C., 1777.—*Miller's Waldoboro, p. 64, State Archives, Vol. 15A, pp. 240-2.*

ROMINGER, Michael, of Broad Bay, Maine; from Germany, before 1764; b. Wurtemburg, 1709; m. Catherine ——; d. Friedland, N. C., 1803. — *Miller's Waldoboro, p. 63.*

ROSE, John, Boston, Mass.; from Great Britain, before 1719; int. m. Katherine Tucker, Jan. 21, 1720.— *Boston Rec. Com., Vol. 28, p. 98.*

Ross, Alexander, of Portland, Me.; from Stroma, Scotland; b. Oct. 19, 1717; m. Elizabeth ——; d. Nov. 24, 1768, in Falmouth, Me.—*Gravestone, East Cemetery, Portland Price Current, July 7, 1877.*

Ross, David, of Bath, Maine; from Great Britain, before 1718; m. Elizabeth —— (see below); at Brunswick, Sept. 4, 1718.—*York Deeds, p. 238.*

Ross, Mrs. Elizabeth, Portland, Me.; from South Ronaldsha, Orkney Islands; b. Jan. 1, 1721; m. Alexander Ross (above); d. March 1, 1798, at Gorham, Me.—*Gravestone, East Cemetery, Portland, Portland Price Current, July 7, 1877.*

Ross, James, of Gorham, Maine; from Scotland, before 1758; m. Hannah Dyer; Children: Mary, Rebecca, Elizabeth, Sarah, Alexander, Walter, Alley, John Fleet, Anna; d. 1780, aged 68. — *McLellan's Gorham, p. 752.*

Ross, Jane, see Isaac Miller.

Ross, John, of Wells, Maine; from Sligo, Ireland, 1720, with his family.—*Bourne's Wells, p. 313.*

ROTCH, William, of Provincetown, Mass.; from Salisbury, England, 1710; b. 1670; m. Hannah ——; Children: Joseph, Benjamin. — *Secomb's Amherst, p. 750.*

ROTH, Richard, of Boston, Mass.; Irish servant of David Stoddard; ran away, 1722; aged 26 in 1722.—*Boston News Letter, July* 9, 1722.

ROTHETT, John, to New England; from Blackburn, Lancashire, 1699, in the "Virginia"; nineteen years old, with seven years to serve.—*N. E. Hist. Gen. Reg., Vol.* 64, *p.* 260.

ROUMAGE, Benjamin, Boston, Mass.; from England, with Captain Thomas, cir. May, 1715; warned out, Nov. 1715.—*Boston Rec. Com., Vol.* 11, *p.* 238.

ROUNSEVILLE, Philip, of East Freetown, Mass.; from England, before 1763; b. in "Hunneton in old England" (Honiton, County Devon); d. 1763, aet 86 years.—*East Freetown Cemetery.*

ROUSO, Samuel, Boston, Mass.; from Newfoundland, before 1712; a Frenchman; int. m. Mary Pereway, July 20, 1713.—*Boston Rec. Com., Vol.* 28, *p.* 93.

ROWLANDS, James, from London to New England, on the ship "Venus," 1774, to settle; taylor, aged 29.—*N. E. Hist. Gen. Reg., Vol.* 63, *p.* 234.

RUBINE, Peter, Boston, Mass.; mason from Philadelphia and Rhode Island, 1711; "subject to fits and now weak in his hands"; warned out June 11, 1711.—*Boston Rec. Com., Vol.* 11, *p.* 135.

RUSEL, Henry, Boston, Mass.; from Great Britain, before 1720; mariner; int. m. Mary Heath, Nov. 1, 1720.—*Boston Rec. Com., Vol.* 28, *p.* 99.

RUSSELL, David, from Scotland to Boston on the "Success," 1774; cooper, aged 25, to settle.—*N. E. Hist. Gen. Reg., Vol.* 63, *p.* 24.

RUSSELL, George, of Chester, N. H.; British soldier, 1775; m. Martha McNeil; Children: John, Dawson, Mary; d. in New Boston.—*Chase's Chester, p.* 584.

RUSSELL, John, Boston, Mass.; from Great Britain, before 1713; int. m. Rachel Morrell, Nov. 10, 1713. —*Boston Rec. Com., Vol.* 28, *p.* 93.

RUTHERFORD, Rev. Robert, of Pemaquid and Cushing, Me.; from Ireland, before 1735; b. 1698; m. ———, d. Feb. 8, 1780; Children: Mary, Lettice, Ann Maria, Elizabeth, Hepsibeth, Hannah; d. Oct. 18, 1758, at Warren, Maine.—*Eaton's Warren, pp.* 97, 423, *new ed., p.* 612.

RUTTER, John, Boston, Mass.; from Bay of Compecha, with John Brewer, 1707.—*Boston Rec. Com., Vol.* 11, *p.* 6.

RYAN, Anthony, of Leicester, Mass.; from Ireland, probably before 1743; m. Margaret ———; Children: John, Mary, Katherine, Sarah, Samuel, Susanna, Daniel, Margaret, Susanna, Hannah. — *Washburn's Leicester, p.* 391, *Leicester Vital Records, pp.* 73, 75, 200.

RYAN, John, of Leicester, Mass.; "a foreigner," 1764; m. Elizabeth Sinclair, of Spencer, int. Jan. 6, 1764. —*Leicester Vital Records, p.* 200.

RYAN, Roger, of Newbury, Mass.; from Ireland; "an Irishman who was hired in the Parish"; d. of the fever, August 9, 1758, aged under 30 years.—*Newbury Vital Records, Vol.* 2, *p.* 713.

RYAN, William, of Boston, Mass.; Irish servant of David Stoddard; aged 23, in 1722.—*Boston News Letter, July* 9, 1722.

ST. BARBE, George, Jr., of Salem, Mass.; from Southampton, England, before 1763; m. Lydia Chapman, Aug. 20, 1763; Child: Elizabeth.—*Salem Vital Records, Vol.* 4, *p.* 283, *Vol.* 2, *p.* 264.

ST. LAWRENCE, Joseph, of Boston, Mass.; from Ireland, before 1737; a merchant.—*Cullen's Irish in Boston, p.* 32.

SALSBURY, Humphrey, of Braintree, Mass.; from Glandiray, Derbyshire, 1699, in the "Virginia"; b. in Evistocke, 1685, son of John and Katharine (Nicholas) Salisbury; nineteen years old, with seven years to serve; m. Mary Milborn, in Boston, July 11, 1707; Child: William; d. July, 1708, in Braintree, Mass.—*N. E. Hist. Gen. Reg., Vol.* 64, *p.* 260, *Boston Rec. Com., Vol.* 28, *p.* 16, *Vol.* 24, *p.* 58, *The House of Salisbury, pp.* 44, 45.

SALTER, Edward, Boston, Mass.; from North Carolina in sloop "Dolphin," 1737; to be educated; bonded by Capt. James Gold; accepted. — *Boston Rec. Com., Vol.* 15, *p.* 44.

SALTMARSH, Thomas, of Watertown, Mass.; from England after 1700; m. 1. Mary Hazen, daughter of Richard Hazen, of Boxford, Mass.; m. 2. Mrs. Anna (Jones) Stone, Hopkinton, Mass., June 11, 1769; Children: Mary, Elizabeth, William, Thomas, John, Abigail, Deborah, Catherine, Isaac.—*Hadley's Goffstown, p. 445, Wyman's Charlestown, Watertown Vital Records, Vol. 2, pp. 100, 106, Vol. 3, pp. 111, 115, 118, 119, N. E. Hist. Gen. Reg., Vol. 32, p. 174, Hopkinton Vital Records, pp. 356, 365.*

SAMUEL, Philip, Boston, Mass.; "a Jew from New York"; warned April 24, 1726.—*Boston Rec. Com., Vol. 13, p. 154.*

SANDEMAN, Robert, of Danbury, Conn.; from Scotland, Oct. 18, 1764, with Captain Montgomery; b. Perth, Scotland, 1718; founder of "Sandemanians"; d. April 2, 1771, aet 51.—*Thomas's History of Printing, Vol. 2, p. 230, Bailey's Danbury, p. 301, Colonial Society, Vol. 6, p. 110 et seq., Gravestone at Danbury, Conn., N. E. Hist. Gen. Reg., Vol. 84, p. 167.*

SANDERS, Thomas, of Boston, Mass.; from Bristol, England, in 1716; blacksmith.—*Boston Rec. Com., Vol. 29, p. 232.*

SAUNDERS, —— (1), of the Isles of Shoals; from Torbay, England; Children: John, Samuel, George, Robert.—*Parsons' Rye, N. H., p. 523.*

SAUNDERS, George, of the Isles of Shoals; from Torbay, England (son of above (1)); m. Sarah Kive, 1756/7, b. 1736; Children: Elizabeth, Sarah, William, Martha, Mercy Haines, George, Samuel, Sarah, Mary, Hannah; d. 1786.—*Parsons' Rye, N. H., p. 523-4.*

SAUNDERS, John, of Isles of Shoals; from Torbay, England (son of above (1)); m. 1. Mary Berry, April 7, 1740; Children: Esther, Robert, Mary, John, George Berry; m. 2. Tryphena Philbrick, 1760; Children: Abigail, William, Sarah, Olly; d. Oct., 1770, in a gale.—*Parsons' Rye, N. H., p. 523.*

SAUNDERS, Robert, of Isles of Shoals; from Torbay, England (son of above (1)); m. Elizabeth Berry; Child: Robert; d. March 7, 1807, aet 92.—*Parsons' Rye, N. H., p. 524.*

SAUNDERS, Samuel, of Isles of Shoals; from Torbay, England (son of (1)); m. Hannah Foss, 1746; Children: Mary, Samuel, Hannah, Elizabeth, Robert, George, Levi Dearborn; d. 1770, in a gale.—*Parsons' Rye, N. H., p. 523.*

SAVAGE, Ebenezer, of Rutland, Mass.; m. Mary Hambleton, Nov. 24, 1726, in Westboro, Mass.—*Vital Records of Rutland, p. 190.*

SAVAGE, Edward, Rutland, Mass.; from Ireland, before 1727; b. Loudoun, Scotland; m. Mary ——, d. Feb. 10, 1767, aet 59; Children: Mary, Edward, Sarah, Seth, Abraham, Isaac, Eunice; Miss Potter calls him brother of Capt. John Savage of Pelham and of Abraham Savage of Chatham, N. Y.—*Merrill's Ackworth, p. 262, Reed's Rutland, pp. 82, 154, Rutland Inscriptions, p. 30, Rutland Vital Records, pp. 86, 246.*

SAVAGE, James, of Boston; "James Savage, his wife and five children, Irish people from small point," in 1723; warned from Boston, Apr. 10, 1723.—*Boston Rec. Com., Vol. 13, p. 112.*

SAVAGE, Capt., John, of Pelham, Mass.; from Ireland, in 1716; m. Eleanor Hamilton, Jan. 15, 1733; called brother of Edward and Abraham Savage.—*Contributed by Miss J. M. Potter.*

SAVAGE, John, Boston, Mass.; from London, April 17, 1727; warned out, April 17, 1727.—*Suffolk Court Files, 20510, Boston Rec. Com., Vol. 13, p. 167.*

SAVAGE, Robert, Boston, Mass.; from Great Britain, before 1712; int. m. Sarah Lewis, April 16, 1712.—*Boston Rec. Com., Vol. 28, p. 92.*

SAWYER, Josiah, of Sharon, N. H.; from Ireland; b. 1721; Child: Josiah; d. 1807, in Sharon.—*Smith's Peterborough, Pt. 2, p. 242.*

SCARLET, Humphrey, Boston, Mass.; from England, April 29th, 1715, with Captain Atwood; butcher; warned out, June 21, 1715; m. 1. Mehitable Peirse, Dec. 2, 1718; Child: Mary; m. 2. Mary Wentworth, Sept. 11, 1733; Child: Humphrey. — *Boston Rec. Com., Vol. 11, p. 229, Vol. 28, pp. 78, 187, Vol. 24, pp. 139, 219.*

SCHEAFFER, John Martin, of "Broad Bay," Me.; from Germany, before 1762.—*Eaton's Warren, p.* 116.
SCHENK, James, Broad Bay, Me.; from Germany, before 1760; a tanner.—*Miller's Waldoboro, p.* 51.
SCHNEIDER, Melchoir, of Broad Bay, Maine; from Germany; removed to North Carolina, 1770.—*Miller's Waldoboro, p.* 67.
SCHOFF, Jacob, Ashburnham, Mass.; from Germany, in the "St. Andrew," 1752, from Hornbery; a baker; m. Mrs. Elizabeth (Darrow) Grapes; Children: Elizabeth, Lena, Jacob, Katherine, John, Daniel, Henry, Isaac; lived in Franconia, Northumberland, Maidstone, Vt., and Brunswick, Me. — *Kingsbury's Surry, p.* 438, *Ashburnham Vital Records, p.* 70.
SCHOMBERG, Roman, Boston, Mass.; from London on the ship "London," 1774; seaman; "for better employment."—*N. E. Hist. Gen. Reg., Vol.* 63, *p.* 21.
SCHROUTENBACH, Conrad, of "Germantown," Braintree, Mass.; from Germany, cir. 1752.—*State Archives, Vol.* 15A, *pp.* 240-2, *Pattee's Braintree, p.* 480.
SCHWERE, Margaret, Lancaster, Mass.; "a German Protestant," 1762.—*Lancaster Vital Records, p.* 320.
SCHUMAKER, Adam, Waldoboro, Maine; from Germany, before 1764; left with wife and 5 children for North Carolina, 1769.—*Miller's Waldoboro, pp.* 67, 64.
SCOTT, Alexander, of Lancaster, Mass.; with his wife, from Ireland, before 1734. — *Lancaster Vital Records, p.* 283.
SCOTT, Janet, of Ellington or Windsor, Conn.; from Ireland, before 1724; sister of Robert Scott; m. James Thompson.—*Stiles' Ancient Windsor, Vol.* 2, *p.* 675.
SCOTT, John, Boston, Mass.; from Ireland, in the ship "Elizabeth," 1719; warned, Nov. 3, 1719.—*Boston Record Com., Vol.* 13, *p.* 63.
SCOTT, John, of Lunenburg, Mass.; from Ireland, before 1729; b. 1702; m. Lydia Thwing, in Boston, 1729, d. 1792; Children: John, Abraham, Edward, Mary, Benjamin, David, Jonathan, Elizabeth; d. cir. 1756 (will).—*Fitchburg Hist. Soc.,* 1900-6, *p.* 98, *Lunenburg Records, p.* 327.

Scott, Joseph, Newbury, Mass.; from White Haven, Great Britain, before 1736; m. Jane Fitzgerald, "an Irish woman," Dec. 28, 1736.—*Newbury Vital Records, Vol.* 2, *p.* 173.

Scott, Robert, of Ellington, Conn.; from Ireland, with Harper, Thompson, McKnight, etc.; "now of Windsor," July 8, 1724; m. Rachel ———; Children: Timothy, Rachel, and another child; d. abt. 1750. — *Stiles' Ancient Windsor, Vol.* 2, *p.* 675.

Scott, Robert, from London, to New England, on the "Venus," 1774, to settle; baker, aged 25. — *N. E. Hist. Gen. Reg., Vol.* 63, *p.* 234.

Scott, Thomas, Boston, Mass.; from the "Barbadoes," with Capt. Bent, Aug. 19, 1718; warned out, Oct. 22, 1718.—*Suffolk Court Files* 12620.

Scott, Thomas, of Halifax, Vt.; perhaps from England; b. 1744; m. Sarah Hale, 1769; Children: Asahel, and others; d. 1802.—*Amer. Ances., Vol.* 3, *p.* 173.

Scott, William, of Hopkinton, Mass.; from Coleraine, Ireland, in 1736; m. Margaret Gregg, 1740, b. 1717, d. 1797; Children: Ellen, Mary, Jean, David, Thomas, Hannah, William, Margaret; d. 1795.—*Smith's Peterborough, Pt.* 2, *p.* 244.

Scott, William, Boston and Lunenburg, Mass.; from Ireland, cir. 1760; b. cir. 1720; Children: Henry; d. 1795 in Lunenburg. — *Fitchburg Hist. Soc., pp.* 97-99, *p.* 263.

Seabury, Rev. Samuel, from England to New England, 1730 (Groton, Conn?); D.D. 1777. — *Emigrant Ministers to America, p.* 54.

Searle, John, Portsmouth, N. H.; from Luppitt, Devonshire, before 1726; m. Anna Benson, Aug. 31, 1726. —*N. E. Hist. Gen. Reg., Vol.* 24, *p.* 358.

Searls, Samuel, of Newbury, Mass.; from Woodbery, County Devon, England, before 1747; int. m. Deborah Hodgkins, Jan. 9, 1747.—*Newbury Vital Records, Vol.* 2, *p.* 235.

Seaton, Andrew, of Andover, Mass., and Amherst, N. H.; from Tellehoague, Ireland, in 1740; b. in Scotland, brother of James and John; m. 1. Jane Blake, in Scotland; m. ? 2. Margaret Wood of Topsfield, Sept.

14, 1741; Children: Andrew, Richard, Sarah, Ismenia, Elizabeth, Anna. — *Seaton Family, pp.* 237-240, *Boxford Vital Records, p.* 197.

SEATON, Andrew, of Amherst, N. H.; from Ireland, in 1740; b. in Scotland or Ireland, son of Andrew and Jane Seaton; m. Betsy Gordon.—*Seaton Family, p.* 245.

SEATON, James, of Andover, Mass.; from Ireland, in 1729; b. 1718, son of John and Jane Seaton; m. Elizabeth Robinson, May 5, 1748; daughter of Joseph and Elizabeth Robinson; Child: Elizabeth.— *Seaton Family, p.* 240, *Andover Vital Records, Vol.* 1, *p.* 328, *Vol.* 2, *p.* 297, *Boxford Vital Records, p.* 84.

SEATON, James, from Ireland, in 1727; brother of John and Andrew.—*Seaton Family, p.* 236.

SEATON, John, of Boxford, Mass.; from Ireland, in 1729; b. in Scotland; m. Jane Edwards, in Scotland; Children: Mary, James, Martha, John, Samuel, Elizabeth, Jane.—*The Seaton Family, pp.* 236, 237, *Boxford Vital Records, pp.* 85, 262, *Andover Vital Records, Vol.* 2, *p.* 297.

SEATON, John, of Boxford, Mass., and Washington, N. H.; from Ireland, in 1729; b. cir. 1724, in Scotland, son of John and Jane Seaton; m. Ismenia Seaton, daughter of Andrew Seaton (q.v.); Children: Elizabeth, Jane, Andrew, Mary, Margaret, Martha, John, Ann, and perhaps Ambrose; d. 1793.—*Seaton Family, pp.* 242, 243, *Andover Vital Records, Vol.* 2, *p.* 297, *Boxford Vital Records, p.* 84.

SEATON, Mary, of Andover, Mass.; from Ireland, in 1729; daughter, of John and Jane Seaton; m. John Mauer.—*Seaton Family, p.* 240, *Andover Vital Records, Vol.* 2, *p.* 297.

SEATON, Samuel, of Andover, Mass., and Amherst, N. H.; from Ireland, in 1729; b. in Scotland, son of John and Jane Seaton; m. Ruth Smith, Dec. 2, 1756; Child: Sarah; d. cir. 1796, in Wenham, Mass.— *Seaton Family, pp.* 243, 244, *Andover Vital Records, Vol.* 2, *p.* 297.

SEAVIL, Rev. James, from England, to New England, 1759.—*Emigrant Ministers to America, p.* 54.

SEAWARD, William, Portsmouth, N. H.; from Devonshire, before 1715; m. Mary Shackford, July 28, 1715.—*N. E. Hist. Gen. Reg., Vol.* 23, *p.* 272.

SEDGWICK, Samuel, of Hartford, Conn.; from England, about 1740; Children: Eben, Gordon, Elijah, Samuel.—*Temple's Palmer, p.* 539. .

SEIDERS, Conrad, of Broad Bay, Maine; from Maine; from Germany, before 1760. — *Miller's Waldoboro, p.* 51.

SEITENBORGER, Matthew, of Broad Bay, Maine; from Germany, before 1764; m. Sussannah. — *Miller's Waldoboro, p.* 64.

SEITZ, John Michael, of Broad Bay, Maine; from Germany, 1759; b. Wurtemburg, 1737; with 3 children left for North Carolina, 1769; m. Elizabeth ——; Children: three; d. Friedland, N. C., 1817.—*Miller's Waldoboro, pp.* 64, 67.

SEITZ, Laurentius, of Broad Bay, Waldoboro, Maine; from Germany, before 1752.—*Mass. Archives, Vol.* 15A, *pp.* 240-2.

SELLHAM, Henry, of Ashburnham, Mass.; from Germany, before 1758; m. Katharine ——; afterwards of Ashby, (as Sellenham), and northern N. H.; Children: Jacob, Anna, Elizabeth, Catherine. — *Stearns, Ashburnham, p.* 893, *Ashburnham Vital Records, p.* 70.

SELLHAM, Jacob, of Ashburnham, Mass.; from Germany, before 1758; Child: Henry; d. 1769, aet cir. 60.— *Stearns' Ashburnham, p.* 893.

SEMPSON, Thomas, Portsmouth, N. H.; from "Boroughsenes," Scotland, before 1718; m. Susan Sever, Sept. 17, 1718.—*N. E. Hist. Gen. Reg., Vol.* 23, *p.* 395.

SENDALL, Darby, of Boston, Mass.; "from Jamaica by way of Martin's Vineyard," 1733; warned out, Jan. 29, 1733.—*Boston Rec. Com., Vol.* 13, *p.* 226.

SEVERWRIT, John, of Boston, Mass.; from Ireland, 1719.
—*Cullen's Irish in Boston, p.* 51.

SEWARD, John, Boston, Mass.; from Great Britain, in the "Rook" Galley, with his family, 1704; warned out, April 24, 1704.—*Boston Rec. Com., Vol.* 11, *p.* 37.

SEWARD, John, Boston, Mass.; from Great Britain, before 1716; int. m. Anna Reed, Jan. 16, 1716 (see above).—*Boston Rec. Com., Vol.* 28, *p.* 95.

SHAEFFER, Rev. John Martin, of Waldoboro, Maine; from Germany, cir. 1753; first German Protestant minister in Waldoboro; he left a wife and children in Germany, seduced another man's wife and brought her with him; deposed from the church; d. April 20, 1794.—*Miller's Waldoboro, pp.* 229-231.

SHARP, John, Boston, Mass.; from Great Britain, before 1712; int. m. Elizabeth Carver, Feb. 14, 1713.—*Boston Rec. Com., Vol.* 28, *p.* 92.

SHAW, David, of Palmer, Mass.; from Ireland, in 1720; b. 1676; d. July 4, 1760, in his 84th year.—*Palmer Vital Records, p.* 231.

SHAW, David, of Brimfield and Palmer, Mass.; from Ireland, 1720; b. Queenstown, Ireland, 1691; m. in Ireland, Mary Blackwood, she d. 1782, aet 85, g. s. her mother, Mary Blackwood, came with them and d. 1775, aet 99; Children: David, James, Catharine, Sarah, William; d. July 4, 1775, aet 84.—*Temple's Palmer, p.* 551, *Palmer Vital Records, pp.* 203, 231, 232.

SHAW, Joshua, of Brimfield, Mass.; from Ireland, 1720; b. Queenstown, Ireland, 1687; Child: Katharine, m. George, son of Seth Shaw.—*Temple's Palmer, p.* 547.

SHAW, Samuel, of Palmer, Mass.; from Ireland, 1720; b. 1672; probably a brother of David Shaw, Sen.; Children: James, Samuel; d. June 1, 1767, aet 94.
—*Temple's Palmer, p.* 551, *Palmer Vital Records, p.* 232.

SHAW, Samuel, of Palmer, Mass.; from Queenstown, Ireland, 1720; b. 1704, son of Samuel Shaw, Sen.—*Temple's Palmer, p.* 547.

SHAW, Seth, Brimfield, Mass.; from Ireland, 1720; b. 1707, in Queenstown; m. Jane Erwin, June 17, 1731; d. 1798; Children: George, Mary, Sarah, David, Seth, Elizabeth, Margaret, Daniel, John, Erwin, Jane; d. March 29, 1798, aet 91.—*Temple's Palmer, pp.* 547, 548, *MS. in N. E. Hist. Gen. Soc., Palmer Inscriptions.*

SHAW, William, from England, to New England, 1714; "clerk."—*Emigrant Ministers to America, p.* 54.

SHAW, William, Palmer, Mass.; from Ireland, 1720; d. soon.—*Temple's Palmer, p.* 547.

SHEARER, James, of Palmer, Mass.; from Antrim, 1720, to Union, Conn., from there to Palmer with the Nevins family, 1726; b. 1678 in County Antrim; m. —— ——, b. in County Derry, 1675, d. 1750, aet 75, in Palmer; Children: John, James, William; d. Jan. 21, 1745, aged 67, g. s.—*Temple's Palmer, p.* 543, *Palmer Vital Records, p.* 233.

SHEDELEY, Jonathan, Portsmouth, N. H.; from Lime, Devonshire, before 1715; m. Mary Seward, July 28, 1715.—*N. E. Hist. Gen. Reg., Vol.* 23, *p.* 272.

SHELDON, William, of Salem, Mass.; from Philadelphia, June 24, 1770; m. Margaret Mansfield (widow of Paul), Nov. 12, 1770, d. March 30, 1824.—*Salem Vital Records, Vol.* 4, *pp.* 59, 309, *Vol.* 6, *p.* 218.

SHEPARDSON, Joseph, Boston, Mass.; from London, April 27, 1727; warned out, July 11 (return).—*Suffolk Court Files* 20510, *Boston Rec. Com., Vol.* 13, *p.* 167.

SHIRLEY, Elizabeth, of Boston, Mass.; sailed from London, February 26, 1733, on the "New Industry"; daughter of Governor William Shirley. — *Colonial Society, Vol.* 8, *p.* 244.

SHIRLEY, James, of Chester, N. H.; from Ireland, cir. 1730; Children: John, James, Thomas and others; d. 1754, aet 105.—*Hadley's Goffstown, p.* 463.

SHIRLEY, James, of Brookline, Mass., and Chester, N. H.; from Ireland, cir. 1730; b. 1700, son of James Shirley q.v.; m. Janet Shirley; Children: James, Margaret, Agnes, John, William; d. May 30, 1796; a "seventh son."—*Hadley's Goffstown, p.* 464.

SHIRLEY, John, of Goffstown, N. H.; from Ireland, cir. 1730; son of James Shirley, q.v.; m. 1. ―― ――; m. 2. Mary Miller, widow of Archibald Miller; Children: James, Mary, Ann, Thomas, Jane, Mary, John, Daniel; d. 1768.—*Hadley's Goffstown, p. 463.*

SHIRLEY, William, of Boston and Roxbury, Mass.; from Sussex, England, Oct. 27, 1731; Governor of Massachusetts, 1741-1756; m. Frances Baker, d. August 31, 1746, aet. 54; Children: William, John, Elizabeth, Harriet; d. March 24, 1771.—*Correspondence of Wm. Shirley, Lincoln, Introduction, Vol. 1, p. 186, N. E. Hist. Gen. Reg., Vol. 28, p. 269.*

SHIRLEY, William, from England, 1731; son of Governor William Shirley; killed in the action on the banks of the Monongahela, July 9, 1755.—*Mass. Hist. Soc., second series, Vol. 16, p. 77.*

SHIRLEY, William, Salem, Mass.; formerly of London, 1759; m. Elizabeth Atkinson, widow, int. April 7, 1759.—*Salem Vital Records, Vol. 4, p. 304.*

SIBSON, John, Portsmouth, N. H.; from Durham, in Cumberland, before 1726; m. Ellenor Lavers, Aug. 15, 1726.—*N. E. Hist. Gen. Reg., Vol. 24, p. 358.*

SIDDELL, Luke, and Eliza, Boston, Mass.; from London, with Captain Eves, August, 1717; warned out, Sept. 10, 1717.—*Boston Rec. Com., Vol. 13, p. 29.*

SIDELINGER, Peter, of Broad Bay, Maine; from Germany, before 1760.—*Miller's Waldoboro, p. 51.*

SIDENSBERGER, Jacob, of Broad Bay, Maine; from Germany, before 1760.—*Miller's Waldoboro, p. 51.*

SIMONS, John, Boston, Mass.; from Great Britain, before 1719; int. m. Sarah Prance, servant to Walter Brown, banns forbidden by Sarah Prance.—*Boston Rec. Com., Vol. 28, p. 98.*

SIMONTON, Andrew, Portland, Me.; from Strabane, Ireland, 1718; admitted an inhabitant, 1727; "probably brother" of William Simonton q.v. — *Willis's Portland, p. 326, Bourne's Wells and Kennebunk, p. 313.*

SIMONTON, William, Portland, Me.; from Strabane, Ireland, 1718; admitted an inhabitant, 1727.—*Willis's Portland, p. 326, Bourne's Wells and Kennebunk, p. 313.*

SIMPSON, Alexander, of Windham, N. H.; from Ireland, cir. 1735, with Adam Templeton; m. Janet Templeton, of Ballywilly; Children: William, Agnes, William, Janet, Sarah, John, Alexander, Samuel; d. 1788, aged 67.—*Morrison's Windham, p.* 761, *Suppl. to Morrison's Windham, p.* 63.

SIMPSON, Andrew, of Deerfield, N. H.; from Scotland, cir. 1720; m. 1. Elizabeth Patten, killed by the Indians, 1742; Children: Thomas, Robert, Josiah, Andrew, "Maj"; m. 2. —— (York) Brown; Children: William, Abigail.—*Cogswell's Deerfield, pp.* 455-6.

SIMPSON, Peter, Portsmouth, N. H.; from the parish of St. Clements Dane, London, before 1733; m. Sarah Daley, Sept. 6, 1733.—*N. E. Hist. Gen. Reg., Vol.* 25, *p.* 120.

SIMPSON, William, of Brunswick, Me.; from County Clare, Ireland, 1735; m. Agnes ——; Children: son, daughter, Jane, William, Robert, Lewis, Josiah, and two sons.—*Wheeler's Brunswick, p.* 851.

SIMPSON, William, of Greenland, N. H.; from Ireland; m. Mary Haynes; Children: Joseph, George.—*Morrison's Windham, p.* 768.

SINCLAIR, William, of Leicester and Spencer, Mass.; from Drumbo, County Down, Ireland; b. 1676.—*History of Spencer,* 1841, *pp.* 114, 132.

SINGER, ——, of Edgecomb, Maine; from Ireland; Child: Faithful; Mrs. Singer later m. Mr. Williams.—*Eaton's Thomaston, p.* 394.

SINGLETON, Ann, to New England; from Firwood [Firgrove?],Lancashire, 1699, in the "Virginia"; twenty-three years old, with seven years to serve; bound to Mr. John Moody.—*N. E. Hist. Gen. Reg., Vol.* 64, *p.* 260.

SINNETT, Michael, of Harpswell, Me.; from Ireland; kidnapped; m. Mary ——, of Hingham, Mass.; Children: Stephen, James. — *Wheeler's Brunswick, p.* 852.

SITGREAVES, William, Boston, Mass.; from North Carolina, before 1756; m. Susannah Deshon, Aug. 4, 1756.—*Boston Rec. Com., Vol.* 30, *p.* 20.

SKILTON, Elizabeth, Boston, Mass.; from Great Britain, before 1711; int. m. Stephen Haise, July 14, 1711. —*Boston Rec. Com., Vol. 28, p. 91.*

SKINNER, Christopher, Portsmouth, N. H.; from Miley, Cornwall, before 1737; m. Sarah Grindle, Dec. 20, 1737.—*N. E. Hist. Gen. Reg., Vol. 26, p. 378.*

SKIP, Dennis, of Boston, Mass.; from Ireland, before 1728; m. Margaret Pollard, in Newbury, Nov. 5, 1728.—*Newbury Vital Records, Vol. 2, p. 405.*

SKOLFIELD, Thomas, of Brunswick, Maine; from Ireland; b. 1707; m. Mary Orr; Children: Rebecca, Richard, Clement, Ann, Thomas, Mary, Martha, John, Joseph, William; d. Jan. 6, 1796.—*Wheeler's Brunswick, p. 852.*

SLADER, Samuel, of Hingham, Mass.; from England, cir. 1725; a tailor; m. Mary Wilder, Dec. 7, 1727, daughter of Jabez and Mary (Ford) Wilder; Children: Samuel, Mary, Samuel, Thomas, Sarah, Edward.—*Merrill's Ackworth, p. 266, History of Hingham, Vol. 3, pp. 151, 152.*

SLARROW, Matthew, of Rutland, Mass.; from Ireland, before 1731; m. Mary ——; Children: Joseph, Martha, Agnes, Jane, Matthew, Mary; d. April 13, 1767. —*Reed's Rutland, p. 82, Rutland Vital Records, pp. 87, 191, 247.*

SLEMMONS, William, of Stroudwater, Me.; from Ireland; Child: William, m. Catherine Porterfield in 1734.— *Smith's and Dean's Journal, pp. 91-92.*

SLOAN, William, of Rutland, Mass.; from Ireland, before 1729; he and wife were church members in Rutland; Child: Sarah.—*Rutland Vital Records, p. 87.*

SMALL, Richard, Portsmouth, N. H.; from Jacobstown [Jacobstowe], Devonshire, before 1719; m. Hannah Moulton, of Hampton, N. H., Nov. 12, 1719.—*N. E. Hist. Gen. Reg., Vol. 24, p. 13.*

SMALLCORN, William, Boston, Mass.; from Great Britain, before 1720; int. m. Sarah Saulter, Aug. 24, 1720. —*Boston Rec. Com., Vol. 28, p. 98.*

SMILEY, see also Smylie.

SMILEY, John, of Haverhill, Mass.; from Ireland, before 1741; m. Sarah Cannon, before 1741; Children:

Hugh, Agnes, Mary, William, Sarah, Betty, David; d. 1774, aged 54.—*Smith's Peterborough, Pt.* 2, *p.* 256; *Haverhill Vital Records, Vol.* 1, *pp.* 277, 281, *Vol.* 2, *p.* 294.

SMITH, Benjamin, of Bedford, N. H.; from the North of Ireland, 1738; m. Catherine McCurdy, b. in the Parish of Billy, County Antrim, d. Dec., 1814, aet 96; Children: Robert, James, John, Elizabeth, Jane, Adam; d. October, 1812, aet cir. 92 years.—*Brown's Bedford, pp.* 1074, 1075.

SMITH, David, of New Boston, N. H.; from Ireland.— *Merrill's Ackworth, p.* 268.

SMITH, Edward, Boston, Mass.; from London, May 6, 1727; warned out, July 11 (return), 1727.—*Suffolk Court Files* 20510, *Boston Rec. Com., Vol.* 13, *p.* 168.

SMITH, Francis, of Haverhill, Mass., and Windham, N. H.; from Ireland, cir. 1755; b. 1728; m. Margaret Smiley, at Strabane, Ireland, 1703, according to the Rev. William Homes; Children: William, Solomon, Margaret, Nancy, Francis; d. 1766, in Windham.—*Morrison's Windham, p.* 772, *Cochran's Francestown, p.* 926.

SMITH, Issabella, see John Cochran.

SMITH, James, of Stratford, N. H.; from Worcestershire, to Derby, Conn., 1714-27; m. Elizabeth ———; Child: John.—*Thompson's Stratford, p.* 446.

SMITH, James, of Needham, Mass.; from Ballykelly, Ireland, 1718, with credentials from the minister there; m. Mary ———; Children: Robert, William, Matthew. —*Bolton's Scotch-Irish Pioneers, p.* 196, *Needham Epitaphs, pp.* 12, 13, 15, 16.

SMITH, James, of Rutland, Mass.; from Ireland, cir. 1720; m. Margaret ———, in 1775; Children: Robert, Andrew, John, James, George, Agnes.—*Rutland Vital Records, p.* 247, *Reed's Rutland, p.* 119, *Rutland Inscriptions, pp.* 30, 31.

SMITH, James, of Boston, Mass.; from Glencairn, Nithsdale, Scotland; m. Ann ———, d. April 15, 1741, aged 83; d. April 2, 1732, aged 63.—*Bridgman's Memorials of the Dead, p.* 138, *King's Chapel Burying Ground.*

SMITH, Jeremiah, of Milton, Mass.; from Ireland, 1726; b. 1705; m. Rachel ——, d. May 8, 1791, aet 85, in Milton, Mass.; d. April 16, 1790, aet 86 years, in Milton. — *Cullen's Irish in Boston, p. 186, Milton Vital Records, p. 243.*

SMITH, John, to New England, from Craven, Yorkshire, 1699, in the "Virginia"; seventeen years old, with seven years to serve.—*N. E. Hist. Gen. Reg., Vol. 64, p. 260.*

SMITH, Joseph, of Windham, N. H.; from Ireland, cir. 1755; brother of Francis Smith, q.v.; b. 1736; m. Isabella Wasson; Children: Hannah, Francis, Anna, Sarah, Robert, Isabel, Molly, Joseph, Peggy, James, Wasson; d. 1805.—*Morrison's Windham, p. 773.*

SMITH, Mary, see Joseph Hedman.

SMITH, Robert, of Palmer, Mass.; from Ireland, 1718; b. North of Ireland, 1672; his father came from England in 1658; (Robert and his wife, 2 sons and their wives, and 2 grandchildren emigrated in 1718); m. 1691; Children: James, Patrick, Margaret, ——, m. Mr. Parkhill and another daughter; d. Dec. 21, 1759.—*Temple's Palmer, p. 532.*

SMITH, Robert, of Lunenberg, Mass.; from Moneymore, Ireland, 1736; son of James Smith; m. Elizabeth Smith, daughter James Smith of England, d. in Lunenburg, Mass.; Children: John, Sarah, Mary, William; d. 1761, aged 85.—*Smith's Peterborough, Pt. 2, p. 265.*

SMITH, Samuel, Boston; from Ireland in the ship "Elizabeth," 1719; warned out, Nov. 8, 1719. — *Boston Rec. Com., Vol. 13, p. 63.*

SMITH, Thomas, of Chester, N. H.; probably from Ireland; m. —— Karr.—*Chase's Chester, p. 593.*

SMITH, William, Boston, Mass.; "from Bristol with Capt. Brisca" "three months ago," 1716; miller "now at Waldo°"; warned out, July 13, 1716.—*Boston Rec. Com., Vol. 13, p. 6, Suffolk Court Files 10961.*

SMOUSE, George, of "Germantown," Braintree, Mass.; from Germany, 1753. — *State Archives, Vol. 15A, pp. 240-2, Pattee's Braintree, p. 481.*

SMYLIE, Francis, of Londonderry, N. H.; from Ireland, before 1720; b. 1688; m. Agnes ——, before 1720, d. in her 99th year, in Old Dunstable, Dec. 23, 1786; Children: John, Hugh, William, David, Margaret, and others, perhaps Alexander; d. March 16, 1763. —*Bolton's Shirley Uplands and Intervales, pp.* 356-7, *Contributed by Mrs. Mary L. Holman.*

SNOW, Thomas, Portsmouth, N. H.; from "Eallfaire Coome" [Ilfracomb], Great Britain, before 1716; m. Elizabeth Clark, Oct. 13, 1716.—*N. E. Hist. Gen. Reg., Vol.* 23, *p.* 393.

SOARE, John, Boston, Mass.; from Virginia, before 1716; int. m. Eliner James, April 30, 1716; int. m. Elizabeth Hutchings, Sept. 18, 1727.—*Boston Rec. Com., Vol.* 28, *pp.* 95, 164.

SOBER, Thomas, Boston, Mass.; from Barbadoes, before 1711; int. m. Hannah Savage, Dec. 25, 1711; banns "forbid by Capt. Savage."—*Boston Rec. Com., Vol.* 28, *p.* 91.

SOELLE, George, of Broad Bay, Me.; from Germany, before 1760; ordained at Rippen, in Schleswig, Sept. 3, 1741; he never married; d. May 4, 1773, Salem, North Carolina. — *Miller's Waldoboro, pp.* 61, 62, 64, 65.

SOUTHGATE, Richard, of Leicester, Mass.; from England, in 1718; b. 1670, at Coombs, County Suffolk; m. Elizabeth Stewart, d. Nov. 3, 1751, aet 75; Children: Stewart, Elizabeth, and probably Mary, Richard, Sarah, Hannah, James; d. April 23, 1758, aet 88.—*Leicester Vital Records, pp.* 84, 85, 209, 210, 275, *Washburn's Leicester, p.* 546, *Temple's Palmer, p.* 546.

SOUTHGATE, Steward, of Leicester, Mass.; from England in 1718; son of Richard and Elizabeth Southgate; b. cir. 1703; m. 1. Elizabeth ——, d. Sept. 19, 1748, aet 34; Children: Robert, Sarah, Mary, Stewart; m. 2. Elizabeth ——, d. June 19, 1814, aet 87; Children: Amos, Ruth, Rebecca, Moses; d. Dec. 18, 1764, aet 61.—*Leicester Vital Records, pp.* 84, 85, 275.

SPARE, Samuel, of Boston and Ponkapog, Mass.; from Devonshire, before 1729; "sawyer"; b. cir. 1683;

m. Elizabeth ——, b. cir. 1694; Children: ——, Samuel,——, dau., John.—*MS. in N. E. Hist. Gen. Soc.*

SPEAKMAN, William, Boston, Mass.; from England, cir April, 1716; bread baker; warned out, August 14, 1716.—*Boston Rec. Com., Vol. 13, p. 9.*

SPEAR, see also Spier.

SPEAR, John, of Woburn, Mass.; from Londonderry, Ireland; m. Catrin ——, d. Nov. 30, 1775, aet 96; Child: Robert.—*Eaton's Warren, p. 618.*

SPEAR, Robert, Warren, Maine; from Ireland, cir. 1735; b. Ireland, Sept. 1714; m. Margaret Turk, daughter of J. McLean; Children: John, Catherine; d. Woburn, March 13, 1776, aet 62 yrs., 6 mos.—*Eaton's Warren, pp. 74, 75, 425, 618.*

SPEED, William, of Boston, Mass.; from Scotland; d. August 21, 1808, aged 53. — *Copp's Hill Burying Ground.*

SPENCE, John, of Palmer, Mass.; b. County Antrim, Ireland, 1665; d. July 23, 1753, aet 88.—*Temple's Palmer, p. 578, Palmer Vital Records, p. 236.*

SPENCE, John Russell, Boston, Mass.; from London, before 1768; m. Mary Hooper, daughter of "the late Rev. Mr. Hooper," —— [Mar. ?] 2, 1768.—*Boston Rec. Com., Vol. 30, p. 399.*

SPENCER, William, Boston, Mass.; from Great Britain, before 1714; int. m. Em Marshall, Oct. 28, 1714.—*Boston Rec. Com., Vol. 28, p. 94.*

SPIER, see also Spear.

SPIER, David, of Windsor, Conn., and Palmer, Mass.; from Ireland, before 1727; b. 1676; "formerly of Coldrear (Coleraine), in County Londonderry, Ireland"; Children: David, Anna,(?) William, John, Calvin, Luther, Sarah; d. Nov. 21, 1760, aet 83.—*Stiles's Ancient Windsor, Vol. 2, p. 698, Temple's Palmer, p. 544, Palmer Vital Records, p. 236.*

SPRAGUE, John, Boston, Mass.; from London, on the "Minerva," 1775, to settle; surgeon; aged 23.—*N. E. Hist. Gen. Reg., Vol. 65, p. 116.*

SPROULE, Adam, Boston, Mass.; from London, on the "Minerva," 1774; "to settle"; merchant; aged 45.—*N. E. Hist. Gen. Reg., Vol. 63, p. 134.*

STAHL, John, of Broad Bay, Maine; from Germany, before 1760.—*Miller's Waldoboro, p.* 51.

STAIN, John, of Dresden, Maine; from France.—*Huguenots in Dresden, p.* 18.

STANDEID, James, Boston, Mass.; from Great Britain, before 1716; int. m. Elizabeth Pain, Feb. 1, 1717.—*Boston Rec. Com., Vol.* 28, *p.* 96.

STANHOPE, Rivers, of Boston; from Great Britain, 1715; dancing master, gentleman. — *Court of Sessions of the Peace,* 1715-17, *Vol.* 2, *p.* 111.

STAR, Paul, Boston, Mass.; from France, before 1710; int. m. Margaret Benuit, May 18, 1710. — *Boston Rec. Com., Vol.* 28, *p.* 32.

STARK, Archibald, of Londonderry and Derryfield, N. H.; from Londonderry, Ireland, 1720; b. 1697 in Glasgow; graduate of the University of Glasgow; m. Elizabeth (or Eleanor?) Nichols; Children: Anna, William, Isabel, John, Archibald, Mary, Jean, Samuel; d. June 25, 1758, at Manchester.—*Caleb Stark's John Stark, pp.* 9, 10, *Parker's Londonderry, p.* 239, *Hadley's Goffstown, p.* 479.

STARKEY, Robert, of Boston, Mass.; from London, cir. 1728; m. Walter Ross, 1718; Children: Elizabeth, Rebecca.—*Thomas's History of Printing, Vol.* 2, *p.* 218, *Boston Rec. Com., Vol.* 28, *p.* 78, *Vol.* 24, *p.* 139, 157.

STARMAN, Rev. John William, Waldoboro, Maine; from Germany, 1786; b. 1775, in Germany; m. Mary Whoboas, b. Waldoboro, 1803, d. 1865 (portrait); ordained in New York; came to Waldoboro, 1812, as pastor; d. Sept. 25, 1854, aged 81 years, in Waldoboro, Maine.—*From a portrait in the church at Waldoboro.*

STARRETT, Hugh, of Warren, Me.; son of William Starrett, q.v.; lost at sea.—*Eaton's Warren, p.* 624.

STARRETT, William, of Pemaquid and Warren, Maine; from Ireland, 1735; b. in Scotland, cir. 1700; m. Mary Gamble, d. Warren, April 17, 1786, aet 83; Children: Margaret, Hugh, David, Thomas, William; d. March 8, 1769, aet 71 yrs., Dedham, Mass. —*Eaton's Warren, p.* 428, *New ed., p.* 624, *Coch-*

ran's Antrim, p. 686, Dedham Church Records, p. 166.

STEELE, Thomas, of Londonderry, N. H.; from Ireland, in 1718; b. 1694, in Londonderry; m. Martha Morison, 1715, daughter of Samuel, d. 1738; Children: Thomas, James, John, David, and two others; d. in Londonderry.—*Parker's Londonderry, p. 44, Early Records of Londonderry, p. 17, Cochran's Antrim, p. 688, Smith's Peterborough, p. 290, Hadley's Goffstown, p. 491.*

STERRETT, James, of Londonderry, N. H.; from County Antrim, Ireland, 1718.—*Parker's Londonderry, p. 44.*

STEVENS, Benjamin, of Bedford, N. H.; from England; b. 1721, in England; m. A—— Johnson; Children: Timothy, Jonathan, Eunice, Benjamin, Abigail, David, Phebe, Mary.—*Brown's Bedford, p. 1083.*

STEVENS, John, of Boston; from Surrinam, in 1716; merchant.—*Boston Rec. Com., Vol. 29, p. 232.*

STEVENS, Samuel, of Boxford, Mass.; from Exeter, England; m. Rebecca Stiles, of Middleton, int. Feb. 22, 1761; Children: Samuel, Mary, Hannah, Rebecca, Sarah; d. 1806, in Chester, Vt.—*Cochran's Francestown, p. 441, Boxford Vital Records, pp. 92, 203.*

STEVENS, William, Boston, Mass.; from Pennsylvania, "6 weeks past," 1716; warned July 30, 1716; "with wife." — *Suffolk Court Files 10961, Boston Rec. Com. Vol. 13, p. 6-7.*

STEVENS, William, from Dublin, Ireland; b. cir. 1710; volunteer against the West Indies, 1740.—*Colonial Wars, 1899.*

STEVENSON, see also Stinson.

STEVENSON, John, Boston, Mass.; from Great Britain, before 1716; int. m. Elizabeth Squire, of Portsmouth, Oct. 11, 1716.—*Boston Rec. Com., Vol. 28, p. 95.*

STEVENSON, John, Boston, Mass.; from Great Britain, before 1720; int. m. Deborah Martyn, Sept. 21, 1720. —*Boston Rec. Com., Vol. 28, p. 98.*

STEVENSON, John, of Boston, Mass.; "a stranger," 1726. *Court of Sessions of the Peace, 1725-32, p. 50.*

STEVENSON, Thomas, of Boston, Mass.; from Scotland, cir. 1763.—*Ancient and Honorable Artillery Co., p. 114.*

STEWARD, Charles, of Boston, Mass.; from Jamaica, before 1707; int. m. Sarah Eliot, Oct. 22, 1707.—*Boston Rec. Com., Vol. 28, p. 31.*

STEWARD, George, of Boston, Mass.; from Ireland, 1727; admitted an inhabitant, June 10, 1727. — *Cullen's Irish in Boston, p. 54, Boston Rec. Com., Vol. 13, p. 164.*

STEWART, Charles, of Londonderry, N. H.; from Ireland, before 1727; m. Mary Eyres, Nov. 15, 1727, in Londonderry, N. H., by the Rev. James McGregor; Children: Elizabeth, Mary, Margaret, William.—*Londonderry Vital Records, pp. 114, 257.*

STEWART, George, of Boston, Mass.; from Scotland, 1711; m. Mary ——, d. 28 May, 1714; Children: Eliza, Charles; m. 2. Ruth Cutler, daughter of Dr. John Cutler; Children: John, Mary, James; a physician or surgeon; d. in expedition under Admiral Vernon. —*Colonial Wars, 1899, p. 85.*

STEWART, Robert, of Andover, Mass.; from Ireland, 1718; b. Glasgow, Scotland; m. Lydia Blair, Feb. 22, 1733; Children: John, Samuel, William, Amherst farmer. — *Andover Vital Records, Vol. 2, p. 317.*

STEWART, William, of Boston, Mass.; from Ireland, in 1736, with Captain Robert Boyd in the brigantine "Booth"; m. Mary ——; Children: 2 children; cooper; admitted surety of Joshua Winslow.—*Cullen's Irish in Boston, p. 33, Boston Rec. Com., Vol. 15, pp. 4 and 9.*

STICKNEY, Sarah, Newbury, Mass.; from Mangerville, Sudbury County, Nova Scotia, before 1776; m. Samuel Bridges, Dec. 18, 1776, at Rowley.—*Newbury Vital Records, Vol. 2, p. 467.*

STIGGIN, William, Portsmouth, N. H.; from Devonshire, before 1727; m. Mehitable Berry, of Newcastle, Me., in Portsmouth, Nov. 7, 1727.—*N. E. Hist. Gen. Reg., Vol. 24, p. 359.*

STILFINN, Michel, of Dresden, Maine; from France.—
Huguenots in Dresden, p. 18.
STINSON, John, of Rutland, Mass.; from Ireland, 1718;
m. Margaret Crossett or Savage; Children: John,
Margaret, James, John; d. 1743.—*Parmenter's Pelham, p.* 448.
STINSON, Captain William, of Dunbarton, N. H.; from
Ireland, cir. 1751; b. March 15, 1725, in Ireland;
m. Agnes Caldwell, 1754; Child: William; d. Aug.
21, 1803, aet 78. — *Parker's Londonderry, p.* 154,
Hadley's Goffstown, p. 502.
STIRLING, John, of Worcester, Mass.; from Ireland, before 1733; a John Stirling of the Presbytery of Londonderry, 1720.—*Perry's Scotch Irish, p.* 14.
STIRLING, Robert, Boston, Mass.; "an Irishman from
Rutland," April 23, 1727; warned out, July 11 (return), 1757. — *Suffolk Court Files* 20510, *Boston Rec. Com., Vol.* 13, *p.* 167, *Perry's Scotch-Irish, p.* 14.
STROBRIDGE, John, Boston, Mass.; from Ireland, in the
ship "Elizabeth," 1719; warned out, Nov. 3, 1719;
m. Elizabeth Andrews, in Dorchester, March 28,
1721.—*Boston Rec. Com., Vol.* 13, *p.* 63, *Vol.* 28,
p. 321.
STOCKDALE, John, Boston, Mass.; from Great Britain,
before 1711; int. m. Eliza Grimstone, Feb. 27, 1712.
—*Boston Rec. Com., Vol.* 28, *p.* 91.
STOLE, John, of Braintree, Mass.; from Germany, 1757;
"Germantown," 1761. — *State Archives, Vol.* 15A,
pp. 240-2.
STONEMAN, John, Portsmouth, N. H.; from Topsom,
Devonshire, before 1731; m. Mary Banfield, Sept.
20, 1731.—*N. E. Hist. Gen. Reg., Vol.* 25, *p.* 118.
STONHOUSE, Robert, Boston, Mass.; from Great Britain,
before 1716; int. m. Mary Pursley, Oct. 12, 1716.
—*Boston Rec. Com., Vol.* 28, *p.* 96.
STORER, Andrew, of Waldoboro, Me.; from Germany; b.
1742; m. Elizabeth, d. Jan. 17, 1815, aet 66; Child:
John; d. Nov. 9, 1799, in Warren, Me.—*Eaton's Warren, p.* 430, *New Ed., p.* 629.

STORER, Christoral, of Broad Bay, Maine; from Germany, 1760.—*Miller's Waldoboro, p.* 51.

STOW, William, of Boston, Mass.; from Great Britain, before 1709; mariner; int. m. Sarah Peck, Nov. 14, 1709.—*Boston Rec. Com., Vol.* 28, *p.* 32.

STRAWBRIDGE, William, of Middleboro, Mass.; from Donaghmore, Ireland, before 1722; m. Margaret ——, d. Dec. 8, 1776, aet 83; d. Nov. 14, 1777, aet 87; a blacksmith. — *Weston's Middleboro, p.* 434, *Bolton's Scotch-Irish Pioneers, p.* 156.

STRINGER, Thomas, to New England; from Buckton, Yorkshire, 1699, in the "Virginia"; twenty-two years old, with seven years to serve.—*N. E. Hist. Gen. Reg., Vol.* 64, *p.* 260.

STRONGMAN, Henry, of Deerfield, Mass.; from Dublin, Ireland, cir. 1736; b. cir. 1716; m. 1. —— ——, in Dublin, N. H.; m. 2. Jeanette Alexander; Children: John, Margaret, William, Richard; a weaver. — *Sheldon's Deerfield, p.* 330.

STUART, Alexander, of Freetown, Mass.; from Ireland, about 1734; b. cir. 1701, in Belfast, Ireland; blacksmith, having lived in the Province 30 years in 1764.

STUART, Charles, of Brunswick, Me.; from Ireland, before 1722; warned from Boston, Aug. 12, 1722; he came to Boston from Brunswick with Hannah, Hannah, Samuel, and Henry, presumably his wife and children.—*Boston Rec. Com., Vol.* 13, *p.* 106.

STUART, John, of Windham, N. H.; from Ireland, 1718; b. 1682, in Scotland; m. Elizabeth ——; Children: Charles, Robert, James, John, Samuel, Mary, Joseph, Margaret; d. 1741.—*Morrison's Windham, p.* 778.

STUART, John, of Londonderry, N. H.; from Ireland, before 1737; m. Jean ——; Children: Thomas, John. —*Cogswell's Henniker, N. H., p.* 744, *Londonderry Vital Records, p.* 114.

STUART, Margaret, Lancaster, Mass.; admitted to full communion, April 22, 1751; recommended from the Presbytery of Bovidy, in Ireland.—*Lancaster Vital Records, p.* 3320.

STUART, Robert, of Amherst, N. H.; from Glasgow, Scotland, before 1719; Children: John, Samuel. — *Secomb's Amherst, p.* 783, *Amherst Records.*

STUART, William, of Lunenburg, Mass.; from Ireland, about 1700; moved to Peterborough, 1750; m. Margaret ———; Children: John, William, Thomas, Charles, Elizabeth; d. Peterborough, N. H., 1753.— *Lunenburg Records, pp.* 322, 323.

STUBING, George Martin, of Braintree, Mass.; from Germany, cir. 1752; "Germantown"; m. Earnestian Gezer, 1753.—*State Archives, Vol.* 15A, *pp.* 240-242, *Pattee's Braintree, pp.* 478, 480, 559.

SULLIVAN, John, of Berwick, Maine; from Limerick, Ireland, cir. 1723; b. Limerick, Ireland, 1692; schoolmaster; m. Margery Browne, of Cork, in 1735, b. 1714, d. 1801; Children: Benjamin, Daniel, John (the Major General in the Revolution), James (Governor of Massachusetts), Mary, Ebenezer.—*N. E. Hist. Gen. Reg., Vol.* 1, *p.* 376, *Amory's John Sullivan of Berwick, p.* 149.

SUMMERS, Henry, Boston, Mass.; from Great Britain, before 1714; int. m. Hannah Curtice, Aug. 7, 1714.— *Boston Rec. Com., Vol.* 28, *p.* 93.

SURAH, John, of Braintree, Mass.; from Great Britain, March, 1753.—*House Journal, Pattee's Braintree, p.* 486.

SUTTON, John, of Boston, Mass.; from the Bahamas, in 1716.—*Boston Rec. Com., Vol.* 29, *p.* 232.

SWIFT, Thomas, of Boston, Mass.; from Ireland, 1716; shoemaker.—*Boston Rec. Com., Vol.* 29, *p.* 232.

SWINDLE, Jane, to New England; from Macclesfield, Cheshire, 1699, in the "Virginia," Edmund Ball, master; twenty-three years old, with seven years to serve.—*N. E. Hist. Gen. Reg., Vol.* 64, *p.* 259.

SYDER, Frederick, of Braintree, Mass.; from Germany, before 1753; m. Christian Solomy Hackvathin, March 20, 1753.—*Pattee's Braintree, p.* 478, *Bates' Braintree Records, p.* 739.

SYMES, John, Portsmouth, N. H.; from Exborn, Devonshire, before 1718; m. Hannah Jackson, Oct. 22, 1718.—*N. E. Hist. Gen. Reg., Vol.* 23, *p.* 395.

TACKELS, Alexander, of Palmer, Mass.; from Ireland, petitioner in 1732; Child: William.—*Temple's Palmer, pp.* 132, 562.

TAGGART, Archibald, of Londonderry and Hillsborough, N. H.; from Londonderry, Ireland; Children: Robert, Archibald, James, Joseph, John, William. — *Brown's Hillsborough, N. H., p.* 556.

TAGGART, Archibald, of Hillsborough, N. H.; from Ireland, in 1738; son of Archibald Taggaret (q.v.); m. Hannah Bradford; Children: Robert, Polly; d. cir. 1810.—*Browne's Hillsborough, p.* 557.

TAGGART, Hugh, of Londonderry, N. H.; from Ireland, before 1723; m. Mary Maccalester, June 17, 1723, in Londonderry, by the Rev. James McGregor.— *Londonderry Records, p.* 258.

TAGGART, John, of Londonderry, N. H.; from Ireland, before 1723; m. Mary ——; Children: Merrian, Agnus, Margaret, Jenneat.—*Londonderry Vital Records, p.* 115.

TAGGART, Robert, of Londonderry, Hillsborough, and Sharon, N. H.; from Ireland, after 1735; son of Archibald Taggart (q.v.); b. 1735, in Ireland.— *Browne's Hillsborough, p.* 557.

TALBUT, Richard, Boston; from London, 1716; blockmaker; disallowed.—*Boston Rec. Com., Vol.* 11, *p.* 2.

TALLANT, Hugh, of Haverhill, Mass., Hampstead, Plainton and Pelham, N. H.; from County Carlow, Ireland, before 1731; m. 1. Abiah Little, 1749, d. 1752; Children: John, Joseph; m. 2. Mary Dodge, of Hampstead, June 28, 1753, d. Feb. 22, 1775; Children: Hugh, Thomas, Abiah, William, David Dodge, Andrew Hugh, George, Andrew, Sarah. — *Lyford's Canterbury, pp.* 323-4.

TANDY, Abel, of Salisbury, N. H.; from Scotland; m. Rachel Smith, Nov. 5, 1751, died choked with sand, 1819; Children: Abel, Samuel, Rachel, Priscilla; d. May 19, 1797.—*Dearborn's Salisbury, p.* 804.

TATE, George, of Falmouth, Me.; mast agent, in Maine, before 1756; b. England, Nov., 1700; Children: Samuel, William, George (the Russian Admiral), Robert; d. 1794.—*Willis's Portland, p.* 840, *Smith and Dean's Journal, p.* 218.

TAYLOR, Abraham, of Boston, Mass.; from "Sandwich nigh London," before 1708; int. m. Cartwright Berry, Feb. 16, 1708.—*Boston Rec. Com., Vol. 28, p. 31.*

TAYLOR, George, Portsmouth, N. H.; from St. Mary's Parish, Limerick, Ireland, before 1736; m. Sarah Phicket, June 23, 1736.—*N. E. Hist. Gen. Reg., Vol. 26, p. 376.*

TAYLOR, James, of Pelham, Mass.; before 1738; m. Margaret ———; settled first at Worcester; d. March 28, 1755. — *Parmenter's Pelham, p. 17, Pelham Vital Records, p. 175.*

TAYLOR, Mary, to New England; from Ratchdale [Rochdale], Lancashire, 1699, in the "Virginia"; twenty-two years old, with seven years to serve; perhaps m. Peter Miers, June 29, 1708.—*N. E. Hist. Gen. Reg., Vol. 64, p. 260, Boston Rec. Com., Vol. 28, p. 20.*

TAYLOR, Matthew, of Derry, N. H.; from Londonderry, Ireland, in 1722; m. Janet ———; Children: John, Matthew, William, David, Adam, Samuel, Sarah, Janet.—*Parker's Londonderry, p. 298.*

TAYLOR, William, Boston, Mass.; from Bristol, England, in 1716; seal maker.—*Boston Rec. Com., Vol. 29, p. 233.*

TEMLETT, Robert, Boston, Mass.; from Great Britain, before 1717; int. m. Sarah Davis, of Cambridge, April 20, 1717; m. Mary ———; Child: Robert.—*Boston Rec. Com., Vol. 28, p. 96, Vol. 24, p. 147.*

TEMPLE, William, of Worcester, Mass.; from Ireland, before 1729; m. Sarah ———; Children: Levy, Stephen, John, Mary, Isaac, Hepsebath and Beulah, Sarah and William, Luce.—*Perry's Scotch-Irish, p. 14, Lancaster Vital Records, pp. 253, 254.*

TEMPLETON, Adam, of Windham, N. H.; from Ballywilly, Ireland, cir. 1735; m. Margaret Lindsay, from County Derry, Ireland, April 12, 1739, in Portsmouth; Children: John, Daniel, James, Matthew; d. 1795, aged 84, in Antrim, N. H.—*Morrison's Windham, p. 783, Cochran's Antrim, p. 705, Suppl. to Morrison's Windham, p. 63, N. E. Hist. Gen. Reg., Vol. 26, p. 380.*

TEMPLETON, Allen, of Chester, N. H.; from Ireland, in 1736 or 7; m. Agnes Craige, d. 1797; Children: Matthew, Jane, Martha; d. 1755.—*Chase's Chester, pp.* 497, 597.

TERRELL, Mary, of Boston, Mass.; from Ireland, 1717, single woman (for having a bastard son), 1720.— *Court of Sessions of the Peace,* 1715-18, Vol. 1, p. 168.

THAITE, Thomas, Boston, Mass.; from Great Britain, before 1720; int. m. Mary Hutchins, Nov. 14, 1720. —*Boston Rec. Com.,* Vol. 28, p. 99.

THEOBOLD, Dr. Ernest Frederick Philip, of Broad Bay, Maine; from Germany, with the Hession Troops, 1777; b. Dec. 2, 1750, at Doernigheim, Germany; graduate of the University of Göttingen, 1772; m. Sally Rittal, at Pownalboro, Me.; Feb. 22, 1781; Child: ——; d. 1829, in Dresden, Me. — *Miller's Waldoboro* p. 237.

THOMAS, Richard, to New England; from Dublin, Ireland, 1699, in the "Virginia"; eighteen years old, with seven years to serve.—*N. E. Hist. Gen. Reg.,* Vol. 64, p. 259.

THOMPSON, Benjamin, of York, Maine; from Ireland, in 1718; brother of James and Thomas Thompson.— *Wheeler's Brunswick,* p. 857.

THOMPSON, Rev. Ebenezer, from England, to New England, 1743.—*Emigrant Ministers to America,* p. 58.

THOMPSON, Hugh, of Ellington, Conn.; from County Derry, Ireland, about 1718; son of William and Margaret Thompson; m. Elizabeth Ellsworth, Jan. 11, 1728; Children: Job, John, William, Hugh, Benoni.—*Stiles' Ancient Windsor,* Vol. 2, p. 755.

THOMPSON, James, to New England; from Scotland, 1699, in the "Virginia," Edmund Ball, master; nineteen years old, with seven years to serve.—*N. E. Hist. Gen. Reg.,* Vol. 64, p. 259.

THOMPSON, James, Boston, Mass.; from the Island of Jamaica, June, 1715; bookseller; warned out, Nov. 22, 1715.—*Boston Rec. Com.,* Vol. 11, p. 238.

THOMPSON, James, of Biddeford and York, Maine; from Ireland, in 1718; brother of Benjamin and Thomas

Thompson; m. Lienie ——; Children: Elizabeth, Samuel.—*Wheeler's Brunswick, p.* 857, *N. E. Hist. Gen. Reg., Vol.* 71, *p.* 131.

THOMPSON, James, of Ellington, Conn.; from County Derry, Ireland, about 1718; b. 1696, son of William and Margaret Thompson; m. Janet Scott, sister of Robert Scott, d. Dec. 29, 1795, aet 88; Children: James, John, Elizabeth, Margaret, Ruth, Miriam; d. Oct. 20, 1776.—*Stiles' Ancient Windsor, Vol.* 2, *pp.* 754, 755.

THOMPSON, John, Boston, Mass.; from New York, August, 1717, with wife and one child; warned out, Oct. 9, 1717.—*Boston Rec. Com., Vol.* 13, *p.* 32.

THOMSON, Capt. John, of Palmer, Mass.; from North of Ireland, 1718; b. 1699; "pitched 1725"; m. 1. Elizabeth ——, d. Oct. 11, 1763, aet 63; Children: Margaret, John, Mary, Jean, Elizabeth, Henry, Noah, Benjamin, Rufus; m. 2. Annie Wilson, int. Oct. 27, 1764; signer of the petition to Governor Shute; d. Jan. 19, 1785, aet 85.—*Temple's Palmer, p.* 563, *Palmer Vital Records, pp.* 79, 186, 238.

THOMPSON, John, of Ellington, Conn.; from County Derry, Ireland, about 1718; son of William and Margaret Thompson; m. Margaret ——, d. Oct. 20, 1769, aet 72; Children: John, Elizabeth.—*Stiles' Ancient Windsor, Vol.* 2, *p.* 755.

THOMPSON, Joseph, of Colrain, Mass.; from Ireland, cir. 1749; m. Jeannette McClellan. — *McClellan's Colrain, p.* 83.

THOMPSON, Joseph, of Ellington, Conn.; from County Derry, Ireland, about 1718; b. 1709; son of William and Margaret Thompson; d. Dec. 2, 1741, aet 32.— *Stiles' Ancient Windsor, Vol.* 2, *p.* 755.

THOMPSON, Margaret, of Ellington, Conn. (widow of William Thompson); from County Derry, Ireland, about 1718; from Scotland to Ireland, 1716; Children: William, Miriam, Samuel, James, Robert, Joseph, John, Hugh, Ruth; d. Jan. 20, 1752, aet 87. —*Stiles' Ancient Windsor, Vol.* 2, *p.* 753.

THOMSON, Robert, of Palmer, Mass.; from North of Ireland, 1718; petitioner to Governor Shute in 1732;

m. Agina ——; Child: Robert.—*Temple's Palmer, p. 563, Palmer Vital Records, p. 185.*

THOMPSON, Robert, of Ellington, Conn.; from County Derry, Ireland, about 1718; b. 1700; son of William and Margaret Thompson; m. Rachel ——, d. June 30, 1785, aet 82; Children: John, Rachel and perhaps Abigail; d. Feb. 26, 1786, aet 85.—*Stiles' Ancient Windsor, Vol. 2, p. 755.*

THOMPSON, Samuel, Ellington, Conn.; from County Derry, Ireland, about 1718; b. 1691; son of William and Margaret Thompson; m. Elizabeth McKinney, d. Oct. 22, 1776, aet 89; Children: James, Samuel, and others; d. Feb. 23, 1782, aet 90.—*Stiles' Ancient Windsor, Vol. 2, p. 754.*

THOMPSON, Thomas, of Biddeford, Me.; from Ireland, about 1718; in Biddeford 1739.—*Wheeler's Brunswick, p. 857.*

THOMPSON, Rev. Thomas, of Londonderry, N. H.; from Tyrone, Ireland, in 1733; m. Frances Cummings, in Ireland, and had one child; minister at Londonderry; d. 1738.—*Parker's Londonderry, p. 140, Morrison's Windham, p. 608.*

THOMPSON, Tobias, Boston, Mass.; from Long Island, with wife and two children; warned out, August 19, 1724.—*Boston Rec. Com., Vol. 13, p. 134.*

THOMPSON, William, Ellington, Conn.; from County Derry, Ireland, about 1718; b. 1686; son of William and Margaret Thompson; m. Esther ——, d. May 14, 1771, aet 82; d. Aug. 3, 1763, aet 76.—*Stiles' Ancient Windsor, Vol. 2, p. 753 re.*

THOMSON, William, of Londonderry, N. H.; m. Hannah, dau. of Abraham Blair, Feb. 21, 1722; Children: David, Sarah, James, Hannah, Ann; will, Sept. 1, 1745.—*Leavitt's Blair Family, p. 150, Londonderry Vital Records, p. 117.*

THONE, Rosamund, of Boston; from Surrinam, in ship "Neptune," in 1716.—*Boston Rec. Com., Vol. 29, p. 230.*

THONE, William, of Windham, N. H.; from Londonderry, Ireland, cir. 1736; b. 1706, in Scotland; m. Elizabeth Weir; Children: Agnes, Jennet, John,

William, Samuel, Isaac, Benjamin; d. 1795, aged 89.—*Morrison's Windham, p.* 787.

THORNTON, Ann, of Boston; lately arrived from Ireland, 1717, in sloop "Elizabeth," John Lawrence, master. —*Court of Sessions of the Peace, 1715-18, Vol.* 2, *p.* 210.

THORNTON or Thornington, James, of Worcester, Mass.; from Londonderry, 1718; spent winter in Casco Bay; b. 1714; Child: Matthew (signer of the Declaration of Independence).—*Lincoln's Worcester, p.* 49, *Parmenter's Pelham, p.* 17, *Wall's Reminiscences of Worcester, p.* 128, *Londonderry Vital Records, p.* 117.

TICKLE, Pierce, to New England; from Limb, Cheshire, 1699, in the "Virginia"; seventeen years old, with ten years to serve; m. Jane Ratleif in Boston, May 26, 1707.—*Boston Rec. Com., Vol.* 28, *p.* 16, *N. E. Hist. Gen. Reg., Vol.* 64, *p.* 260.

TILLET, Edward, Boston; from England, in the "Mast fleet"; wife and 2 children; Mr. Callender, bondsman.—*Boston Rec. Com., Vol.* 11, *p.* 118.

TILLEY, John; from Bristol, England, 1716; rope maker. —*Boston Rec. Com., Vol.* 29, *p.* 233, *See also Wm. Tilley, Jr., Vol.* 75, *pp.* 181-2.

TODD, Alexander, of Boston, Mass.; from Ireland, in 1720; brother of Andrew and Samuel Todd; a graduate of Edinburgh University; m. Elizabeth ———; Children: Abigail, Elizabeth, and one other daughter.—*Parker's Londonderry, p.* 301, *Boston Rec. Com., Vol.* 24, *pp.* 153, 162.

TODD, Andrew, of Londonderry, N. H.; from Ireland, in 1720; b. 1697; son of James and Rachel (Neilson) Todd; m. Beatrix Moore, daughter of John Moore; Children: Alexander, John, James, Andrew, Rachel, Samuel, and a daughter; d. 1778, at Peterborough, aged 80 yrs.—*Parker's Londonderry, p.* 301, *Cochran's Antrim, p.* 713, *Smith's Peterborough, Pt.* 2, *p.* 316, *Moore Family, p.* 4.

TODD, James, of Nutfield, N. H.; from Ireland, cir. 1720; m. Rachel ———, d. August 18, 1746, aet 85; Children: Alexander, Andrew, Samuel, Sarah. —

Willey's Nutfield, p. 349, Parker's Londonderry, p. 301, Cochran's Antrim, p. 713, Smith's Peterborough, Pt. 2, p. 316.

TODD, John, Boston, Mass.; from London, April 25, 1727; warned out, July 11 (return), 1727.—*Suffolk Court Files* 20510, *Boston Rec. Com., Vol.* 13, *p.* 167.

TODD, Margaret, to New England; from Ingleton, Yorkshire, 1699, in the "Virginia"; nineteen years old, with seven years to serve.—*N. E. Hist. Gen. Reg., Vol.* 64, *p.* 260.

TODD, Samuel, of Boston, Mass.; from Ireland, 1720; brother of Alexander and Andrew Todd; graduate of University of Edinburgh; d. unm., in Jamaica.—*Parker's Londonderry, p.* 381, *Essex Inst. Coll., Vol.* 41, *p.* 269.

TODD, William, of Chester, N. H.; from Ireland; Children: Mary, William, Daniel.—*Chase's Chester, p.* 598.

TOLFORD, John, of Chester, N. H.; from Londonderry, Ireland, before 1724; b. July, 1701 (or May); m. Jean McMurphy, Jan. 8, 1734, b. Oct., 1710 or 11, d. Dec. 29, 1792; Children: Mary, Susanna, Joshua, Rebecca, Jane, Rebecca, Anna, Hugh, John; he was major in the militia; d. May 10, 1790.—*Chase's Chester, p.* 598, *Hadley's Goffstown, p.* 528.

TOLFORD, William, of Chester, N. H.; from Ireland; brother of John Tolford; m. 1. Isabel McMurphy; m. 2. Agnes ——; Children: Elizabeth, John, Mary, David, Margaret; d. 1792, aged 92.—*Chase's Chester, p.* 599.

TOMB, Andrew, Portsmouth, N. H.; from Minehead, Somersetshire, before 1730; m. Elizabeth Shackford, Nov. 12, 1730.—*N. E. Hist. Gen. Reg., Vol.* 25, *p.* 118.

TOMSON, Elizabeth, see Daniel McCleres.

TOMSON, Mary, see Isaac Miller.

TONKIN, Ralph, Boston, Mass.; from Great Britain, before 1709; int. m. Elizabeth Harris, April 20, 1709. —*Boston Rec. Com., Vol.* 28, *p.* 31.

TOOGOOD, William, Boston, Mass.; from Great Britain, before 1715; int. m. Eliza Chapin, Jan. 4, 1716.— *Boston Rec. Com., Vol.* 28, *p.* 95.

TORPEE, Francis, Boston, Mass.; from Ireland, before 1720; int. m. Mary Smith, Nov. 25, 1720.—*Boston Rec. Com., Vol. 28, p. 99.*

TOREY, Lydia, and Dorothy, of Boston, Mass.; from London, England, 1716; orphans, bound out for five years to Pleasant, wife of George Brownell; the ministers of Boston bought their indentures, and they were declared free.—*Court of Sessions of the Peace, 1715-18, Vol. 2, p. 166.*

TOUT, Henry, Portsmouth, N. H.; from Dartmouth, Great Britain, before 1714; m. Hannah Layton, Sept. 30, 1714.—*N. E. Hist. Gen. Reg., Vol. 23, p. 270.*

TOWNSEND, Benoni, Boston, Mass.; from England, August 28, 1717; a baker; warned out, Sept. 4, 1717. —*Boston Rec. Com., Vol. 13, p. 29.*

TOWNSLEY, Micah, of Springfield, Mass.; came from —, as a licensed exporter; m. Hannah Stebbins, of Springfield, 1712-3. — *Hist. Coll. of Brimfield, p. 462.*

TRAIL, John, of Boston, Mass.; from Kirkwall, Orkney Islands, before 1750; merchant; d. before 1750.— *Goldthwaite Records, Ms. in the Boston Athenæum.*

TRAIL, Robert, of Boston; from Orkney Islands, before 1756; nephew of John Trail; merchant. — *Goldthwaite Records,- Ms. in the Boston Athenæum.*

TREUPFEL(?), Conrad, of Broad Bay, Waldoboro, Maine; from Germany, before 1752.—*Mass. Archives, Vol. 15A, pp. 340-2.*

TRIST, Arthur, Boston, Mass.; from Plymouth, in Great Britain, 1716; warned from Boston, July 3, 1716. —*Boston Rec. Com., Vol. 13, p. 5, Suffolk Court Files 10961.*

TROUTBECK, Rev. John, from England, to Massachusetts Bay, 1754; son of George Troutbeck, of Blencow, Cumberland.—*B. A., 1741, Emigrant Ministers to America, p. 60.*

TRUDE, Thomas, Portsmouth, N. H.; from Tiverton, Devonshire, before 1732; m. Anna Mills, Dec. 14, 1732.—*N. E. Hist. Gen. Reg., Vol. 25, p. 119.*

TUCKEY, Joshua, Boston, Mass.; from England, June, 1717; a twiner; warned out, Aug. 6, 1717.—*Boston Rec. Com., Vol. 13, p. 24.*

TUFFS, John, of Brookfield, Mass.; b. about 1711 [45 in 1756]; yeoman; m. Agnes ———; Children: Sarah, and probably John and Thomas.—*Mrs. H. S. Tufts, Deed of Belfast, Me.,* 1769, *Brookfield Vital Records, p.* 213.

TURNBULL, John, of Newcastle, Maine; from Scotland; b. Jan. 29, 1759; m. Hulda Glidden, in Newcastle, b. Jan. 5, 1764; Children: Margaret, John, Eleanor, Elizabeth, James, William, Robert, Charlotte, Lydia. —*Cushman's Ancient Sheepscot and Newcastle, pp.* 428, 429.

TURNER [or Tornier], Alexander, of Pelham, Mass.; from Great Britain, before 1738; m. Mary ———; Children: Alexander, and probably James.—*Parmenter's Pelham, p.* 17, *Pelham Vital Records, p.* 77.

TURNER, James, Portsmouth, N. H.; from Kingsbury, Somersetshire, before 1730; m. Mary Mills, Nov. 3, 1730.—*N. E. Hist. Gen. Reg., Vol.* 25, *p.* 118.

TURNER, Joseph, of Peterborough, N. H.; from Ireland; m. Rachel ———; Children: Thomas, Joseph, William; d. 1783, aged 77.—*Smith's Peterborough, Pt.* 2, *p.* 320.

TYGARD, William, from Ireland; bricklayer; b. cir. 1716; volunteer against the West Indies, 1740.—*Colonial Wars,* 1899.

TYLER, Rev. John, from England, to Connecticut, 1768. —*Emigrant Ministers to America, p.* 60.

UKKELY, Bernhard, of Broad Bay, Maine; from Germany, before 1760.—*Miller's Waldoboro, p.* 51.

ULMER, John, of Warren, Maine; from Germany, in 1740; b. 1736; acting minister; m. Catherine Remilly; Children: George, Mary, John, Margaret, Hannah, Jacob, Matthias, Mary, Philip, Andrew, Sarah, Martin, Catherine; d. 1809, aged 73.—*Eaton's War-*

ren, p. 62 (1st Ed.), State Archives, Vol. 15A, pp. 240-2, Bettinger's Germans in Colonial Time, Millers Waldoboro, pp. 20, 27, 51.

ULMER, John Jacob, of Broad Bay, Maine; from Germany, before 1752.—*Miller's Waldoboro, p. 51, State Archives, Vol. 15A, pp. 240-2.*

ULRICK, John, Dresden, Maine; Huguenot.—*Huguenots in Dresden, p. 19.*

UMBERHINE, Charles, of Broad Bay, Maine; from Germany, before 1760.—*Miller's Waldoboro, p. 51.*

UNDERWOOD, Anthony, Boston, Mass.; sadler, from England, with his wife, June 1720; warned out, June 22, 1720.—*Boston Rec. Com., Vol. 13, p. 72.*

UNWIN, Mr. Martin, Boston, Mass.; from London, 1737; stationer and bookbinder; he was granted liberty to open a shop.—*Boston Rec. Com., Vol. 15, p. 53.*

URQUHART, The Rev. John, of Warren, Me.; from Scotland, 1774; m. ——, whom he left in Scotland.— *Eaton's Warren, p. 154 (1st Ed.), p. 166 (2d Ed.) et seq.*

VAUSTOPE, Michll, Boston, Mass.; mariner; a Dutchman, from Antiago, with Capt. Lowder, in 1716; warned out, Oct. 15.—*Boston Rec. Com., Vol. 13, p. 11.*

VEIW, Daniel, Boston, Mass.; from France, before 1718; int. m. Elizabeth Swan, Dec. 20, 1718.—*Boston Rec. Com., Vol. 28, p. 97.*

VELDEN, Thomas, Boston, Mass.; with his wife from Newfoundland, Nov. 5, 1716, with Captain Dench; warned out, Nov. 15.—*Boston Rec. Com., Vol. 13, p. 13.*

VERSTILLE, Peter, of Hartford, Conn.; b. July 11; 1734, in Parish of St. Luke, London, Co. Middlesex; son of Wm. Verstille; in Boston, 1752; in Wethersfield, Conn., 1761; m. Nov. 30, 1756, Naomi Gedney, dau. of Samuel Ridgeway; Child: William, b. Boston, Sept., 1757, he d. June 30? 1778, at Hartford. —*Stiles's Ancient Windsor, Vol. 2, p. 770.*

VICAR, Mr., see Mrs. Hamilton Hathorne.

VICKERS, Samuel, from London, 1716; servant; m. Abigail Newman, Dec. 24, 1716.—*Boston Rec. Com., Vol. 29, p. 234, Vol. 28, p. 96.*

VICTORY, John, of Deerfield, Mass.; from Venice, Italy, before 1764; baptised a Protestant in 1764.—*Sheldon's Deerfield, Vol. 2, p. 350.*

VINCENT, Ambrose, of Boston, Mass.; from England; b. 1713; m. Ann Bleigh, before 1736; Children: Anna, Ambrose; d. 1800.—*Bridgman's Memorials of the Dead, p. 146, Boston Rec. Com., Vol. 24, pp. 227, 235.*

VINCENT, Ambrose, Boston, Mass.; from Philadelphia, in the sloop "Humbird," 1737 (see above).—*Boston Rec. Com., Vol. 15, p. 39.*

VINCENT, James, of Boston, Mass.; silk dyer, from London; at the "Blew Dog and Rainbow," Cambridge St., 1729.—*News Letter, April 3, 1729.*

VINCENT, William, of Boston, Mass.; from Bristol, England, 1716; joiner.—*Boston Rec. Com., Vol. 29, p. 233.*

VINECUT, George, Portsmouth, N. H.; from "Northlen," Devon, before 1723; m. Mary Wiatt of Boston, in Portsmouth, Dec. 19, 1723.—*N. E. Hist. Gen. Reg., Vol. 24, p. 17.*

VINER, John, of Rutland, Holden, Princeton, and Westminster, Mass.; from Buckington, Somerset, England, cir. 1777; b. 1750, in "Buckington"; m. Sarah Chard, Nov. 17, 1786, alive 1826; clothier; Children: George, Charlotte, John, Isaac, Joseph, Susanna, James, William, Betsy; d. Sept. 4, 1826.—*Heywood's Westminster, Mass.; Rutland Vital Records, p. 201, Westminster Vital Records, pp. 90, 91, 250.*

VOGLER, John Philip, of Broad Bay, Maine; from Germany, before 1752; b. in the Palatinate, 1725; m. Catherine ——; removed to North Carolina, 1770; d. Bethania, N. C., 1790.—*Miller's Waldoboro, p. 63, State Archives, Vol. 15A, p. 240-2.*

VOGLER, Philip Christopher, of Broad Bay, Maine; from Germany, 1742.—*Miller's Waldoboro, p. 79.*

VOOHAN, Henry, from "Plimo in Eng."; husbandman; b. cir. 1695; volunteer against the West Indies, 1740.—*Colonial Wars, 1899.*

VORBACK, Philip, of Ashburnham, Mass.; from Germany, 1758; m. Lois ——; Children: Susannah, Lois,

Philip, John, Catherine, Mary, Jacob, Henry, William; d. after 1780.—*Stearn's Ashburnham, p.* 927, *Ashburnham Vital Records, p.* 78.

VOSE, David, of Braintree, Mass.; from Germany, cir. 1752; "Germantown," 1753.—*State Archives, Vol.* 15A, *pp.* 240-2, *Pattee's Braintree, p.* 481.

WAGHORNE, John, of Boston, Mass.; from England, before 1739; teacher of "vocal Psalmody" and japaning, at his house "opposite the great trees, at the South End" of Boston.—*Boston Gazette, July* 9/16, 1739, *Old-Time New England, Vol.* 18, *p.* 90.

WAKLEY, John, Waltham, Mass.; from Great Britain, 1769; m. Abigaiel Meriam, in Lynn, 1770 (he called "a stranger"); "one infant."—*Lynn Vital Records, Vol.* 2, *p.* 251.

WALCK, Christorer, of Broad Bay, Maine; from Germany, before 1760.—*Miller's Waldoboro, p.* 52.

WALES, James, Portsmouth, N. H.; from Dublin, Ireland, before 1718; m. Mary Saunders, Jan. 16, 1718. —*N. E. Hist. Gen. Reg., Vol.* 23, *p.* 394.

WALKER, Ane, Boston, Mass.; from London, April 25, 1727; warned out, July 11 (return), 1727.—*Suffolk Court Files* 20510, *Boston Rec. Com., Vol.* 13, *p.* 167.

WALKER, John, to New England; of Titherington, Cheshire, 1699, in the "Virginia," Edmund Ball, master; nineteen years old, with seven years to serve.—*N. E. Hist. Gen. Reg., Vol.* 64, *p.* 259.

WALKER, John, of Boston, Mass.; from Ireland, Nov., 1719; with wife and three children; warned out, Dec. 5, 1719.—*Cullen's Irish in Boston, p.* 51, *Boston Rec. Com., Vol.* 13, *p.* 64.

WALKER, Joseph, Boston, Mass.; from London, April 25, 1727; warned out, July 11, 1727.—*Suffolk Court Files* 20510.

WALKER, Thomas, of Boston, Mass., and Pemaquid, Maine; from Ireland, August, 1718; warned out of Boston, Oct. 22, 1718; in the will of Thomas Walker of Pemaquid, Me., he mentions his wife Jane, now in Ireland; Child: John, now in Ireland; d. 1741. *Maine Wills, p.* 547, *Cullen's Irish in Boston, p.* 51, *Boston Rec. Com., Vol.* 13, *p.* 46, *Suffolk Court Files,* 12620.

WALKER, William, of Worcester, Mass.; from Ireland; m. Mary ———; Children: Adam, John, Robert, Joseph, Isabella, Mary, Nancy; will, 1760; [he built the house later owned by George Bancroft, the historian].—*From Mrs. C. F. White, Warren St., Brookline.*

WALKEY, Andrew, Boston, Mass.; from Ireland, in the ship "Elizabeth," 1720; warned, Nov. 3, 1720; farmer.—*Boston Rec. Com., Vol. 13, p. 63.*

WALLACE, see also Wallas, Wallis, Wallise.

WALLACE, Benoni, of Lunenburg, Mass.; from Ireland before 1740; son of William and Eleanor Wallace; m. Rebecca Brown of Lynn, July 2, 1755; Children: Benjamin, Curwin, David, Molly, Ebenezer, Frederick.—*Lunenburg Records, pp. 260, 330.*

WALLACE, John, of Londonderry, N. H.; b. cir. 1695; from Colerain, County Antrim, Ireland, in 1719 or 1720; m. Annis Barnett, or Barnard, 1721; Children: James, Rebecca, William, John, Janet, Samuel, Ann, Sarah; d. March 29, 1777, aet 82.— *Parker's Londonderry, pp. 90, 302, Cochran's Antrim, p. 730, Brown's Bedford, p. 1106, Documentary History of Maine, p. 24, Londonderry Vital Records, pp. 118, 262, 316.*

WALLACE, John, of Londonderry, N. H.; from Ireland, before 1726; brother of Joseph Wallace; m. Janet Steele; Children: Jane, Mary, Elizabeth, Margaret, Janet, Ann.—*Londonderry Vital Records, p. 118.*

WALLACE, John, of Boston, Mass.; from Ireland, before 1736, with Capt. Beard; taken into the house of John White, cordwainer, as a journey-man.—*Boston Rec. Com., Vol. 13, p. 318.*

WALLACE, John, of Londonderry, N. H.; from Ireland, about 1750; b. cir. 1698; m. Janet Lindsey, Nov. 28, 1725, in Londonderry, d. 1802, aged 97; Children: Martha, Agnes, James, Matthew, Jonathan, George, James; d. about 1798, aged about 100.— *N. E. Hist. Gen. Reg., Vol. 56, p. 185, Merrill's Ackworth, p. 277, Londonderry Vital Records, pp. 118, 262.*

WALLACE, Jonathan, of Londonderry, N. H.; from Ireland, before 1725; m. Agnes ———; Children: William B., Jonathan, Thomas.—*Londonderry Vital Records, p.* 118.

WALLACE, Peter, Newbury, Mass.; from Glasgow, "of ye ship Apollo"; d. 1748, aged about 18, in Newbury.—*Newbury Vital Records, Vol.* 2, *p.* 746.

WALLACE, Robert, of Londonderry, N. H.; should be John, q.v.—*Merrill's Ackworth, p.* 277.

WALLACE, Thomas, of Londonderry and Bedford, N. H.; from Coleraine, Ireland, in 1726; brother of John Wallace; m. Jean Wallace, a sister of Joseph Wallace of Milford, N. H.; Children: James, Joseph, William, John, Janet, Margaret, Ann, Betsey.— *Parker's Londonderry, p.* 303, *Merrill's Ackworth, p.* 276.

WALLACE, Thomas, of Londonderry, N. H.; from Ireland, 1732; b. Bush Mills, Northern Ireland, 1673; m. Barbary Cochran, 1704, b. 1677, d. Sept. 2, 1771; d. Aug. 22, 1754, Londonderry. — *Hadley's Goffstown, p.* 538.

WALLACE, Thomas, of Londonderry, N. H.; from County Antrim, Ireland; a nephew of John Wallace; m. Jean ———; Children: Robert, Thomas, William, James, Mary, Jennat, Joseph, Margaret, Ann, John. *Parker's Londonderry, p.* 305, *Londonderry Vital Records, p.* 118.

WALLACE, William, of Worcester, Mass.; from Ireland, before 1740; m. Eleanor ———; Children: Elizabeth, Elenor, Sarah, Benoney, William.—*Worcester Vital Records, p.* 260.

WALLAS, Matthias, of Worcester, Mass.; from Ireland; m. Eleanor ———, d. April 16, 1767, in her 85th year, at Shirley, Mass.; Children: Elizabeth, Eleanor, Jane.—*Bolton's Shirley Upland and Intervales, pp.* 60, 61, *Middlesex County Probate,* 16881, *Shirley Vital Records, p.* 209, *Chandler's Shirley, p.* 502.

WALLAS, William, of Lunenburg, Mass.; from Ireland; m. Elizabeth ———; Children: Jane, Elizabeth, Martha, Mary, Margaret, Anne, Susanna, Samuel, Hannah, William, David, Sarah.—*Lunenburg Records, p.* 329, 330.

WALLEAZOR, Christopher, of Broad Bay, Maine; from Germany, before 1760.—*Miller's Waldoboro, p.* 51.

WALLER, Rev. William, from England, to New England, 1764.—*Emigrant Ministers to America, p.* 61.

WALLISE, Daniel, Boston, Mass.; a sick man from "ye Isle of May" [Man?], May, 1719; warned out, July 22, 1719.—*Boston Rec. Com., Vol.* 13, *p.* 57.

WALLIS, Oliver, of Worcester, Mass.; from Ireland, before 1733.—*Perry's Scotch-Irish, p.* 14.

WALLIS, Robert, from Brunswick, Maine; warned from Boston, Aug. 12, 1722, with Martha Wallis, John Wallis, and Anbah Wallis.—*Boston Rec. Com., Vol.* 13, *p.* 107.

WALSH, William, of Thomaston, Me.; from Dublin, Ireland, 1774; b. 1765; m. Sarah Pressy; Children: James, Lawrence, William, John, Robert, Sarah, Alice; schoolmaster; d. 1837.—*Eaton's Thomaston, p.* 449.

WALT, Jacob, of Broad Bay, Maine; from Germany, before 1752.—*State Archives, Vol.* 15A, *pp.* 240-2.

WALTER, William, of Boston, Mass.; from Bristol, Eng., 1716; carpenter; m. ? Amy Morecock, July 27, 1726; Child?: William, "Jr."—*Boston Rec. Com., Vol.* 29, *p.* 233, *Vol.* 28, *pp.* 135, 175, 180.

WALTON, John, of Canterbury, N. H.; from Yorkshire, England, 1753; m. Eliza Clark; Children: George, John.—*Lyford's Canterbury, p.* 330.

WANTELL, Henry, of Braintree, Mass. (or Wansell); "Germantown," 1757. — *State Archives, Vol.* 15A, *pp.* 240-2, *Pattee's Braintree, p.* 480.

WARBURTON, Rev. Charles, of Boston, Mass.; from England; d. July 1, 1814, aged 30.—*Copp's Hill Burying Ground.*

WARIN, William, Portsmouth, N. H.; from Devonshire, before 1716; m. Mary Brittain, Jan. 8, 1716.—*N. E. Hist. Gen. Reg., Vol.* 23, *p.* 392.

WASHAR, John, of Middletown, Mass.; from England, aged 10; m. Hannah Wilkins, 1735; Children: Amy, Stephen, Anna, dau., dau., Susannah, John. — *Secomb's Amherst, p.* 813.

WASON, James, Portsmouth, N. H.; from the Parish of Bellemanus (Balleymena?), County Antrim, before 1736; m. Hannah Calwell, also of "Bellemanus," in

Portsmouth, Nov. 30, 1736.—*N. E. Hist. Gen. Reg., Vol. 26, p. 377.*

WASON, Thomas, of Chester, N. H.; from Ireland, before 1738; Children: Thomas, Robert, John, James; d. 1801, aged cir. 100.—*Chase's Chester, p. 609.*

WASSON, Isabel, see Calwell.

WATERHOUSE, Joseph, of Portsmouth, N. H.; from England, before 1730; m. —— ——; Child: Joseph. —*Southgate's Scarborough, p. 226.*

WATKINSON, Roger, Boston, Mass.; from Great Britain, before 1712; int. m. Mary Towt, Aug. 29, 1712.— *Boston Rec. Com., Vol. 28, p. 92.*

WATSON, Charles, of Providence, R. I.; from London, England, before 1711; m. Mary Morey, daughter of Thomas Morey, of Roxbury, Mass.—*Goldthwaite Records, Ms. in the Boston Athenæum.*

WATSON, John, Boston; from Ireland, in the ship "Elizabeth"; warned out, Nov. 3, 1719; farmer.—*Boston Rec. Com., Vol. 13, p. 63.*

WATSON, John, of Leicester, Mass.; from Coleraine, Ireland, in 1718; b. 1716, son of Matthew and Mary (Orr) Watson; m. Mary Blair, dau. of Robert Blair, int. m. Nov. 20, 1743, d. July 21, 1795, aet 70; Children: John, Mary, Sarah, William, Patrick, Samuel; d. Nov. 9, 1795, aet 80.—*Leicester Vital Records, pp. 227, 280, Spencer Vital Records, pp. 110, 112, 271, 273.*

WATSON, Matthew, of Leicester, Mass.; from Coleraine, Ireland, 1718; b. England?; m. Mary Orr, 1695; Children: Matthew, Samuel, Patrick, Robert, William, Elizabeth, Margarette, John, Oliver; d. 1720. —*Watson's Hist. and Gen. of Spencer, Mass., Draper's History of Spencer.*

WATSON, Matthew, of Leicester, Mass.; from Coleraine, Ireland, 1718; son of Matthew and Mary (Orr) Watson.

WATSON, Oliver, Boston, Mass.; from Ireland, in the ship "Elizabeth"; warned, Nov. 3, 1719; farmer.—*Boston Rec. Com., Vol. 13, p. 63.*

WATSON, Oliver, of Leicester, Mass.; from Ireland, 1718; b. on the voyage, 1718, son of Matthew and Mary (Orr) Watson; m. Elizabeth Blair, dau. of Robert

Blair, of Worcester, Mass., int. Dec. 4, 1742, d. Oct. 31, 1779, aet 54; Children: Abigail, Elizabeth, James, James, Martha, Mary, Oliver, Robert, Simeon, Thankful; m. 2. Hannah ——, d. March 6, 1808, aet 84; d. Dec. 20, 1804, aet 86.—*Leicester Vital Records, pp.* 100, 101, 227, *Spencer Vital Records, pp.* 109, 110, 112, 271-273, *Draper's History of Spencer,* p. 264.

WATSON, Patrick, of Spencer, Mass.; from Ireland; b. 1706; m. Elizabeth ——, d. Feb. 22, 1751, aet 36; d. March 31, 1754, aet 48.—*Spencer Vital Records, pp.* 271, 272.

WATSON, Samuel, of Leicester, Mass.; from Coleraine, Ireland, 1718; b. 1698, son of Matthew and Mary (Orr) Watson; m. Margaret ——, d. Aug. 6, 1780, aet 77; Children: Elizabeth, William, Samuel, John, Daniel; d. March 9, 1776, aet 78.—*Leicester Vital Records,* p. 102.

WATSON, William, of Rutland, Mass.; from Ireland, before 1728; church member in Rutland; m. Anne ——; Children: James, William, Elizabeth.—*Rutland Vital Records,* p. 99.

WATSON, William, of Falmouth, Scarboro, and Thomaston, Maine; from Ireland; m. twice; Children: 1. John, William, Jane, Mary, Margaret; 2. James, Elizabeth, Matthew, David; d. Sept. 21, 1768.—*Eaton's Thomaston,* p. 454, *Eaton's Warren,* p. 639.

WATTS, John, Boston, Mass.; from Great Britain, before 1720; int. m. Dorothy Frothingham, April 12, 1720; forbid by her mother, Mrs. Mary Knock.—*Boston Rec. Com., Vol.* 28, p. 98.

WATTS, "Josep," Boston, Mass.; planter, from South Carolina, Feb., 1719; warned out, Feb. 24, 1719.—*Boston Rec. Com., Vol.* 13, p. 52.

WATTS, William, of Boston, Mass.; from Ireland, cir. 1719; m. Margaret McLellan, of Casco (m. 2. Samuel Gilchrist); Children: John, Samuel, Elizabeth. —*Eaton's Warren,* p. 430, *Eaton's Thomaston,* p. 451, *new ed.,* p. 639.

WAUGH, Joseph, of Windham, N. H.; from Great Britain, cir. 1733; m. Janet ——; Child: William; d. 1771, aged 78.—*Morrison's Windham,* p. 807.

WAY, Captain Robert, of Boston, Mass.; from Pennsylvania, before 1733; m. Mrs. Mary Brewster, of Boston, Oct. 23, 1733, in Newbury; Child: Robert.—*Newbury Vital Records, Vol. 2, p. 502, Boston Rec. Com., Vol. 24, p. 224.*

WEAVER, Arthur, of Boston, Mass.; from "Tanton, Dean," England, before 1726; woolen manufacturer; m. Alice Miller, of Boston, Oct. 12, 1726, in Newbury, Mass.—*Newbury Vital Records, Vol. 2, p. 329.*

WEBB, ——, of Woolwich, Maine; from Scotland; settled in Scituate; Children: Nathaniel, Susan, Ruth, Jane, Luther, Martha; d. cir. 1763, by the fall of a tree. —*Ancient Sheepscot and Newcastle, p. 430.*

WEBB, Samuel, of Windham, N. H., and Gorham, Maine; from Redrift, England, cir. 1713; b. Dec. 25, 1696; son of Samuel and Susanna Webb; m. Mary McIntire, of Tiverton, R. I., or the daughter of Captain John Randall, of Weymouth, Mass., in 1718; Children: Samuel, Thomas; first school teacher of Windham; m. 2. Bethiah (Farrah) Spear, d. Nov. 3, 1770, aet 62; Children: David, Ezekiel, John, Seth, Susanna, Eli, James, Josiah, Abigail, Elizabeth; d. Feb. 15, 1785, at Deer Isle, Maine.—*McLellan's Gorham, p. 815.*

WEBB, Stephen, Boston, Mass.; from Great Britain, before 1712; int. m. Elizabeth Olkerson, Feb. 9, 1712. —*Boston Rec. Com., Vol. 28, p. 91.*

WEER, Anne, of Wells, Me.; from Ireland, in 1729.— *Bourne's Wells and Kennebunk, p. 313.*

WEIR, Robert, of Londonderry, N. H.; from Ireland, in 1718.—*Parker's Londonderry, p. 44.*

WELBEC, Charles, Boston, Mass.; "a sick man who came Last New found Land, Nov., 1719"; warned out, Dec. 15, 1719.—*Boston Rec. Com., Vol. 13, p. 64.*

WELCH, John, of Brunswick and Bath, Maine; from Ireland, before Sept. 4, 1718; a linen weaver; Children: John, Patrick, William, Samuel.—*York Deeds, Vol. 9, p. 238, Cochran's Monmouth and Wales, pp. 602, 603.*

WELCH, Thomas, Portsmouth, N. H.; from Dungarvin, Waterford, Ireland, before 1731; m. Olive Carn of

Kittery, Me., cir. 1731.—*N. E. Hist. Gen. Reg., Vol. 25, p. 118.*

WELENEN, Charles, Boston, Mass.; from Bristol, England, April 27, 1727; warned out, July 11, 1727.—*Suffolk Court Files, 20510.*

WELLS, John, at York, Maine; from Suffolk, England, before 1723; a soldier; d. 1723 (will).—*Maine Wills, p. 254.*

WELLS, William, Boston, Mass.; from Great Britain, before 1718; int. m. Sarah Parrington, June 25, 1718. —*Boston Rec. Com., Vol. 28, p. 97.*

WELT, John, of Broad Bay, Maine; from Germany, before 1760.—*Miller's Waldoboro, p. 52.*

WENTON, Dorothy, widow, Boston, Mass.; from Carolina to New York, and then to Roxbury, 1716; warned out, July 15, 1716.—*Boston Rec. Com., Vol. 13, p. 6, Suffolk Court Files, 10961.*

WERNER [Varner and Vannah], George, Broad Bay, Me.; from Germany, 1753; Children: dau., m. —— Kinsell, dau., m. —— Achorn.—*Miller's Waldoboro, p. 51.*

WESCOM, John, Portsmouth, N. H.; from Tiverton, Devonshire, before 1716; m. Elizabeth Lang, July 28, 1716.—*N. E. Hist. Gen. Reg., Vol. 23, p. 392.*

WEST, Mary, Boston, Mass.; from New York, 1727; warned out, April 15, 1727.—*Boston Rec. Com., Vol. 13, p. 167.*

WEST, Thomas, of Salem, Mass.; from Blyth, Northumberland, before 1763; m. Hannah Browne, June 26, 1763.—*Salem Vital Records, Vol. 4, p. 455.*

WHEATLEY, Phillis, of Boston, Mass.; from Africa, 1761; b. Africa, 1753; "the African poetess"; m. John Peters, April, 1778; Children, three, all of whom died young; d. Boston, Dec. 5, 1784.—*Mass. Hist. Soc.,* 1863-4, *pp.* 166, 267-279, 1864-5, *p.* 461.

WHEELER, Rev. Wolland, from England, to Massachusetts, 1766 or 68.—*Emigrant Ministers to America, p. 63.*

WHITE, Mrs. Elizabeth, of Lunenburg, Mass.; b. Makery, County Monaghan, Ireland, cir. 1687; wife of John White q.v.; d. 1753, aet 66.—*Fitchburg Hist. Soc.,* 1897-9, *p.* 266.

WHITE, Hannah, Boston, Mass.; from the Island of Orecock in North Carolina; wife of Thomas White; brought by Mr. Thomas Mill.—*Boston Rec. Com., Vol. 13, p. 291.*
WHITE, John, Boston, Mass.; from Ireland, in the ship "Elizabeth," warned out, Nov. 3, 1719; "an Irishman from Dedham"; warned out, July 11, 1727; warned again April 6, 1727.—*Suffolk Court Files,* 20510, *Boston Rec. Com., Vol. 13, p. 63, 167.*
WHITE, John, of Lunenburg, Mass.; b. Glasgow, Scotland, 1672; to Ireland, 1723; m. Elizabeth ———, q. v.; Children: John, Patrick; d. 1739, aet 67.—*Fitchburg Hist. Soc.,* 1897-9, *p. 266-7.*
WHITE, John, of Lunenburg, Mass.; from Ireland, after 1723; son of John and Elizabeth White; m. Mary Wallis, Dec. 9, 1747; Children: John, Charles, William; m. 2, Feb. 22, 1753, Mary Whitney of Lunenburg; Children: David, Elizabeth.—*Lunenburg Vital Records, pp. 260, 331.*
WHITE, Miriam, of Boston, Mass.; from Jamaica, in the sloop "Ann," John Beney, master; admitted an inhabitant, Sept. 24, 1730.—*Boston Rec. Com., Vol. 13, p. 201.*
WHITE, Patrick, of Lunenburg, Mass.; from Ireland; b. 1710, son of John and Elizabeth White; m. Jane White, int. Dec. 24, 1741, of "Chesher"; Children: John, Elizabeth, Mary, William, Jane, Eleanor, James, David, Thomas; d. 1778, in Peterborough.—*Smith's Peterborough, Pt. 2, p. 335, Lunenburg Records, pp.* 113, 137, 157, 162, 163, 176, 180, 182, 190, 193, 215, 240.
WHITE, Peter, of Berwick, Maine; from Canada, after the fall of Quebec, 1759; m. ———; Children: five. —*Southgate's Scarborough, p. 176.*
WHITE, Samuel, of Marblehead, and Salem, Mass.; from Wiltshire, England, before 1771; m. Elizabeth Emery, Dec. 26, 1771; Child: Sarah. — *Salem Vital Records, Vol. 2, p. 420, Vol. 3, p. 334, Vol. 4, p. 462.*
WHITE, Sarah, see Henry Keese.
WHITE, William, of Londonderry, N. H.; from Londonderry, Ireland, in 1725; b. 1687, in England; m. in

Ireland; Children: Henry, James, Jane, Robert, David, Thomas, William.—*Chase's Chester, p.* 614.

WHITE, William, of Lancaster, Mass.; from "Dumbo" [Drumbo?], Ireland; m. Elinor ——; Children: Samuel, 1730, Katharine, William and Margaret (twins), Isaac, Jane.—*Lancaster Vital Records, pp.* 280, 282-284, *Carter's Pembroke, p.* 312.

WHITFIELD, William, Boston, Mass.; from Great Britain, before 1709; int. m. Mary Faulkner, Nov. 10, 1709. —*Boston Rec. Com., Vol.* 28, *p.* 32.

WHITTEMORE, Nathaniel, from Hitcham, Hertfordshire, England; Child: Nathaniel.—*Smith's Peterborough, Pt.* 2, *p.* 344.

WHITTIER, Reuben, of Exeter, and Newtown, N. H., from Scotland, cir. 1730; b. cir. 1712; m. Mary Smith; Children: Moses, Richard, Josiah, Reuben, Mary, Joseph, Daniel, Deborah, Sarah, Miriam, Phineas, Aaron, Clark.—*Cogswell's Deerfield, pp.* 492, 495, 496.

WHITTIER, William, of Deerfield, N. H.; from Scotland, cir. 1730; b. 1710; m. Abigail Morrill; Children: Abigail, Isaac, Nathaniel, Phebe; m. 2. Sarah Huntington.—*Cogswell's Deerfield, pp.* 492-3.

WHITTLE, Richard, from London, to New England; on the "Venus," 1774, to settle; taylor; aged 24.— *N. E. Hist. Gen. Reg., Vol.* 63, *p.* 234.

WIDDOP, Paul, to New England; from Halifax, Yorkshire, 1699, in the "Virginia," Edmund Ball, master; twenty-six years old, with seven years to serve. —*N. E. Hist. Gen. Reg., Vol.* 64, *p.* 259.

WIDEMAN, Christian, Boston, Mass.; from Germany, before 1751; m. Arenstien Gross, also from Germany, Dec. 28, 1751.—*Boston Rec. Com., Vol.* 28, *p.* 341.

WILDRAGE, Mrs. Isabella, Portland, Me.; from Island of South Ronaldsha, North Britain; b. 1740; m. Captain James Wildrage; d. Sept. 23, 1780, aet 40 yrs. —*Gravestone, East Cemetery, Portland, Portland Price Current, July* 7, 1877.

WILKE, ——, of Warren, Maine; from Scotland, 1753. —*Eaton's Warren, p.* 85.

WILKER, Jacob, of Boston and Ashburnham, Mass.; b. Germany, 1731; m. Anna Barbary Roberts, Boston,

d. April 16, 1803, aet 71; Children: Elizabeth, George, Susan, Catherine; d. Nov. 3, 1816, aet 85. —*Stearns' Ashburnham, p. 976, Ashburnham Vital Records, pp. 87, 165, 211, 212.*

WILKINS, Thomas, from Northampton, to Boston, 1774, in the ship "Mary Ann," "to settle"; "gentleman," aet 43; w. Temperance, aet 46; Children: Ann, Mary, Frances, John, Temperance, William.—*N. E. Hist. Gen. Reg., Vol. 63, p. 22.*

WILKISON, Thomas, Portsmouth, N. H.; from London, before 1715; m. Elizabeth Caverly, July 28, 1715. —*N. E. Hist. Gen. Reg., Vol. 23, p. 272.*

WILLIAMS, Edward, Boston, Mass.; from Great Britain, before 1719; int. m. Tabatha Mitchell, Sept. 9, 1719; forbidden by her.—*Boston Rec. Com., Vol. 28, p. 98.*

WILLIAMS, John, Portsmouth, N. H.; from Wansworth, Surrey, before 1714; m. Cathrine Lucy, Sept. 30, 1714.—*N. E. Hist. Gen. Reg., Vol. 23, p. 270.*

WILLIAMS, John, of Boston, Mass.; from Ireland, 1716; m. Elinor ———; two children; joyner.—*Boston Rec. Com., Vol. 29, p. 232.*

WILLIAMS, John, of Boston; from London, before 1733; son of John and Elizabeth Williams.—*Tyley Manuscript in the Boston Athenæum.*

WILLIAMS, John, 2d, Salem, Mass.; from Pool, England, before 1770; m. Anna Gray, widow, June 17, 1770, d. April 10, 1826, aet 99; Children: Hittee Phelps, Betty, Patty, John.—*Salem Vital Records, Vol. 4, p. 475, Vol. 2, pp. 430, 432, 434, Vol. 6, p. 335.*

WILLIAMS, Matthew, to New England, from Blew Morrice, Wales, 1699, in the "Virginia"; twenty-six years old, with seven years to serve.—*N. E. Hist. Gen. Reg., Vol. 64, p. 260.*

WILLIAMS, Richard, Boston, Mass.; from London, before 1727; tallow chandler; admitted a resident, May 3, 1727; security £100, by Elisha Cook and Captain Demerick.—*Boston Rec. Com., Vol. 13, p. 163.*

WILLIAMS, Rev. Simon, of Windham, N. H.; from England, cir. 1760; b. 1729, in Trein, County Meath, Ireland, m. Maria Floyd; Children: Adam, George, Catherine, Nancy-Ann, Gilbert Tennent, Simon Finley, Mary, John Floyd, Elizabeth; d. 1793.—*Morrison's Windham, p.* 813.

WILLIAMS, Thomas, Boston, Mass., "a lame man from Virginiah"; warned out, Aug. 31, 1723. — *Boston Rec. Com., Vol.* 13, *p.* 120.

WILLIAMSON, James, convict, assigned to Apthorp and Hancock, July 18, 1747, from Wm. Cookson of Hull. —*Suffolk Court Records.*

WILLIAMSON, Jonathan, of New Castle, Me.; from the West of England.—*Sullivan's History of the District of Maine, p.* 168.

WILLIS, Dennes, from Ireland; laborer; b. cir. 1716; volunteer against the West Indies, 1740.—*Colonial Wars,* 1899.

WILLIS, Thomas, Boston, Mass.; "a lame man from Carolina," July, 1717; warned out, August 14, 1717.—*Boston Rec. Com., Vol.* 13, *p.* 29.

WILSON, Adam, Londonderry, N. H.; from Ireland; b. North of Ireland, 1723; m. Elizabeth ———; Children: Thomas, and others.—*Cogswell's Henniker, p.* 787.

WILSON, Alexander, of Windham, N. H.; from Londonderry, Ireland, 1719; yeoman; Child: James (see Londonderry, N. H.); d. March, 1752, aged 93; owned an "exempt" farm.—*Parker's Londonderry, p.* 257, *Deed of Belfast, Me., Morrison's Windham, p.* 818, *Cochran's Francestown, p.* 984.

WILSON, John, of ———, R. I.; from County Kilkenny, Ireland, before 1775; b. cir. 1753.—*Murray's Irish Rhode Islanders, p.* 28.

WILSON, Robert, Boston, Mass.; from North Carolina, May 6, 1727; warned out, July 11 (return), 1727. —*Suffolk Court Files,* 20510, *Boston Rec. Com., Vol.* 13, *p.* 167.

WILSON, Capt. Thomas, of Topsham, Maine; from Ireland; to Boston, then to Topsham, 1752; m. Ann Cochran, of Londonderry, N. H.; Children: William, James, Thomas, Lettice, Margaret, Mary, Elizabeth. —*Wheeler's Brunswick, pp.* 823, 861.

WILSON, William, Boston, Mass.; from England, April 1, 1710, with his wife; warned out.—*Boston Rec. Com., Vol.* 11, *p.* 106.

WILSON, William, of Townsend, Mass.; from Tyrone, Ireland, 1737; m. ——; Children: Robert, one daughter.—*Smith's Peterborough, Pt.* 2, *p.* 350.
WINCHENBACK, Jacob, Waldoboro, Maine; from Germany, before 1760.—*Miller's Waldoboro, p.* 107.
WINDROW, see Winter.
WINGATE, Rev. Joseph, from England, to New England, 1763.—*Emigrant Ministers to America, p.* 64.
WINNINGTON, Philip, Boston, Mass.; from New York, April 23, 1727; warned out, July 11 (return), 1727. —*Suffolk Court Files,* 20510, *Boston Rec. Com., Vol.* 13, *p.* 167.
WINTER, Capt. Abraham, Newbury, Mass.; from Topsham, Devonshire, England, before 1724; m. Rachel Jarvott, of Boston, June 23, 1724, in Newbury.— —*Newbury Vital Records, Vol.* 2, *p.* 259.
WINTER, Andrew, of Braintree, Mass.; "Germantown," 1757.—*State Archives, Vol.* 15A, *pp.* 240-2, *Pattee's Braintree, p.* 481.
WINTER, Andrew (his name was Windrow at first), of Ashburnham, Mass.; from Germany, before 1758; m. Mary ——, d. March 14, 1814, aet 91; Children: Philip Henerck, John, Jacob, Andrew, Mary, Margaret, Catherine; d. 1792, aet 70.—*Pattee's Braintree, p.* 481, *Stearns' Ashburnham, p.* 998, *Ashburnham Vital Records, pp.* 90, 213.
WISDOM, Stephen, Portsmouth, N. H.; from Limerick, Ireland, before 1733; m. Sarah Thompson, of Colrain, Ireland, in Portsmouth, Sept. 17, 1733.—*N. E. Hist. Gen. Reg., Vol.* 25, *p.* 120.
WISWALL, Rev. John, from England, to Massachusetts Bay, 1765.—*Emigrant Ministers to America, p.* 64.
WITHERSPOON, John, of Chester, N. H.; from Ireland, (probably) before 1741; Children: Daniel, Alexander, James, David, Robert, Mary.—*Chase's Chester, p.* 619, *Cochran's Francestown, p.* 987.
WOLTZ, John, of Broad Bay, Maine; from Germany, before 1760.—*Miller's Waldoboro, p.* 51.
WOLTZGRUBER, Christobal, of Broad Bay, Maine; from Germany, before 1760.—*Miller's Waldoboro, p.* 51.
WOOD, Michal, of Boston, Mass.; late from London, clothier; admitted an inhabitant with liberty to open

a shop, Jan. 22, 1719.—*Boston Rec. Com., Vol. 13, p. 64.*

WOODBURN, David, of Londonderry, N. H.; from Ireland, cir. 1720; son of John Woodburn,? q. v.; m. ——, and had two daughters; drowned.—*Parker's Londonderry, p. 307.*

WOODBURN, John, of Londonderry, N. H.; from Ireland, cir. 1720; m. 1. Mary Boyd; m. 2. Mary Taggart; Children: Nancy, Margaret, Sarah, Mary, David, John, Betsey, Hannah; d. 1780.—*Parker's Londonderry, p. 307.*

WOODCOCK, Job, of Boston, Mass.; "from Great Britain, since of Boston, a soldier lately deceased," 1761.—*News Letter, Feb. 5, 1761.*

WOODEN, John, Portsmouth, N. H.; from London, Surrey, before 1723; m. Easter Griffiths, May 22, 1723; Children: Hannah, Mary; Easter, the widow, m. 2. John Greeley.—*N. E. Hist. Gen. Reg., Vol. 24, p. 16.*

WOODSIDE, Rev. James, Brunswick, Me.; from "Derry Lough," Ireland, before 1714; returned before 1726; recommended by the Presbytery of Route, in the Bann Valley.—*Wheeler's Brunswick, p. 354, 823, Bolton's Scotch-Irish, pp. 220-7, Colonial Wars, 1899, p. 85.*

WOODSIDE, William, Brunswick, Maine; from England, before 1719; m. ——; Child: James; d. 1764.—*Colonial Wars, 1899, p. 85.*

WOOLET, Edmond, Portsmouth, N. H.; from Eltham, Kent, before 1716; m. Mary Polloy, Nov. 1, 1716. —*N. E. Hist. Gen. Reg., Vol. 23, p. 393.*

WOOLFE, Henry, of North Yarmouth, Me.; from England; m. Rachel ——; Children: Elizabeth, Mary, Rachel; (grandchildren: Henry, Elizabeth Moxey); d. 1759 (will).—*Maine Wills, p. 872-4.*

WORKMAN, John, of Colraine, Mass.; from Ireland, before 1750; son of Mary (McCrillis) (Foster) (Workman) (Henry) Ellis; m. Phoebe Stewart, daughter of James Stewart.—*McClellan's Colraine, p. 75.*

WORTHLEY, Thomas, Salem, Worcester, Mass., Londonderry and Goffstown, N. H.; from England, 1705; b. 1691, Bedfordshire; m. 1. Mehitable Yarrow, of Worcester; m. 2. Mehitable Ordway, of Hopkinton;

Children: Timothy, Thomas, John, Mehitable, Molly, Susanna, Jonathan; d. aged 108 years.—*Hadley's Goffstown, p. 571.*

WOSTER, David, of Vinal Haven, Maine; from England, cir. 1744; b. 1732.—*Hundredth Anniversary of Vinal Haven, p. 52.*

WRIGHT, Michael, of "Seacunnet," R. I.; from Mountmellick, Queens County, Ireland, before 1775; b. cir. 1739.—*Murray's Irish Rhode Islanders, p. 33.*

WRIGHT, Thomas, Portsmouth, N. H.; from London, before 1716; m. Hepsibar Seavey, Nov. 4, 1716.—*N. E. Hist. Gen. Reg., Vol. 23, p. 393.*

WYLIE, Robert, of Boothbay, Maine; from Great Britain, before 1740; b. about 1703; m. Martha ———, d. 1799, aet 92; Children: John, Martha, William, Mary, Sarah, Robert, Samuel, Catherine, Easter, Neal, Jean, Alexander; d. 1770, aet 67.—*Greene's Boothbay, p. 643.*

WYLLIE, John, of Damariscotta, Maine; from North Ireland; m. Jane (Bell) Harkness; Children: Walter (d. in Ireland), John, James, Robert, Thomas, Elizabeth.—*Eaton's Warren, p. 436, new ed., p. 649.*

YOUNG, David, of Worcester, Mass.; from Londonderry, Ireland, 1718; son of John Young (q.v.); born in Taughboyne, County Donegal, Ireland; m. Martha Boyd? d. at Worcester, Oct. 26, 1749, aged 65; Child: William; d. Dec. 26, 1776, aged 94.—*Perry's Scotch-Irish, p. 11, Worcester Inscriptions, p. 67, Wall's Reminiscences of Worcester, p. 128.*

YOUNG, David, Boston, Mass.; from Ireland, with Captain Dennis, Nov., 1719; farmer.—*Boston Rec. Com., Vol. 13, p. 64.*

YOUNG, James, Boston, Mass.; "a North Britain," 1726; warned, April 26, 1726.—*Boston Rec. Com., Vol. 13, p. 134.*

YOUNG, John, of Brunswick and Bath, Maine; from Ireland, before Sept. 4, 1718; Katherine, Margaret, Mary, Easter and Sarah Young were warned from Boston, August 12, 1722, having been brought from Brunswick with others.—*York Deeds, Vol. 9, p. 238, Boston Rec. Com., Vol. 13, p. 106.*

Young, John, of Worcester, Mass.; b. Isle of Bert, Londonderry, Ireland, 1718; Child: David; d. June 30, 1730, aet 107 or 93.—*Perry's Scotch-Irish, p.* 11, *Worcester Inscriptions, p.* 67, *Wall's Reminiscences of Worcester, p.* 128.

Young, John, Boston, Mass.; from Ireland, with Capt. Dennis, Nov., 1719; farmer. — *Boston Rec. Com., Vol.* 13, *p.* 64.

Young, Robert, Boston, Mass.; from Great Britain, cir. 1711; int. m. Rachel Killum, Nov. 7, 1711.—*Boston Rec. Com., Vol.* 28, *p.* 91.

Young, Thomas, of Boston; from Glasgow, in 1716, on the snow "Amity."—*Boston Rec. Com., Vol.* 29, *p.* 232.

Young, William, of Worcester, Mass.; from Ireland, in 1718.—*Lincoln's Worcester, p.* 49.

Zinger, John, Boston, Mass.; from Philadelphia, May 9, 1727; warned out, July 11 (return), 1727.—*Suffolk Court Files,* 20510, *Boston Rec. Com., Vol.* 13, *p.* 168.

CORRECTION

Anthoine, Nicholas, of Marblehead, Mass.; probably son of Richard Anthoine of Philadelphia, and grandson of Richard Anthoine and his wife Sarah, who came to Philadelphia from the Isle of Jersey in 1700; Nicholas Anthoine married Rachel, not Anne Hawkes.—*Communicated by Miss Amy L. Anthoine of Portland, Maine.*

ADDENDA

Allen, Edward, of Salem, Mass.; from Berwick-on-Tweed, England, before 1759; m. Ruth Gardner, Jan. 18, 1759.—*Salem Vital Records, Vol.* 3, *p.* 404.

Armstrong, James, of Falmouth, Maine; from Ireland, before 1720; m. Mary ——; Children: Thomas, John, James.—*Portland Records, MS. in the N. E. Hist. Gen. Soc., p.* 67.

Beaver, John, to New England; from Hepworth, Yorkshire, 1699, in the "Virginia"; twenty-two years old, with seven years to serve.—*N. E. Hist. Gen. Reg., Vol.* 64, *p.* 260.

BEDENALL, Elizabeth, Newbury, Mass.; "a jearsey woman"; d. Feb. 3, 1695, in Newbury.—*Newbury Vital Records, Vol.* 2, *p.* 548.

BISHOP, Margaret, to New England; from Loughborough, Leicestershire, 1699, in the "Virginia"; twenty-five years old, with seven years to serve.—*N. E. Hist. Gen. Reg., Vol.* 64, *p.* 260.

BLAIR, Peter, Salem, Mass.; from Cockburnsmith, Great Britain, before 1752; m. Sarah Baker, of Marblehead, in Salem, Oct. 5, 1752.—*Salem Vital Records, Vol.* 3, *p.* 113.

BOLE, Peter, to New England; from Paynton, Cheshire, 1699, in the "Virginia"; twenty years old, with seven years to serve.—*N. E. Hist. Gen. Reg., Vol.* 64, *p.* 260.

BORDEN, Hope, see Edward Hankin.

BOUDRIX, Claude, of Biddeford, Maine; from Canada, after the fall of Quebec, 1759; m. ———; Children: Joseph, John, Mary, Margaret (assigned to Scarborough) and one other.—*Southgate's Scarborough, p.* 176.

BOYDELL, John, Boston, Mass.; from England, in 1716; grocer; secretary to Governor Shute; Register of Probate for Suffolk County, 1717-1739; m. Hannah; Children: Edward, John, Martha, Mary; d. Dec. 11, 1739.—*Mass. Hist. Soc., second series, Vol.* 16, *pp.* 48-52.

BOYER, Mr. James, of Boston, Mass.; from London, before 1723; a jeweller living at Mr. Eustones in Key Street, Boston; m. Marian Johonnot, June 22, 1724; Children: Peter, Susanna, James, Daniel, Peter.—*New England Courant, Dec.* 31/*Jan.* 7, 1723, *Old-Time New England, Vol.* 18, *p.* 39, *Boston Rec. Com., Vol.* 28, *p.* 160, *Vol.* 24, *pp.* 174, 180, 190, 195, 201.

BROAD, Francis, of Salem, Mass.; from England, before 1730; pub-int. to Elizabeth Barton, Aug. 29, 1730; banns forbidden as "Robt. Williams & wife can Testifie that they have often heard the said Broad say that he was a married man and had a wife and two children in England."—*Salem Vital Records, Vol. 3, p.* 138.

BROWN, John, of Salem, Mass.; from Wenyaw, South Carolina, before 1770; m. Elizabeth David, Aug. 20, 1770.—*Salem Vital Records, Vol. 3, p.* 147.

BROWNE, William, of Salem, Mass.; from Exeter, England, before 1745; m. Lydia Dart, April 27, 1745.—*Salem Publishments, p.* 38.

BROWNING, James, of Rutland, Mass.; from Scotland; b. 1672; d. Feb. 3, 1749, aged 77.—*Rutland Vital Records, p.* 217, *Rutland Inscriptions, p.* 7.

BURGISS, Mr. Abraham, Boston, Mass.; from London, England, with Captain Calif, Oct. 7, 1772.—*N. E. Hist. Ben. Reg., Vol.* 84, *p.* 360.

BURKE, William, of Salem, Mass.; from Ireland, before 1769; m. Mercy Masury, Dec. 12, 1769; Children: William, Mercy, Polly.—*Salem Vital Records, Vol.* 4, *p.* 74, *Vol.* 1, *p.* 140.

BYNG, John, of Salem, Mass.; from Portsmouth, England, 1769; m. Abigail Sarl, int. Nov. 25, 1769.—*Salem Vital Records, Vol.* 4, *p.* 286.

CAMPBELL, Daniel, of Rutland, Mass.; from Scotland, in 1716; b. cir. 1696; murdered March 8, 1744, in his 48th year, by Edward Fitzpatrick.—*Rutland Vital Records, p.* 218, *Rutland Inscriptions, p.* 10.

CAPE, Nathaniel, of Boston, Mass.; from London, before 1757; a white-smith, near the New Brick Meeting House.—*Boston Gazette, Aug.* 15, 1757, *Old-Time New England, Vol.* 18, *p.* 94.

CAREW, William, Boston, Mass.; from Barbadoes, before 1753; m. Martha Gooch, Aug. 29, 1753. — *Boston Rec. Com., Vol.* 30, *p.* 8.

CHADDOCK, James, to New England, from Rochdale, Lancashire, 1699, in the "Virginia," Edmund Ball, master; twenty-two years old, with seven years to serve.—*N. E. Hist. Gen. Reg., Vol.* 64, *p.* 259.

CHEEVOR, Rev. Israel, Boston, Mass.; from Liverpool, Nova Scotia, before 1762; m. Susannah Nichols, May 3, 1762.—*Boston Rec. Com., Vol.* 30, *p.* 46.

CLARK, James, of Rutland, Mass.; from Ireland; killed by the Indians, August 3, 1724. — *Rutland Vital Records, p.* 219.

CLARKE, James, to New England; from Newtown heath, Cheshire, 1699, in the "Virginia"; seventeen years old, with seven years to serve.—*N. E. Hist. Gen. Reg., Vol. 64, p. 260.*

CLEW, Daniel, to New England; from Manchester, Lancashire, 1699, in the "Virginia"; twenty-one years old, with seven years to serve.—*N. E. Hist. Gen. Reg., Vol. 64, p. 260.*

CLIFFORD, Benjamin, of Salem, Mass.; from Charleston, South Carolina, before 1750; m. Mrs. Dorothy Frost, int. March 17, 1750.—*Salem Vital Records, Vol. 3, p. 221.*

CLIFTON, John, of Salem, Mass.; from County Norfolk, England, before 1766; m. Elizabeth King, August 19, 1766; Child: John.—*Salem Vital Records, Vol. 1, p. 185, Vol. 3, p. 571.*

CLOWS, Daniel, to New England; from Asterfield, Staffordshire, 1699, in the "Virginia," Edmund Ball, master; twenty-three years old, with six years to serve.—*N. E. Hist. Gen. Reg., Vol. 64, p. 259.*

COLE, Robert, Newbury, Mass.; from Great Britain, before 1715; m. Abigail Tenney, of Rowley, Aug. 31, 1715, at Newbury, Mass.—*Newbury Vital Records, Vol. 2, p. 476.*

CONDY, Rev. Jeremy, Boston, Mass.; from London, England, with Captain Folger, July 3, 1761.—*N. E. Hist. Gen. Reg., Vol. 84, p. 157.*

COOK, Edward, to New England; from Hope Parish, Derbyshire, 1699, in the "Virginia"; nineteen years old, and seven years to serve.—*N. E. Hist. Gen. Reg., Vol. 64, p. 259.*

CORNISH, Captain James, of Newbury, Mass.; from Bristol, England, before 1730; m. Mrs. Mary Woodbridge, Oct. 12, 1730, d. Oct. 25, 1735; Child: Hester.—*Newbury Vital Records, Vol. 1, p. 128, Vol. 2, pp. 124, 576.*

COTTON, William, of Salem, Mass.; from York River, Virginia, in 1771; m. Hannah Cook, daughter of James Cook, Oct. 9, 1772.—*Salem Vital Records, Vol. 3, p. 247.*

CROOKSHANKS, James, of Salem Mass.; from Airth, Scotland, before 1750; m. Martha Allen, Jan. 26, 1750.—*Salem Publishments, p.* 38.

CUNNINGHAM, James, of Rutland, Mass.; from Ireland, in 1737; m. Mary ——, d. Dec. 29, 1824, aet 91; d. Feb. 20, 1786, aet 73.—*Rutland Vital Records, p.* 221.

DAVIS, Mrs. Mary, of Ipswich and Salem, Mass.; from Newfoundland, before 1756; m. Samuel White, March 8, 1756.—*Salem Vital Records, Vol.* 4, *p.* 462.

DAWSON, Mary, to New England; from Leeds, Yorkshire, 1699, in the "Virginia," Edmund Ball, master; twenty-two years old, with seven years to serve.—*N. E. Hist. Gen. Reg., Vol.* 64, *p.* 259.

DE DAMOS, Antonio, of Salem, Mass.; from Parinhu, Brazil, before 1768; m. Abigail Horton, June 7, 1768.—*Salem Vital Records, Vol.* 3, *p.* 519.

DELLEWARE, Anna, Newbury, Mass.; from France, before 1768; m. Amos Le Favour, Dec. 25, 1768.—*Marblehead Vital Records, Vol.* 2, *p.* 260.

DENECORE, Joseph, of Arundel, Maine; from Canada, after the fall of Quebec, 1759; m. ——; Child.—*Southgate's Scarborough, p.* 176.

DONOVAN, Dennis, Boston, Mass.; in Boston, before 1745; m. Jean Dicky, Nov. 5, 1745.—*Boston Rec. Com., Vol.* 28, *p.* 340.

DOUSSET, Francis, of York, Maine; from Canada, after the fall of Quebec, 1759; m. ——; Children: nine. —*Southgate's Scarborough, p.* 176.

ELLISON, Mr. Abraham, Boston, Mass.; from London, England, with Captain Calef, Oct. 7, 1772.—*N. E. Hist. Gen. Reg., Vol.* 84, *p.* 360.

ERSKIN, Christopher, of Bridgewater, Mass., from Ireland in 1729; m. Susanna Robinson or Robertson, daughter of Gain Robertson, q. v.—*N. E. Hist. Gen. Reg.,* 1845, *p.* 13.

FAUX, Edward, to New England; from Flint, Wales, 1699, in the "Virginia"; nineteen years old, with seven years to serve.—*N. E. Hist. Gen. Reg., Vol.* 64, *p.* 260.

GLEDDALE, Mary, to New England; from Hepworth, Yorkshire, 1699, in the "Virginia," Edmund Ball, master; twenty years old, with seven years to serve. —*N. E. Hist. Gen. Reg., Vol.* 64, *p.* 259.

GLOVER, Edward, to New England; from Manchester, Lancashire, 1699, in the "Virginia"; twenty years old, with seven years to serve.—*N. E. Hist. Gen. Reg., Vol.* 64, *p.* 260.

GRAY, John, of Biddeford, Maine (see before); from London, England, in 1716; the son of Joseph Gray, linen draper, of London; m. Elizabeth Tarbox; Children: Elizabeth, Mary, Olive. — *N. E. Hist. Gen. Reg., Vol.* 71, *p.* 211.

HARVEY, James, of Haverhill, Mass., and Derry, N. H.; from Ireland, 1726; m. Ann ———; Children: Robert, Rachel, Thomas, Margaret, Grizel, Rose, Mary, Elizabeth; d. May 4, 1742.—*McCrillis MS., pp.* 31, 32.

KING, John, of Kittery, Maine; from Canada, after the fall of Quebec, 1759; m. ———; Children: eight.— *Southgate's Scarborough, p.* 176.

LABLANC, Paul, of Falmouth, Maine; from Canada, after the fall of Quebec, 1759; m. ———; Children: eleven. —*Southgate's Scarborough, p.* 176.

LEBLAND, Francis, of Needham, Mass.; "French neutrals" from Canada; m. Margaret ———; Children: Peter, Simon, Sibbel (sent to Boston), Ann (sent to Stoughton), (there seem to have been eleven children in all, four of whom stayed in Needham, and seven who were sent to Stoughton).—*Clarke's History of Needham, pp.* 555, 556.

McDONALD, Patrick, of Salem, Mass., from Ireland; m. the widow Abigail Gilpin, Feb. 18, 1748.—*Salem Publishments. p.* 38.

LEWIS, Maudlin, to New England, from Carmarthen, Wales, 1699, in the "Virginia"; fifteen years old, with seven years to serve.—*N. E. Hist. Gen. Reg., Vol.* 64, *p.* 260.

MITCHELL, John, of Wells, Maine; from Canada, after the fall of Quebec, 1759; m. ———; Children: four. —*Southgate's Scarborough, p.* 176.

INDEX

Aberlock, John, 149.
Abott, Abitt, James, 52.
  Sarah, 157.
Achorn, ——, 211.
Adams, Agnes, 33.
  Esther, 42.
  Hester, 19.
  Jannet, 37.
  Thomas, 19.
Aiken, Anna, 164.
  Margaret, 74.
Albee, Ann, 109.
Alcock, Anna, 73.
Alcott, Elizabeth, 99.
Alexander, Jeanette, 190.
  Margaret, 74.
  Mary, 46, 166.
Allen, Edward, 219.
  Martha, 223.
Allison, Catherine, 140.
  Jane, 54.
Alman, Philip, 43.
Anderson, Martha, 138.
Andrews, Elizabeth, 190.
Anthoine, Nicholas, 219.
  Richard, 219.
  Sarah, 219.
Apthorp and Hancock, 7, 43, 60, 64, 98, 215.
Arbuckle, Elizabeth, 153.
Archibald, Matthew, 61.
Armstrong, James, 219.
  John, 219.
  Mary, 219.
  Sarah, 52.
  Thomas, 219.
Arnold, Capt., 56.
  Benedict, 6, 56.
  Seth, 30.
Arrixson, Mary, 66.
Arwin, George, 57.
Ashwell, Isabella, 66.
Asten, Thomas, 20.
Atkinson, Elizabeth, 180.
Atwood, Capt., 173.
Ayres, Isabella, 114.

Baird, Jeanette, 29.
Baker, Frances, 180.
  Sarah, 159, 220.
Ball, Edmund, 90, 99, 100, 139, 147, 152, 160, 192, 195, 204, 213, 221-224.
  Hannah, 67.
  Joanna, 91.
Ballock, Jane, 161.
Bancroft, George, 205.
Banfield, Mary, 190.
Barnard, Annis, 205.
  Sarah, 93.
Barnett, Annis, 205.
  James, 135.
Barr, Beatress, 12.
  Jennet, 59.
  John, 96.
  Matthew, 59.
Bartlett, Lydia, 157.
  Mary, 56.
Barton, Elizabeth, 220.
Bason, Mary, 55.
Bass, Priscilla, 164.
Batt, Sarah, 59.
Beal, Mary, 25.
Beard, Capt., 167, 205.
Beath, Jennett, 65.
  Walter, 65.
Beauchamp, Beauchamp, Katherine, 109.
  Marian, 109.
  Mary, 161.
Beaver, John, 219.
Bedenall, Elizabeth, 220.
Bedonah, Lydia, 41.
  Thomas, 41.
Belknap, Jane, 136.
Bell, Jane, 218.
  John, 164.
  Letitia, 53.
  Mary, 153, 164.
  Sarah, 12.

Beney, John, 212.
Beninton, Sarah, 71.
Benson, Anna, 175.
  Parthenia, 158.
Bent, Capt., 175.
Benuit, Margaret, 187.
Berry, Cartwright, 194.
  Elizabeth, 172.
  Mary, 172.
  Mehitable, 189.
Bishop, Elizabeth, 43.
  Margaret, 220.
Bixby, Solomon, 34.
Black, Elinor, 50.
  Martha, 28.
Blackston, Mary, 17.
Blackwood, Mary, 178.
Blair, ——, 122.
  Abraham, 197.
  Elizabeth, 208.
  Hannah, 197.
  John, 31.
  Lydia, 189.
  Mary, 8, 117, 208.
  Peter, 220.
  Robert, 208, 209.
  Sarah B., 220.
  William, 8, 76.
Blake, Jane, 175.
Bleigh, Ann, 203.
Blood, ——, 46.
  Abigail, 153.
  Ebenezer, 153.
Boarn, Joanna, 146.
Bole, Peter, 220.
Bolton, Thomas, 41.
Bonaparte, Jerome, 16, 18.
Bond, Capt., 115.
  Susan, 54.
Boon, Sarah, 54.
Borden, Hope, 82, 220.
  Joseph, 82.
Boudrix, Claude, 220.
  John, 220.
  Joseph, 220.
  Margaret, 220.
  Mary, 220.

(225)

INDEX

Boulderson, Elizabeth, 62.
Bourn, Joanna, 146.
Bowdoin, Sarah, 141.
Bowen, Elizabeth, 39
Mary, 67.
Boyce, Mary, 23, 72.
Samuel, 23.
Boyd, Andrew, 76.
Martha, 218.
Mary, 132, 217.
Robert, 189.
Boydell, Edward, 220.
Hannah, 220.
John, 220.
Martha, 220.
Mary, 220.
Boyden, Mehitable, 6.
Boyer, Daniel, 220.
James, 220.
Marion J., 220.
Peter, 220.
Susanna, 220.
Boyle, Margaret, 117, 118.
Boyleston, Joanna, 108.
Bradbury, Anne, 106.
Bradford, Hannah, 193.
Bradley, Elizabeth, 3.
Breens, Sarah, 23.
Brewer, John, 171.
Brewster, Mary, 210.
Briard, Abigail, 44.
Brickett, Elizabeth, 104.
Brickley, Bathsheba, 64.
Bridge, Bridges, Esther, 47.
Samuel, 189.
Sarah, 84.
Brinley, Deborah, 144.
Britton, Brittain, Mary, 207.
Ruth, 129.
Broad, Francis, 220.
Brooks, Elizabeth, 162.
William, 93.
Broughton, Elizabeth, 92.

Broughton, Sarah, 167.
Brown, Browne, Elizabeth D., 221.
George, 6.
Hannah, 110, 211.
Isabella, 134.
John, 134, 221.
Joseph, 149.
Louisa, 126.
Lydia D., 221.
Margaret, 108.
Margery, 192.
Martha, 105.
Rebecca, 205.
Sybella, 134.
Walter, 180.
William, 221.
Brownell, George, 200.
Pleasant, 200.
Browning, James, 221.
Brunton, Capt., 74.
Buckingham, Jonas, 119.
Temperance, 26.
Bull, Elizabeth, 159.
Burgiss, Abraham, 221.
Burke, Mercy, 221.
Mercy M., 221.
Polly, 221.
William, 221.
Burnside, Margaret, 125.
Burpee, Hepsibah, 112.
Burt, Esther, 158.
Buskby, Christian, 35.
Bussell, Jane, 156.
Buzwell, Mehitable, 93.
Byles, Josias, 15.
Byng, Abigail S., 221.
John, 221.

Caldwell, Agnes, 190.
Calef, Calif, Capt., 221, 223.
Calhoun, Samuel, 80.
Callender, ——, 198.
Calwell, Callwell, Hannah, 207.
Jane, 123.

Calverly, Elizabeth, 214.
Calzik, David, 29.
Cameron, Janette, 118.
Campbell, Daniel, 62. 221.
Elizabeth, 94.
John, 94.
Margaret, 130.
Mary, 72.
Mollie, 106.
Sarah, 19, 122.
Cannon, Sarah, 182.
Cape, Nathaniel, 221.
Carew, Martha G., 221.
William, 221.
Cargil, Cargill, Annis, 134.
Janet, 78.
Marion, 133.
Maryann, 133.
Carlisle, Lettice, 125.
Carlton, Elsie, 68.
Carmack, Elener, 72.
Carn, Olive, 210.
Carr, Jane, 12.
Carroll, Carrell, John, 26, 32, 107, 159.
Nathaniel, 70.
Carson, ——, 61.
Carter, Jane, 37.
Carver, Elizabeth, 178.
Caswell, Margaret, 65.
Cavalear, Mary, 92.
Chaddock, James, 221.
Chandler, Lucretia, 144.
Chopin, Eliza, 199.
Chapman, Lydia, 171.
Chard, Sarah, 203.
Chardon, Ann, 48.
Chase, Sarah, 7.
Cheever, Cheevor, Chever, Israel, 221.
Lydia, 56.
Susannah N., 221.
Childs, Elizabeth, 71.
Christie, Margaret, 130.

INDEX

Churchill, Martha, 105.
Cinae, Dinish, 32.
Clap, Margaret, 35.
Clark, Clarke, ——, 54, 66.
Eliza, 207.
Elizabeth, 185.
James, 221, 222.
Jane, 163.
Philadelphia, 17.
Rachel, 41.
Sarah, 85, 161.
Clay, Elizabeth, 30.
Clayland, Elizabeth, 35.
Clement, Agnes, 135.
Clew, Daniel, 222.
Clifford, Benjamin, 222.
Dorothy F., 222.
Clifton, Elizabeth K., 222.
John, 222.
Clogstone, Miriam, 70.
Cloutman, Elizabeth, 132.
Clows, Daniel, 222.
Cobb, Deborah, 31.
Elizabeth, 107.
Isabella, 168.
Cochran, Cochrane, Cockran, Ann, 168, 215.
Barbary, 206.
Janet, 134, 145.
Jean, 2, 137.
Letitia, 34.
Margaret, 2.
Cole, Abigail T., 222.
Robert, 222.
Collar, Priscilla, 66.
Collins, Sarah, 159.
Combs, Combes, Anna, 48.
Elizabeth, 48.
John, 48.
Condy, Jeremy, 222.
Connor, Polly, 40.
Cony, Susanna, 93.
Cook, Edward, 222.
Elisha, 214.
Hannah, 222.
James, 222.
Jean, 63.
Sarah, 73.
Cookson, Wm., 7, 43, 60, 64, 98, 215.
Coolbroth, Susannah, 63.
Cooper, Sarah, 64.
Copley, Mary, 155.
Copstick, Susanna, 153.
Cornish, Hester, 222.
James, 222.
Mary W., 222.
Cotton, Hannah, 222.
Sarah, 146.
William, 222.
Cowdin, Thomas, 76.
Craige, Craig, Agnes, 195.
Hannah, 40.
James, 40.
Janet, 40.
Jean, 4.
Mary, 16, 18.
Craighead, Janet, 20.
Katherine, 90.
Cranch, Mary, 151.
Crane, Jerusha, 136.
Crawford, Margaret, 107.
Rose, 137.
William, 13.
Critchfeeld, Silence, 143.
Crookshanks, James, 223.
Martha A., 223.
Cross, George, 53.
Lydia, 113.
Margaret, 52, 53.
Crossett, Margaret, 41, 190.
Cummings, Annie, 97.
Francis, 46, 197.
Molly, 9.
Cunningham, Catherine, 96.
James, 223.
Mary, 223.
William, 61.
Curtice, Hannah, 192.
Cushing, Hannah, 87.
Cutler, John, 189.
Ruth, 189.
Daggett, Jemima, 26.
Daley, Sarah, 181.
Dalrymple, Margaret, 103.
Daniels, Joanna, 103.
Darrow, Elizabeth, 174.
Dart, Lydia, 221.
David, Elizabeth, 221.
Davis, Dorothy, 38.
John, 159.
Mary, 40, 223.
Rebecca, 44.
Sarah, 194.
Dawson, Mary, 223.
Deags, Barbara, 77.
Dean, Josiah, 24.
Mary, 24.
Ruth, 24.
De Damos, Abigail, 223.
Antonio, 223.
Defew, Rachel, 59.
Dellerware, Anna, 223.
Demerick, Capt., 214.
Dench, Capt., 202.
Denecore, Joseph, 223.
Deneford, Elizabeth, 81.
Denett, Elizabeth, 81.
Dennis, Capt., 3, 5, 19, 42, 43, 53, 72, 74, 82, 87, 109, 131, 154, 155, 158, 218, 219.
Derby, Polly, 79.
Deshon, Susannah, 181.
Devett, Sarah, 118.
Dew, Nathaniel, 98.
De Wose, Capt., 109.
Dickey, Dickie, Elizabeth, 13.
Jane, 136.
Jean, 223.
John, 49.
Margaret, 98.
Mary, 74.
Nancy, 49.
Dickinson, Mary, 144.
Dillarock, Eliza, 19.

228 INDEX

Dillarock, Philip, 19.
Dinsmore, Elizabeth, 91.
Ditchfield, Margrait, 166.
Dixson, Edward, 94.
Dobbin, Polly, 132.
Dodge, Mary, 193.
Donovan, Dennis, 223.
Jean D., 223.
Dousset, Francis, 223.
Douglas, Capt., 71.
Draper, Rachel, 158.
Drumer, Mary, 87.
Drummond, Frances, 28.
Duncan, Anna, 162.
Dunkin, John, 53.
Dunlap, ——, 161.
Mary, 85.
Dunnell, Sarah, 86.
Dunsmoor, William, 137.
Dupee, Martha, 68.
Duty, Mehitable, 81.
Dyer, Hannah, 169.

Eastwick, Grizzell, 5.
Eaton, Elizabeth, 82.
Edwards, Barbara, 1.
Jane, 176.
John, 55.
Egbear, Elizabeth, 146.
Ela, David, 61.
Eliot, Eliott, Elliott, Martha, 113.
Richard, 137.
Sarah, 189.
Ellery, Mary, 110.
Ellis, Mary, 217.
Richard, 86, 126.
Ellison, Abraham, 223.
Ellsworth, Elizabeth, 195.
Elton, Mary, 108.
Emery, Elizabeth, 212.
Erickson, Mary, 66.
Erskin, Christopher, 223.

Erskin, Susanna R., 223.
Erwin, Jane, 179.
Eustone, ——, 220.
Evans, Mary, 78.
Eves, Capt., 9, 22, 180.
Eyres, Mary, 189.

Fairfield, Elizabeth, 136.
Farrand, Andrew, 154.
Farrar, Farrah, Bethiah, 210.
Hepzibah, 51.
Farrell, Robert, 57.
Faulkner, Mary, 213.
Faux, Edward, 223.
Ferguson, Ann, 168.
Isabel, 107.
James, 6.
Fisher, Elizabeth, 128.
Fitzgerald, Jane, 175.
John, 62.
Martha, 62.
Fitzpatrick, Edward, 28, 221.
Flagg, Ebenezer, 56.
Sarah, 57.
Flanders, Jacob, 16, 17.
Tabitha, 16, 17.
Flint, Capt., 108.
Florence, Charles, 108.
Flowers, Charles, 110.
Floyd, Maria, 214.
Folger, Capt., 222.
Foosheron, Anna, 98.
Ford, Mary, 182.
Foss, Hannah, 173.
Foster, ——, 86, 126.
Elizabeth, 122, 128.
John, 71.
Margaret, 4.
Mary, 217.
William, 83.
Fowler, Mary, 159.
Freeland, Rachel, 106.
Frost, Dorothy, 222.
Frothingham, Dorothy, 160, 209.

Fullerton, Jean, 140.
Margaret, 11.
Wm., 11.
Fulton, Elizabeth, 14.
Furber, Elizabeth, 50.

Gaat, ——, 68.
Galloway, Isabella, 66.
Galt, ——, 68.
Gamble, Mary, 187.
Gardner, Ruth, 219.
Garrison, William Lloyd, 114.
Gaskill, Mary, 82.
Gautier, Mary, 63.
Gedney, Naomi, 202.
Gerrish, Capt., 8.
Gezer, Earnestian, 192.
Gibbons, Hannah, 66.
Gibbs, ——, 8.
Gilchrist, Samuel, 209.
Gileris, Annie, 145.
Giles, John, 119.
Gilmore, Margaret, 128.
Gilpin, Abigail, 128, 224.
Girton, Mary, 84.
Gleddale, Mary, 224.
Glenn, Martha, 123.
Glidden, Hulda, 201.
Glover, Edward, 224.
Glyn, Martha, 123.
Godfrey, Sarah, 150.
Godstead, Anna, 163.
Gold, James, 171.
Gooch, Martha, 221.
Goodin, Gooding, Edward, 83, 88.
Edwin, 69.
Mary, 47.
Goodman, Elizabeth, 82.
Goose, Elizabeth, 62.
Gordon, Gordin, Betsey, 176.
Janet, 164, 165.
Joanna, 60.
William, 118.
Gott, ——, 68.
Gouchy, Susanne, 27.

INDEX

Gove, Elizabeth, 82.
Hannah, 144.
Graham, Esther, 64.
Margaret, 63.
Mary, 42, 63.
Grapes, Elizabeth, 174.
Gray, Anna, 214.
Anne, 83.
Easter, 91.
Elinour, 130.
Elizabeth, 128.
Elizabeth T., 224.
Experience, 40.
Jean, 102.
John, 224.
Joseph, 224.
Mary, 15, 134, 224.
Matthew, 102, 130.
Olive, 224.
Rebecca, 130.
Sarah, 8.
Susannah, 60.
William, 15.
Greeley, John, 217.
Green, Jonathan, 66.
Gregg, Gragg, Elizabeth, 89.
John, 78.
Margaret, 89, 175.
Griffin, Jean, 59.
Simon, 23.
Susanna, 29.
Griffiths, Griffeth, Capt., 37.
Easter, 217.
Grimstone, Eliza, 190.
Grindle, Sarah, 182.
Gross, Arenstein, 213.
Mary, 89.
Gurney, Elizabeth, 114.
Gyles, Elizabeth, 156.

Hackvathin, Christian Solony, 192.
Hahn, Hans George, 148.
Margaret, 165.
Haise, Stephen, 182.
Hale, Sarah, 175.
Hall, Daniel, 10.
Elisha, 58.
Elizabeth, 122.
Henry, 89.
Hall, Jane, 101.
Mary, 89.
Percival, 122.
Stephen, 110.
Halyday, ——, 86.
Ham, Mercy, 18.
Hamberton, Priscilla, 142.
Hamilton, Hambleton, Eleanor, 173.
Frances, 155.
John, 86.
Martha, 44.
Mary, 124, 173.
Hancock, Handcock, ——, 110.
Mary, 97, 110.
Hankin, Edward, 220.
Hardwick, John Peter, 82.
Hardwig, Elizabeth, 22.
Harkness, Jane, 218.
Mary, 112.
Harper, Hepsibar, 218.
Rachel, 72.
Harper, ——, 175.
Harrington, John, 136.
Harris, Elizabeth, 199.
John, 40.
Hart, Bathshaba, 64.
Katherin, 48.
Harvey, Ann, 85, 126, 224.
Dorothy, 154.
Elizabeth, 224.
Grizel, 224.
James, 126, 224.
John, 154.
Margaret, 126, 224.
Mary, 224.
Rachel, 224.
Robert, 224.
Rose, 224.
Thomas, 224.
Haskell, Andrew, 129.
Haston, Rebecca, 122.
Hatch, Mehitable, 96.
Hathorne, ——, 13.
Hawes, James, 53.
Hawkes, Anne, 5, 219.
Rachel, 219.
Hay, Margaret, 126.
Haynes, Mary, 181.
Hazen, Mary, 172.
Richard, 172.
Heath, Mary, 170.
Henderson, Margaret, 4.
Hendery, Malcam, 119.
Hennesy, James, 61.
Henry, Jane, 122.
John, 86, 126.
Margaret, 140.
Mary, 74, 141, 142, 217.
Hepworth, Elizabeth, 112.
Heselton, ——, 9.
Hetton, Ann, 114.
Hewet, Grace, 157.
Hicks, Mary, 74.
Rose, 147.
Hildreth, Ephraim, 87.
Hill, Dorothy, 69.
Mary Langdon Storer, 124.
Hilt, Margaret, 116.
Hinds, Elizabeth, 52.
Hinsdale, Mary, 11.
Hitchcock, Abigail, 5.
Hix, Sarah, 55.
Hodgkins, Deborah, 175.
Holgrave, John, 90.
Holmes, Homes, John, 103.
Mary, 103, 139, 140.
William, 98, 122.
Holt, Rebecca, 79.
Holton, Susanna, 1.
Hooper, ——, 186.
Mary, 186.
Hopkins, Experience, 149.
Horton, Abigail, 223.
Houdlette, Louis, 31.
Howard, Jane, 64.
Mary, 105.
Hudson, Dorcas, 21.
Huggins, Mercy, 97.

INDEX

Hughs, Bethia, 98.
Hull, Elizabeth, 84.
Hume, Janet, 74.
Humphrey, James, 61.
 Jane, 29.
 Jannet, 29.
Hunking, Mary, 51.
Hunt, Mercy, 79, 105.
Hunter, Alice, 21.
Huntington, Capt., 88.
 Sarah, 213.
Huston, ——, 55.
Hutchins, Hutchings, Elizabeth, 185.
 Mary, 195.

Jackson, Elizabeth, 71.
 Hannah, 192.
 Mary, 157.
 Sarah, 101.
James, Eliner, 185.
Jamison, Mary, 158.
Jarvott, Rachel, 216.
Jefferds, Susanna, 94.
Jerould, James, 68.
Johnson, Ann, 59.
 Florence, 153.
 Issable, 30.
 Susannah, 99.
Johonnot, Marion, 220.
Joiner, Susanna, 165.
Jones, Anna, 172.
 Elizabeth, 26.
 Jonathan, 26.
Joslin, Susanna, 24.

Kaler, Catherine Elizabeth, 116.
Karr, ——, 2.
Keel, Sarah, 86.
Keen, Mary, 147.
Kellock, ——, 100.
Kellyhorn, Katherine, 38.
Kelsey, Jane, 141.
 Jean, 126.
 Margaret, 126.
 William, 126.
Kelso, Agnes, 69.
 Ann, 102.
 Margaret, 28.
Kendall, James, 103.

Kennedy, Elizabeth, 49.
 Jane, 113.
 Mary Ann, 70.
Kenney, John, 125.
 Tabitha, 39.
Kilgore, Lily, 36.
Killum, Rachel, 219.
King, Elizabeth, 222.
 John, 224.
 Margaret, 88.
 Martha, 106.
Kinsell, ——, 211.
Kive, Sarah, 172.
Klaus, Polly, 88.
Knock, Mary, 209.
Knot, Susana, 79.
Kraus, ——, 44.

Lablanc, Paul, 224.
Lambeth, Mary, 56, 153.
Lang, Elizabeth, 211.
Langdon, John, 3.
Larrabee, Elizabeth, 143.
 Isabel, 10.
 Samuel, 10.
Lavers, Ellenor, 180.
Law, Anna, 151.
Lawless, Mary, 114.
Lawrence, Hannah, 27.
 John, 198.
Layton, Hannah, 199.
Lebland, Ann, 224.
 Francis, 224.
 Margaret, 224.
 Peter, 224.
 Sibbel, 224.
 Simon, 224.
Leby, Agnis, 22.
Lee, Grace, 142.
Le Favour, Amos, 223.
 Anna, 223.
Le Grow, Rebekah, 5.
Leishman, John, 89, 105.
Leitch, Elizabeth, 42.
Lewis, Alice, 26.
 Elizabeth, 147.
 Lucy, 81.
 Lydia, 160.
 Maudlin, 224.
 Sarah, 143, 173.

Libby, Lydia, 142.
 Rhoda, 141.
Lillie, Capt., 102.
Lindsey, Lindsay, Janet, 205.
 Margaret, 194.
Linehan, Elizabeth, 50.
Linsley, Lydia, 104.
Lithcoo, Margaret, 133.
Lithgow, Susanna, 144.
 William, 144.
Little, Abiah, 193.
 Eunice, 160.
 Jane, 65.
 Thomas, 35.
Livingston, Mary, 30.
Logan, Elizabeth, 61.
Love, Robert, 15.
Lowder, Capt., 202.
Lucy, Cathrine, 214.
 Elizabeth, 32.
Lunt, Judith, 151.
Lyde, Catherine, 22.
 Deborah, 22.
 Edward, 22.
Lym, John, 21.
Lynde, Benjamin, 89.
Lyndhurst, ——, 39.

McAffee, Ann, 69.
McAlister, Maccalester, Martha Ann, 139.
 Mary, 193.
McCarter, Maccarter, Margaret, 86.
 Rebecca, 60.
 William, 119.
McCartney, Margaret, 46.
McClanathan, Elizabeth, 144.
McClellan, McClellam, McLellan, Cary, 121.
 Elizabeth, 121.
 Hugh, 41, 152.
 James, 41.
 Jane, 152.
 Jeannette, 196.
 John, 98.
 Margaret, 209.
 Mary, 158.

INDEX

McClintin, William, 123.
McCloud, Jennett, 14.
McClure, David, 71.
Jean, 65.
McCobb, Isabella, 168.
McColley, Margaret, 143.
McCollo, Margaret, 136.
McConnell, Jane, 148.
McCordy, Elizabeth, 27.
McCormack, Elsie, 101.
McCrellis, McCrillis, Martha, 141.
Mary, 86, 217.
McCulloch, Sarah, 110.
McCurdy, Catherine, 183.
Jane, 113.
McDaniel, Sarah, 60.
McDonald, Abigail G., 224.
Patrick, 224.
McFadden, Andrew, 54.
McFarland, Duncan, 119.
Elenor, 91.
George, 131.
Martha, 102.
McGathery, Robert, 132.
McGlauthlin, ——, 153.
McGregor, James, 34, 129, 189, 193.
Margaret, 28.
McHenry, Jane, 96.
McIntire, Mary, 210.
McKean, McKeen, Elizabeth, 145.
J., 46.
James, 145.
Janet, 145.
Jennie, 36.
MacKertney, Elizabeth, 37.
McKinney, Elizabeth, 197.
McKinstrey, John, 13.
McKnight, ——, 175.
McKolney, Margery, 130.
McLean, J., 186.
Mary, 33.
McMaster, Jno., 60.
McMurphy, Isabel, 199.
Jean, 199.
McNear, Margaret, 111.
McNeil, Adam, 58.
Catherine, 58.
Martha, 170.
Macpheden, Sarah, 141.
McPherson, Ann, 9.
McQuaid, Jane, 25.
McQuesten, McQuisten, Anna, 26.
David, 61.
Maddin, Sarah, 38.
Mahier, Richard, 63.
Malcolm, Anne, 4.
Mallard, Priscilla, 167.
Malvern, Pasco, 148.
Mann, Man, Anna, 39.
Elinor, 87.
Manning, Hannah, 148.
Mansfield, Margaret, 179.
Paul, 179.
Marr, John, 56.
Marrow, Mary, 104.
Marshall, Em, 186.
Emme, 63.
Marston, Abigail, 27.
Benjamin, 27.
Martin, Martyn, Deborah, 188.
Sarah, 73.
Mason, Anna, 100.
Elizabeth, 39.
Masury, Mercy, 221.
Mauer, John, 176.
Maule, Thomas, 103.
Maxwell, Maxwill, Ann, 126.
Hannah, 65.
Mayheer, Richard, 63.
Maynard, Elizabeth, 92.
Simon, 92.
Means, Mary, 152.
Robert, 152.
Meder, Lydia, 55.
Meek, Alice, 110.
Meinzeis, John, 143.
Melendy, Hepzibah, 60.
Melony, Martha, 49.
Meriam, Abigaiel, 204.
Merrill, Damaris, 67.
Merrow, Martha, 62.
Mickleroy, Mary, 82.
Miers, Peter, 194.
Mighill, Margaret, 46.
Milborn, Mary, 171.
Mill, Thomas, 212.
Miller, Millar, Alice, 210.
Anne, 117, 118.
Archibald, 180.
Hannah Nickels, 124.
Jance, 65.
Janet, 23.
Mary, 83, 118, 119, 180.
Sarah, 85.
Mills, Anna, 200.
Mary, 201.
Tamozine, 85.
Miltmore, Priscilla, 153.
Mitchell, Mitchill, Eleanor, 73.
Elizabeth, 73.
Janet, 163.
John, 224.
Larance, 73.
Lettice, 33.
Martha, 99, 164.
Ruth, 137.
Tabitha, 33, 214.
Monks, George, 162.
Montgomery, Capt., 172.
Agnis, 80.
Anne, 144.
Mary, 51.
Robert, 31, 144, 152.
Moodey, Hannah, 116.

INDEX

Moodey, John, 181.
Moore, Moor, Moer,
  Beatrix, 198.
  Elizabeth, 89.
  Hugh, 89.
  Isaac, 150.
  Isabella, 14.
  James, 89.
  Jane, 32.
  Joanna, 60.
  John, 198.
  Margaret, 124.
  Mary, 26, 89.
  Sarah, 156.
  Thomas, 89.
  William, 89.
Mooty, Elizabeth, 128.
Morecock, Amy, 207.
Moreton, Matthew, 139.
Morey, Mary, 208.
  Thomas, 208.
Morrill, Morrell, Abigail, 213.
  Rachel, 170.
Morris, Martha, 44.
Morrison, Morison,
  Hugh, 126.
  Jane, 138.
  Jenny, 91.
  Martha, 188.
  Mary, 90.
  Samuel, 139, 188.
Morse, Lydia, 56.
  Mary, 136.
Morton, Martha, 69.
Moses, Thomas, 155.
Mould, Capt., 58.
Moulton, Hannah, 182.
Mounier, Jeanne, 158.
Moxey, Elizabeth, 217.
  Henry, 217.
Mugeridge, Mary, 115.
Mullican, Mary, 121.
Munden, Judith, 161.
Murray, Jean, 144, 162.
  John, 162.
Murriner, Mary, 68, 75.
Muzzey, ——, 39.

Nason, Sarah, 50.
Nazro, Dr., 12, 67.
Neal, Joseph, 53.
  Martha, 53.
Needham, Mary, 45, 55.
Neilson, Rachel, 198.
Neland, Abigail, 124.
Nesbe, Sarah, 157.
Nevins, Mary, 78.
Newberry, Newbery,
  Martha, 46.
  Mary, 38.
Newbit, Abigail, 91.
Newman, Abigail, 202.
Newton, Hannah, 116.
Nexon, Mary, 162.
Nicholas, Katherine, 171.
  Eleanor, 187.
  Elizabeth, 79, 187.
  Susannah, 221.
Nicholson, Elizabeth, 106.
Norcott, Patience, 119.
Norman, Elizabeth, 55.
  John, 55.
  Sara, 55.
Norris, Capt., 6.
North, Lydia, 39.
Norton, Susanna, 120.

Oakes, Edward, 6.
Odell, Capt., 65.
Olkerson, Elizabeth, 210.
Ordway, Mehitable, 217.
Orne, Anna, 27.
  Joseph, 27.
Orr, Margaret, 132.
  Mary, 182, 208, 209.
  Samuel, 42.
Osborn, Capt., 1.
Osgood, Abigail, 30.
Otis, David, 103.
Oysterbanks, Mary, 11.

Paden, Anie, 112.
Paige, ——, 5.

Paine, Pain, Elizabeth, 187.
  William, 162.
Palmer, Esther, 44.
Parkhill, ——, 184.
Parlin, John, 136.
Parrington, Sarah, 211.
Parsons, Sarah, 139.
Partridge, Mary, 137.
  Rachel, 67.
Patrick, Mary, 129.
Patten, Elizabeth, 181.
  Letitia, 36.
  Nancy, 49.
Patterson, ——, 154.
  Agnes, 166.
  Anne, 166.
  Elizabeth, 16, 18.
  Paul, Hannah, 77.
Peard, Samuel, 11.
Pearson, John, 40.
  Mary, 40.
Pease, Mary, 143.
Pebbels, Sarah, 127.
Peck, Sarah, 191.
Peggee, Bethiah, 80.
Peiret, Susannah, 74.
Peirse, Mehitable, 173.
Pemberton, Hannah, 56.
Pereway, Mary, 170.
Perkins, Abiel, 126.
  Mary, 49.
  Thomas, 126.
Perks, Stephen, 93.
Perry, Elizabeth, 101.
Peters, John, 211.
Phicket, Sarah, 194.
Philbrick, Tryphena, 172.
Philpot, Capt., 69.
Pickman, Abigail, 56.
  Anna, 143.
Pico, Susanna, 103.
Pierce, Rebecca, 129.
Pilkenton, Mercy, 149.
Pilsbury, Ann, 25.
Pinkerton, Mary, 119
Pitman, Ruth, 116.
  Sarah, 154.
Pitts, ——, 52.
  Capt., 45.

INDEX

Player, Eliza, 93.
Plumb, Samuel, 10.
Susanna, 10.
Pollard, Margaret, 182.
Polloy, Mary, 217.
Pope, Margaret, 95.
Porter, Capt., 64, 160.
Elizabeth, 57.
Porterfield, Catherine, 182.
Powell, Mary, 19.
Prance, Sarah, 180.
Press, Elizabeth, 18.
Pressy, Sarah, 207.
Preston, Elizabeth, 17.
Mary, 161.
Susanna, 151.
Prindle, Sarah, 110.
Proctor, Eliza, 54.
Puffer, Ruth, 51.
Pullen, Elizabeth, 156.
Pulsafer, Margaret, 119.
Pursley, Mary, 190.
Pushard, Jean, 157.

Quick, Charity, 159.

Rainey, Robert, 149.
Ralston, Alexander, 27.
Rand, Elizabeth, 77.
Randall, John, 210.
Ranger, Mary, 95.
Rankin, David, 14.
Esther, 35.
Isabella, 14.
Joan, 44.
Rattliff, Ratleif, Eunice, 51.
Jane, 198.
Ray, Elizabeth, 88.
Redmond, William, 72.
Reed, Andrew, 144.
Anna, 178.
Henry, 110, 127.
Jean, 144.
Remilly, Catherine, 201.
Rich, Susana, 23.
Richardson, Hepzibah, 51.

Ridgeway, Samuel, 202.
Riggs, Rachel, 155.
Rijan, Joan, 102.
Rittal, Sally, 195.
Roach, John Walter, 107.
Roberts, Ann, 70.
Anna Barbary, 213.
Mary, 142.
Robinson, Robertson, Elizabeth, 176.
Gain, 223.
Isabella, 85.
Joseph, 176.
Margaret, 166.
Susanna, 223.
Rogers, Beatrice, 124.
George, 124.
Martha, 123.
Sarah, 146.
Ross, Walter, 187.
Rowell, Elsie, 39.
Russell, Abigail, 39.

Samuel, Elizabeth, 130.
Sandlin, Anna, 94.
Sante, Hannah, 57.
Sarl, Abigail, 221.
Sastero, Dorothy, 109.
Saulter, Sarah, 182.
Saunders, Sanders, ———, 55.
Anna Mary, 89.
Mary, 204.
Savage, Capt., 185.
Edward, 119, 144.
Hannah, 185.
John, 81.
Margaret, 190.
Scarlet, Hannah, 77.
Schenk, Sophia, 62.
Scott, Janet, 196.
Margaret, 66.
Robert, 196.
Scribner, Martha, 167.
Seadon, Sarah, 24.
Seaford, Joan, 9.
Sever, Hannah, 78.
Susan, 177.
Seward, John, 51.
Mary, 179.

Shackford, Elizabeth, 199.
Mary, 177.
Shaddock, Elenor, 53.
Shapley, Betsy, 158.
Sharp, Elizabeth, 77.
Shaw, Martha, 119.
Seth, 57.
Sheehan, Catherine, 116.
Sheffield, Nathaniel, 87.
Sigourney, Susanna, 22.
Simonds, Simons, Mary, 100.
Sarah, 112.
Sinclair, Elizabeth, 171.
Singleton, John, 39.
Mary, 39, 155.
Skinner, Elizabeth, 23.
Skolfield, Susan, 148.
Smallage, Martha, 30.
Smiley, Margaret, 183.
Smith, Abigail, 60,
Elizabeth, 16, 17.
George, 122.
Issabella, 36.
Hugh, 16, 18.
James, 16.
Jedidah, 149.
Jeremiah, 16, 17.
Mary, 42, 85, 101, 133, 140, 200, 213.
Nathan, 100.
Phebe, 59.
Rachel, 193.
Ruth, 176.
Sarah, 5.
William, 42.
Snelling, Jonathan, 141.
Snow, Elizabeth, 156.
Esther, 72.
Soyle, Marg, 110.
Spaulding, Joanna, 97.
Spear, Bethiah, 210.
Spencer, Elizabeth, 154.
Thomas, 13.

INDEX

Sprague, Jonathan, 72.
Lydia, 72.
Squire, Elizabeth, 189.
Stanwood, David, 105.
Mary, 105.
Stark, Anne, 66.
Starling, James, 38.
Starrett, Mary, 147.
Stebbins, Hannah, 200.
Steele, Janet, 140, 205.
Jeanette, 140.
Stevens, Elizabeth, 52, 149.
Mary, 32.
Stevenson, Margaret, 1.
Stewart, Ann, 132.
Elizabeth, 185.
James, 217.
Phoebe, 217.
Stiles, Rebecca, 188.
Stinson, Elizabeth, 132.
Stoddard, David, 170, 171.
Mehitable, 95.
Stone, Anna, 172.
William, 34.
Strathearn, Rachel, 120.
Strong, Lydia, 87.
Swan, Elizabeth, 202.
Syle, Margaret, 95.

Taggart, Mary, 217.
Tarbox, Elizabeth, 75, 224.
Taylor, Jane, 61.
Samuel, 61.
Sarah, 61.
Temple, ——, 149.
Capt., 53, 99.
Templeton, Adam, 181.
Allen, 148.
Janet, 181.
Martha, 148.
Tenney, Tenny, Abigail, 37, 222.
Terrance, Margaret, 131.

Thing, Love, 72.
Thomas, Capt., 99, 170.
Lucy, 77.
Thompson, Tomson, ——, 175.
Elizabeth, 130.
Frances, 46.
James, 174.
Margaret, 125.
Sarah, 19, 216.
Thorn, Thorne, ——, 56.
Margaret, 121.
Thwing, Lydia, 174.
Tilden, Christopher, 15.
Tillet, Sarah, 149.
Tippin, Mary, 159.
Tobey, Catherine, 23.
Todd, Elizabeth, 12.
James, 12.
Rachel, 12, 53.
Tolman, Susanna, 64.
Tout, Sarah, 108.
Townsend, Massie, 165.
Towt, Mary, 208.
Tucker, Katherin, 156, 169.
Turk, Margaret, 186.
Tusker, Margaret, 62.
Tuttle, Joanna, 58.
Lydia, 93.
Tyler, Joanna, 155.
Molly, 81.
Thomas, 146.
Tyley, Sarah, 108.
Tyng, Capt., 84.

Ulmer, Mary, 44.
Uran, Mehitable, 61.

Vale, Mary, 70.
Vernon, Admiral, 189.
Vibert, Jane, 103.
Vicar, ——, 84.

Wadsworth, Benjamin, 60.
Wakefield, Ann, 65.
Dorcas, 51.
Walden, Mary, 91.

Walker, Capt., 162.
Isabella, 101.
Mary, 148.
William, 148.
Wallace, Wallis, Elizabeth, 35, 114.
Margaret, 142.
Mary, 212.
Matthias, 114.
Susanna, 35, 114.
William, 35.
Wansell, Henry, 207.
Ward, Eliza., 150.
Prudence, 63.
Wardwell, Elizabeth, 121.
Warren, Elizabeth, 41.
Wasson, Isabel, 28.
Isabella, 184.
Waters, Abigail, 52.
Robert, 52, 101.
Watson, Margaret, 134, 167.
Watts, Margaret, 69.
Sarah, 127.
Waugh, Elizabeth, 29.
Margaret, 151.
Wayman, Sarah, 99.
Webber, John, 45.
Webster, Mary, 39, 158.
Weir, Elizabeth, 197.
Wells, Elizabeth, 162.
Wentworth, Capt., 21.
Katharine, 146.
Mary, 173.
Whiden, Sarah, 116.
White, Elizabeth, 18, 69.
John, 205.
Martha, 141.
Mary, 223.
Patrick, 169.
Samuel, 223.
Sarah, 101.
Whitehead, Christine, 96.
Chrystal, 96.
Whitney, Mary, 212.
Whitridge, Mary, 108.
Whoboas, Mary, 187.

Wiatt, Mary, 203.
Wilder, Aaron, 34.
  Jeranthneel, 34.
  Mary, 182.
Wildes, ——, 48.
  Nathaniel, 48.
Wiley, Janet, 6.
  Sarah, 76.
Wilkins, Hannah, 207.
  Sarah, 37.
Wilkinson, Elizabeth, 97.
Willard, Elizabeth, 72.
  Jacob, 72.
Williams, ——, 181.
  John, 95.
  Robert, 220.
  Ruth, 104.
  Tabitha, 10.
Wilson, Alexander, 117.
  Annie, 196.

Wilson, Eleanor, 92, 117.
  Elizabeth, 101.
  Grisey, 153.
  Jane, 75, 137.
  Janet, 2.
  Mary, 135.
  William, 137.
Wimble, James, 115.
Windrow, Andrew, 216.
Winslow, Joshua, 189.
  Mary, 128.
Winthrop, Anne, 109.
Wire, Mary, 122.
Wolfe, Catherine, 104.
Wood, Woods, Esther, 151.
  Margaret, 175.
Woodbridge, Mary, 222.

Woodcock, Mary, 36.
Woodend, Margaret, 167.
Wooster, Patience, 108.
Workman, ——, 86.
Worthylak, Mary, 103.
Wright, Anna, 47.
Wye, Sarah, 45, 91.
Wyer, Mary, 103.
  William, 148.
Wyman, Sarah, 168.

Yarrow, Mehitable, 217.
Young, ——, 2, 44.
  Deborah, 109.
  Eleanor, 151.
  Mary, 101.
  Sarah, 70.
  Susannah, 165.
Yuran, Eleanor, 116.

www.ingramcontent.com/pod-product-compliance
Lightning Source LLC
Chambersburg PA
CBHW051046160426
43193CB00010B/1083